CHANGE AND APATHY

CHANGE AND APATHY

Liverpool and Manchester during the Industrial Revolution

FRANÇOIS VIGIER

THE M.I.T. PRESS
Cambridge, Massachusetts, and London, England

Copyright © 1970 by
The Massachusetts Institute of Technology
Designed by Dwight E. Agner. Set in Linotype Janson
by Publishers Composition Service, Inc.
Printed and bound in the United States of America
by The Colonial Press Inc.

ISBN 0 262 22012 1 (hardcover)
Library of Congress catalog card number: 70-91607

Contents

List of Illustrations

List of Tables

CHANGE AND APATHY

CHAPTER ONE

Introduction

It is only in recent years that the urban phenomenon has become a topic of general interest to the public and a subject for careful investigation by the social scientist. While the nineteenth century accumulated demographic information on cities in order to show their proliferation and growing importance in an industrializing world, contemporary research has attempted to arrive at a more detailed understanding of the forces shaping the urban environment, of its social and functional dynamics. The purpose of these efforts is not only to remedy the inadequacies inherited from the past and to guide future development but to isolate the intricate relationships between the public and private actions that have encouraged urbanization and given rise to particular functional and land-use patterns. Indeed, it is only through a growing understanding of these relationships, considered both from a historical and a contemporary point of view, that we can hope eventually to achieve the modicum of control that will enable us to create an urban pattern satisfactory to the needs of society. Careful examination of the relatively recent past can be useful insofar as it may bring to light sequences of events whose consequences are still felt today. Far from being a castigation of the private entrepreneurs and public officials whose decisions created, sometimes inadvertently, sometimes through lack of concern, the very conditions that we are still trying to remedy, this book attempts to identify and describe the chain of circumstances, be they external or intrinsic to the institutional characteristics of Liverpool and Manchester, that resulted in a specific pattern of urbanization. It is hoped that the value of such an examination will be to enhance our comprehension of the role of local government in shaping the urban environment during a period of far-reaching and rapid change.

Selection of the closing decades of the eighteenth century and the first half of the nineteenth as a period for investigation seems natural enough for two reasons: the obvious parallel between the social, economic, and political transformations that accompanied the industrial revolution in England and the alteration of traditional institutions now taking place in our urban areas; and the intrinsic interest of that era as a field of historical analysis, resulting not only from its dynamism but from the presence of a fair body of statistical and other descriptive evidence. Much has already been written about the general process of industrialization: social and economic historians, students of politics and public administration, reformers, and novelists have commented upon most, if not all, of the facets of the century or so when the "old order" was replaced by new social and functional characteristics. Yet we know relatively little about the dynamics of the process that caused the emergence of that complex locus of activity, the large industrial city. Similarly, we know little about the circumstances that created the less desirable features of industrialization and urbanization—the pollution of air and water, the crowded and unsanitary living conditions of the poor, the utilitarian ugliness of the environment.

It is simple to illustrate the historical analogy between the transformations that took place during the early years of the industrial revolution and many contemporary changes. *Technologically*, the effects of the introduction of machinery and steam power upon the production of goods were as intensely felt as the effects of automation today in the developed countries. In both instances, the utility of traditional skills decreases or even disappears as more efficient means of production are introduced and large segments of the labor force are faced with the necessity of finding alternative employment, learning new skills, or adjusting their standard of living to the comparatively lower wage scales paid in traditional undertakings.

Economically, the introduction of new means of transport— first the canals, later the railroads—generated a hitherto unknown level of regional and national activity. The diminishing costs of moving raw materials and heavy goods over relatively large distances brought about a growing interdependence between manufacturing establishments. The result was the formation of economic metropolitan areas, that is, clusters of industrial cities functioning in concert; these differed from our contemporary metropolitan areas, however, in that movement between them was restricted largely to goods and did not include people. Together with increased productive capacity made possible by the new machines, cheaper and more efficient means of transport led to the creation of industrial concentrations, such as textiles in Lancashire and metals in the Midlands, whose products were sold throughout England and the world. The extension of the production chain of goods and the localization of industrial activity are also features of today's growing economic specialization, which is itself in part the result of improvements in transportation such as the truck-railroad "piggy-back," containerization, and the use of air freight for low-weight, high-value goods.

Socially, the industrial revolution created two new urban classes: that of the entrepreneurial manufacturer, whose vision of the profits to be reaped from the bounties of the new age allowed him to emerge as the economically dominant element of the middle class, and that of industrial worker, from whose toil many fortunes were made but who found in the factory opportunities that were often more attractive than the slow starvation he had faced in the Irish bogs or the Lancashire freeholds. Indeed, the rural migrants who swelled the population of England's industrial cities during the closing decades of the eighteenth and the first half of the nineteenth centuries were moved by the same dream of a more prosperous way of life as the contemporary American Negro (or, for that matter, his nineteenth-century predecessor, the European farmer), leaving the rural South for New York's Harlem, Detroit, or Chicago. That the dream of these urban migrants was, and still is, often rudely terminated in the stagnation of a slum was as much the consequence of their lack of skills and their inability to compete in a system whose values differed from those that had regulated their former life as of the inherent economic or social harshness of the system itself.

The choice of Liverpool and Manchester as examples of cities undergoing major structural change as a result of industrialization seemed almost inevitable. Not only did Lancashire experience the industrial revolution at an early date, since it was the home of many of the technological innovations that made it possible, but the impact of industrialization and urbanization changed its appearance within less than a century.[1] Moreover, both cities performed roughly similar regional economic functions before, during, and after the industrial revolution—Liverpool was the gateway for Irish, American, and West Indian trade, and Manchester, the marketing center of the county's textile trade—thus isolating technological change as a variable whose effects could be studied. The two towns also had contrasting forms of government. Since this book is concerned with the ability of existing institutions to respond to the process of rapid urbanization as well as with the changes in the urban pattern resulting from the enlarged role imposed on the public sector, the institutional differences between the two towns added a welcome dimension to the investigation.

Liverpool was granted its first royal charter by King John in 1208, when its right to self-government as an independent borough was firmly established. The structure of its governing body—a common council composed of a mayor, two bailiffs, and thirty-eight members elected for life by the assembly of freemen—was established in 1695 under the charter of William III. Liverpool thus possessed, at least in theory, the powers to legislate locally and to take any measures necessary to deal with the problems of rapid urbanization without recourse to Parliament, except in cases where it wanted an extension of its normal powers. It is thus representative of the other 177 English boroughs, whose political institutions came under close scrutiny and were finally radically altered by the Municipal Reform Act of 1835.

Manchester, on the other hand, remained without self-government until 1838, its baronial Court Leet being an anachronistic and "tattered remnant of the old jurisdiction of the Manor," responsible for local government through a cumbersome procedure of suppressing nuisances by imposing fines upon violators and realizing such common responsibilities as maintaining the King's

[1] "The growth of Liverpool during the eighteenth and nineteenth century, the rise of the cotton trade, centering in the town of Manchester, and the development of the coal and iron areas of the county, made Lancashire, in the course of less than a century, the largest center of population outside the London Metropolitan area." Louis W. Moffit, *England on the Eve of the Industrial Revolution* (London: P. S. King & Son, 1925), p. 128.

highway and keeping the peace.[2] Manchester was therefore obliged to develop a series of *ad hoc* institutions to deal with the problems of urbanization, each intended to deal with a specific aspect, each needing justification locally and nationally in order to receive parliamentary sanction. Once established, each institution had to formulate its scope of action in the light of both rapidly changing circumstances and direct competition from other institutions. The multitude of special-purpose committees under the police commissioners, as well as the rivalry between the commissioners, the Court Leet, and the parish vestry, are examples of the overlapping and competing sets of institutions developed in Manchester. Whereas Liverpool illustrates the ability of a traditional borough government to adapt its existing (and theoretically adequate) institutions to new circumstances, Manchester illustrates the propensity of a rapidly urbanizing area to discard its old, essentially rural institutions and to forge new ones designed specifically to meet urban problems.

Any historical investigation that delves into social and economic issues is fraught with the temptation of judging past institutions according to current values. It is indeed easy to castigate the English ruling classes for their very real indifference to the living conditions of the growing numbers of urban poor during the industrial revolution, and to condemn them for their unwillingness to use public powers to prevent the spread of slums. It is equally easy, for that matter, to take our modern urban governments to task for their inability to ensure large segments of the population an adequate standard of housing, for the poor quality of education, and for the

---

[2] Sidney and Beatrice Webb, *The Manor and the Borough* (Hamden, Conn.: Archon Books, 1963), 1:9, 21 ff. Although largely the instrument of the manor (it was presided over by the lord's steward), the Court Leet was empowered to make and enforce new bylaws binding on all the residents within its jurisdiction, either at the steward's or the inhabitants' request. This was an important power, acquired by tradition; to what extent it would have been upheld by the King's courts always remained a point of contention.

The Webbs' praise of the Manchester Court Leet (ibid., pp. 99 ff.) as "an example of a Lord's Court continuing to serve as an *active* local governing authority for a vast population and one of the greatest of English provincial towns" seems totally unwarranted. It is shown in Chapter 5 of the present work that the Manchester court was more notorious for its phlegmatic unawareness of local conditions than "remarkable for its highly developed organization."

lack of employment opportunities for unskilled migrants. Yet it is likely that the fault does not lie entirely with these established authorities. Any form of government is the result of a dialogue, however limited, between the people and their institutions. Public policy is either the result of arbitrary interpretation of what is desirable for the community at large or the translation of objectives supported by the community into governmental action. The inability of the public sector to formulate appropriate policies to guide the development of a community—in modern terms, to plan—can be ascribed to a variety of factors: the lack of a clear understanding of the characteristics of the situation, inappropriate institutions, and inadequate resources, as well as an unwillingness to act.

It can readily be seen that the difficulties facing urban governments during the early years of the industrial revolution were not dissimilar to those we are attempting to solve today. Then, as now, a new scale of economic and functional determinants was beginning to influence urban and regional systems. Then, as now, a new urban lower class of unskilled migrants had to be socially and economically integrated into the community through a congeries of public and private actions. Then, as now, the ability of institutions to adapt themselves to a period of rapid change was perhaps the most important prerequisite for success. Hence, a large part of my discussion of the industrial revolution will be focused on urban governmental institutions, their composition, the powers at their disposal, their relation to other levels of government, and their reaction, as institutions, to change.

The close relation that exists between an institution's structure and its ability to plan needs further elaboration. Theoretically, it is the function of government to realize the community's concept of a desirable way of life.[3] Its role is not only to arbitrate the functioning of the community but to stimulate discussion of and agreement upon issues facing the community. Regardless of whether the insti-

[3] The argument set forth here closely follows the ideas expressed by Arthur Maass on the relationship between the planning process and democratic government. See "System Design and the Political Process: A General Statement," in Arthur Maass et al., *Design of Water-Resources Systems* (Cambridge: Harvard University Press, 1962), pp. 565 ff. Although written in a different context, Professor Maass's emphasis on the need for proper communication between the public and the decision makers as a prerequisite for planning requires only minor change to be suitable for a historical discussion.

tution under consideration is national or local, democratic or autocratic, this definition of the relation between government and the community required for planning implies the following patterns of interaction: (1) Government must be able to apprehend the external forces affecting the community and to translate them into local issues suitable for community discussion. The resources of government must be used to gather information, to analyze it, to determine its consequences, and to present it in a shape suited to a partially informed electorate. (2) A proper forum must exist for community discussion and choice. (3) Further channels must be available through which the community's choices can be transmitted to government. Normally, at least in contemporary Western society, this is achieved through the electoral process. (4) Government must be able to formulate and carry out a series of action-oriented policies representative of the communal choice and, simultaneously, to transmit information about the nature and intended consequences of these policies to the public. (5) The community must support public action and have an opportunity to reevaluate issues and objectives in the light of practical experience, in order to formulate new objectives or to reinforce previous choices.

This structure (illustrated in Figure 1) assumes the need for a continuous dialogue leading to cooperative action between government and the community. As is evident, this dialogue can pertain either to relatively commonplace matters—such as the operation and maintenance of the community's capital plant, the provision of the usual public services, or the drafting of town ordinances and bylaws, for example—or to considerably broader policies on welfare and economic development.

A definition of the constitution and size of the community has purposely been omitted, since both varied greatly during the industrial revolution. Regardless of whether one is examining the relation between the community and a closed oligarchy (such as the freemen of Liverpool and their corporation) or a more representative government (such as the parish vestry of Manchester and its police commissioners), the need to formulate community objectives, to gather and clarify information, and to arrive at specific action-oriented policies and programs still remains the basic ingredient of the planning function. The political nature of the community whose vision of the good life is translated into planning objectives is

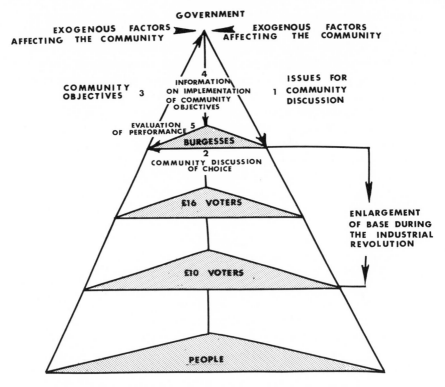

Figure 1. Hypothetical Model of the Planning Process

somewhat incidental to the main line of this argument, at least insofar as it does not cease to represent the desires of the population at large. For example, the process just described is applicable to the internal structure of government: substitute "parliament" or "city council" for "community," and "executive" for "government," and the same need for information, discussion and resolution of issues, and determination of policies and programs still remains.

The advantage of this conceptual model is that it provides a framework within which to evaluate the adequacy of the planning function while remaining generalized enough to admit different circumstances and institutions. In other words, the effectiveness of planning can be measured relative to the expression of societal goals, the mechanisms through which they are interpreted, and the resources at the disposal of the community, rather than by some arbitrary present-day standard. The success or failure of the planning function can be ascribed to an institutional breakdown that cuts off proper communication between the community and government, or to an inability or unwillingness on the part of either party to carry out its share of the responsibility. But neither the actors and their objectives nor the institutional framework needs to be defined before the fact. The flexibility of this model proved advantageous because of the far-reaching changes brought about by the industrial revolution and the differences between the governmental institutions of the two towns selected for detailed study.

The method of analysis employed is akin to that utilized by planners today—that is, a synthesis of interdisciplinary variables—but the emphasis has been empirical and descriptive rather than predictive. I have sought to understand how and why a particular process of urban development occurred rather than to predict the course of future development. I have worked from both primary and secondary sources, attempting to systematize and interrelate the numerous excellent historical, social, and economic studies that exist on the industrial revolution in England. The physical descriptions of Liverpool and Manchester, however, have all been collected from contemporary descriptions and mapped as generalized land-use diagrams.

CHAPTER TWO

Industrialization and Urbanization

In order to provide an appropriate setting for a detailed investigation of Liverpool and Manchester, it is necessary to summarize briefly the conditions that prevailed in England during the second half of the eighteenth century. The early years of the industrial revolution were a period of intense diplomatic success for England. Ushered in by the acquisition of a vast new empire in the East, by an expanding role in Africa, and by the disappearance of French power in North America and most of the West Indies, it may well have seemed the beginning of a new golden age.[1] Yet, within twenty years, not only would England be embroiled in deep political trouble at home and in a colonial war that would result in the loss of a major portion of her American colonies; she would also be on the verge of several decades of military involvement on the Continent. Simultaneously, the English economy would be transformed by technological advances, and the concomitant need for new

---

[1] "When George III succeeded his grandfather (in 1760), the name of Britain was held, perhaps, in higher esteem by the nations of the world than ever before or since. Her free institutions, imperfect as we know them to have been, were regarded with envy by the European nations of that day. No 'anti-English' tradition had yet arisen: the Irish were quiet and forgotten; the American colonies were still united to the mother country and devoted to Pitt. England and 'the Great Commoner' were as much admired as they were feared by the French themselves, a generous and philosophic nation, at that time thoroughly out of love with their own institutions which had brought them to such a pass. The English race was at the top of golden hours." George M. Trevelyan, *History of England*, 3rd ed. (London: Longmans, Green, 1947), p. 545.

markets would necessitate a substantial shift in England's foreign trade pattern, in spite of the rapidly changing and often chaotic international situation.

The severe fluctuations in the British economy that accompanied the industrial revolution were due as much to external political causes as to the inevitable disruption brought about by the new technology.[2] In spite of these fluctuations, the secular economic trend was positive, and as early as 1800 British manufactured goods represented 55 percent of the total value of all exports; by 1850, they accounted for 90 percent of the value of domestic exports, which had more than doubled.[3] The utilization of the new technology in manufacturing—perhaps best exemplified by Arkwright's "water-frame" (1769), Crompton's "spinning mule" (1779), Cartwright's power loom (1785), James Watt's stationary steam engine (1769), and Stevenson's steam locomotive (1815)—not only created a new scale of production, a spurt in industrial output somewhat independent of cyclical effects,[4] but also generated a new pattern of specialized urban functions. The forces that prompted rapid urbanization and a new hierarchy of urban functions, what Pred calls a new set of "external relations,"[5] can be summarized as follows.

1. Selected industries tended to concentrate in specialized locations, while their operational scale and plant size were increased by innovations in manufacturing techniques and transportation. At least during the early years of the industrial revolution, this was a highly selective process. For example, the production of cotton goods in

[2] See, among others, E. B. Schumpeter, "English Prices and Public Finance, 1660–1822," *Review of Economic Statistics* 20 (1938):21–37; Arthur D. Gayer, Walt W. Rostow, and Anna J. Schwartz, *The Growth and Fluctuation of the British Economy: 1790–1850*, 2 vols. (Oxford: Clarendon Press, 1953).

[3] Gayer, Rostow, and Schwartz, *British Economy*, 1:39 and 2:757.

[4] Speaking of the European economy between the end of the eighteenth century and the First World War, Alexander Gerschenkron states: "In a number of major countries of Europe industrial development did not proceed at an even pace. On the contrary, after a lengthy period of fairly low rates of growth came a moment of a more or less sudden increase in the rates which then remained at the accelerated level for a considerable period. That was the period of the great spurt in the respective countries' industrial development." "On the Concept of Continuity in History," *Proceedings of the American Philosophical Society* 106, no. 3 (June 1962):206.

[5] Allan R. Pred, *The External Relations of Cities During "Industrial Revolution"* (Chicago: University of Chicago Press, 1962).

England increased by a factor of 11 between 1785 and 1812, while that of pottery, paper, and glass, all industries that were not affected by technological change, grew by factors of only 2 to 2½.[6]

2. The strict limitations imposed upon the routes of canals and railroads by topography and natural watercourses for the former and, for the latter, by topography and the willingness of property owners to suffer the crossing of their lands by the "iron horse" determined the locational advantages (or disadvantages) of individual cities. The enormous reductions in transportation costs[7] resulted in a potentially greater economic diversification for cities that were located within reach of a canal or, later, a railroad. Raw materials for manufacturing could be brought in over long distances, while the expansion of potential markets spurred the growth of mass-production techniques, spelling the demise of handicraft industries. In these cities, the population tended to grow faster than in those less advantageously located.

3. Reductions in transportation costs favored the larger existing firms since their higher productive capacity could expand faster and capture additional, more distant markets. Although the historical pattern of strong local interdependence between raw materials, production, and marketing was negated, allowing the birth of new industrial activities, existing manufacturing tended to consolidate and grow faster than any potential rival that might theoretically have taken advantage of lower transportation costs. Hence, the continued predominance of such preindustrial complexes as the woolen industry in Yorkshire, the cotton industry in Lancashire, and the steel manufacturing complex of the Midlands.[8]

4. The emergence of these large industrial complexes, clustered within a tight urban pattern, tended to direct the migratory movement of peasants toward a few selected areas rather than to the city in general.

5. The industrial revolution was preceded and accompanied by

[6] Heinrich E. Friedlaender and Jacob Oser, *Economic History of Modern Europe* (New York: Prentice-Hall, 1953), p. 73.

[7] The Duke of Bridgewater's canal halved the cost of coal in Manchester. In the 1850s the long-distance haulage charge for coal was reduced by an additional factor of ¼ by canals and railroads alike. Christopher I. Savage, *An Economic History of Transport* (London: Hutchinson, 1959), pp. 49 ff.

[8] The same phenomenon can be observed on the European continent: for example, in the Ruhr and the French textile centers of Lille, Roubaix, and La Madeleine.

an agricultural revolution, which caused not only a quantitative increase in the production of food, allowing the growth of ever-larger urban areas, but a qualitative one as well. While manufacturing processes were being affected by the first wave of technological improvements, eighteenth-century English agriculture was also undergoing drastic structural changes. These can be divided into two interrelated categories: the virtual disappearance of the small landowner (at least in terms of his relative importance as a producer) and an increasing specialization in agricultural production. Indeed, the gradual extinction of the small farmer—freeholder or copyholder—was a necessary prerequisite for the transformation of agriculture from subsistence to profit, an indispensible step toward feeding a growing urban population. The eighteenth-century enclosure movement, whatever individual hardships it may have caused or whatever opposition it may have aroused, was an efficient mechanism for realizing the economies of scale needed to take advantage of new crop and rotation techniques.[9] The resulting increase in eighteenth-century agricultural productivity is striking: the average weight of a fattened ox at Smithfield market was 800 pounds in 1795, compared to 370 pounds in 1710.[10] The yield of crops, in general, was perhaps four times what was prevalent during the Renaissance and most of the Middle Ages. Moreover, the increase in urban buying power that took place during the second half of the nineteenth century resulted in an increase in the purchase of such luxury goods as fruit, tea, and coffee.

The industrialization of England was accompanied by extraordinary demographic changes. There was an almost simultaneous in-

[9] "The enclosure movement is the crown and completion of the changes in the economic structure of the industry. At the same time it is the channel through which the new commercial and individualistic spirit found its full expression. Enclosures meant the abandonment of the wasteful methods of the open-field system for a system in which economy of management and the new technical progress could reap their full reward. When farming became primarily a source of profit for the community, open fields were doomed and enclosures were already on the horizon. They mark the completion of the transition from the manorial organization where the lord of the manor was the head, social as well as economic, of a largely self-sufficing community, to the capitalistic organization where the landlord is the apex of an industry organized for profit." Louis W. Moffit, *England on the Eve of the Industrial Revolution* (London: P. S. King & Son, 1925), p. 55.

[10] Paul Mantoux, *The Industrial Revolution in the Eighteenth Century*, 2nd ed. (New York: Harcourt, Brace, 1929), p. 161.

crease in the country's total population (owing partly to natural causes and partly to the Irish migration) and a dramatic shift in the balance between urban and total population (see Figure 2). Throughout the eighteenth century, there was a sharp rise in the birth rate, which was probably caused by the earlier marriage age made possible by the gradual discontinuance of the long apprenticeship period.[11] Simultaneously, there was a lowering of the death rate, which can be traced to the improvement in medical techniques after the introduction from Europe, around 1725, of the clinical method of training physicians and to the extensive experimentation in hygiene in the navy and in the army, leading to the development of improved sanitary techniques. The spectacular drop in infant mortality was the result of the increasingly widespread acceptance of basic methods of cleanliness and the improved availability of hospitals within urban areas. Between 1700 and 1818, no fewer than 47 general hospitals and 50 dispensaries were constructed in England. At the British Lying-in Hospital in London, for example, infant mortality fell from 66 per thousand in 1749–1758 to just over 10 per thousand in 1799–1808; the maternal mortality rate declined correspondingly, from 24 to 4½ per thousand.[12] It should be noted that, although these rates are derived from a small sample of the population, they are nevertheless indicative of a general trend to the extent that hospital births, at the time, were restricted largely to so-called "difficult" cases.

By the beginning of the nineteenth century, England was feeling the full impact of a steady and fairly rapid population increase of approximately 2 percent per annum. As in the case of developing countries today, it was not the result of better living conditions but of a higher survival rate.[13] Indeed, there is strong evidence that,

[11] See T. H. Marshall, "The Population Problem during the Industrial Revolution," *Economic History Review* 1, no. 4 (1929):429–456, for an excellent discussion of demographic trends during this period.

The birth rate reached a peak of 37.7 per thousand around 1780 (ibid., p. 433). The national death rate was dropping steadily from 35 per thousand in 1750 to 28 in 1780, 25 in 1800, and 20 in 1815. Mabel Craven Buer, *Health, Wealth and Population in the Early Days of the Industrial Revolution* (London: G. Routledge and Sons, 1926), p. 267.

[12] Buer, *Health, Wealth and Population*, p. 145.

[13] The nineteenth-century Malthusian concern with the population explosion showed a keen awareness of contemporary conditions. The population increase and the food shortages that were prognosticated as its inevitable

in spite of increased agricultural and industrial production, living conditions may have deteriorated during the second half of the eighteenth century, particularly in the towns. Although wages tended to vary according to geographic location and type of work, whatever increases did take place were marginal, like the basic wages themselves. It was not until the turn of the century that the Elizabethan statutes regulating wages were finally repealed. Average urban wages outside London may have risen about 30 percent at best, from 9 shillings per week to 12 shillings in 1800, while, in the same period, the cost-of-living index had risen by 120 percent.[14]

In addition to the overall increase of the population, the second half of the eighteenth century saw some remarkable changes in its geographical distribution and in the ratio of urban to rural population. Before the beginnings of industrialization, over three-fifths of England's population lived in the southern counties, between the Bristol Channel and the Suffolk coast. Starting about 1750, the center of gravity of population moved toward the northwestern coal deposits and the manufacturing centers that were beginning to

---

consequence were attributed to the artificial encouragement of childbearing, notably by the Poor Laws and the demand for child labor in the new industries. In addition to the works of Malthus himself, those of his contemporaries illustrate the socioeconomic concerns of English demographers during the early years of the industrial revolution. See, for example, Patrick Colquhoun, *A Treatise on Indigence* (London: J. Hatchard, 1806) and *A Treatise on the Wealth, Power, and Resources of the British Empire* . . . (London: J. Mawman, 1814); William T. Comber, *An Inquiry into the State of National Subsistence* . . . (London: T. Cadell and W. Davies, 1808); Sir Frederick Morton Eden, *An Estimate of the Number of Inhabitants in Great Britain and Ireland* (London: J. Wright, 1800); Joseph Lowe, *The Present State of England in Regard to Agriculture, Trade and Finance* (New York: E. Bliss and E. White, 1824); Joshua Milne, *A Treatise on the Valuation of Annuities* . . . , 2 vols. (London: Longman, Hurst, Rees, Orme and Brown, 1815); Richard Price, *Observations on Reversionary Payments*, 4th ed., 2 vols. (London: T. Cadell, 1783); Williams Wales, *An Inquiry into the Present State of Population in England and Wales* (London: C. Nourse, 1781).

[14] James E. T. Rogers, *Six Centuries of Work and Wages* (New York: G. P. Putnam, 1884), p. 494. Elizabeth W. Gilboy points out that there were significant local differences due to poor communications and variations in industrial development. "Regional differences in the course of real wages in eighteenth century England are very evident." While there was a decline in real wages over much of the country, and in London in particular, "in the north of England, money wages and prices rose almost simultaneously. From 1760 to 1775, prices went up 40 per cent, while wages increased approximately 70 per cent." "The Cost of Living and Real Wages in Eighteenth Century England," *Review of Economic Statistics* 18 (1936):141–142.

grow around them, and by 1801 almost half of England's population lived in these industrial counties. There was a parallel trend in the percentage of the population living in urban areas: although most cities remained quite small until the end of the nineteenth century, the number of people living in urban areas[15] starts increasing sharply from 1775 on. Prior to the introduction of the new manufacturing techniques and their repercussion on urban functions, the proportion of urban dwellers had remained at a steady 27 percent of the total population. By 1800, however, when the initial impact of industrialization had been widely felt, the ratio of urban to rural population had reached 35 percent and continued to increase steadily: 40 percent in 1825, 50 percent in 1850, 64 percent in 1875 (see Figure 2).

What may be an even more striking change can be observed in the distribution of city sizes, shown in Figure 3. If all urban areas except metropolitan London (which will be excluded from the rest of this discussion because of its atypical character as a "primate" city) are taken into account, the "median" English city had a population of 2000 to 5000 until well into the 1840s. Not until after 1800 does there appear more than an occasional city with a population larger than 50,000; as late as 1851, only 24 out of 460 English cities had populations in excess of 50,000, only 5 in excess of 100,000, and only 3 in excess of 200,000. However, the total number of urban areas had grown from 159 in 1750 to 460 in 1851.

It is apparent that there were two distinct cycles of urbanization. The first, from 1750 to about 1821, consisted of a substantial increase in the total number of urban areas, although the relative rank-size distribution remained essentially the same. This was the time when former villages acquired "urban" characteristics, mainly as a result of the influx of people attracted by the sudden increase in employment opportunities offered by rapidly expanding smaller-

---

[15] "Urban areas" have to be defined somewhat arbitrarily in order to provide a comparative continuum. Using a limiting criterion of density (10 persons per gross acre or more), places having a population of 2000 or more were considered to perform urban functions. Although this number may seem small today, it must be remembered that until the beginning of the Renaissance, 700 to 1000 inhabitants were sufficient to ensure an appropriately "urban" diversity of functions, and this number increased only marginally during the Renaissance itself. See Roger Mols, *Introduction à la démographie historique des villes d'Europe du XIVième au XVIIIième siècle*, 3 vols. (Gembloux, Belgium: J. Duculot, 1954–1956).

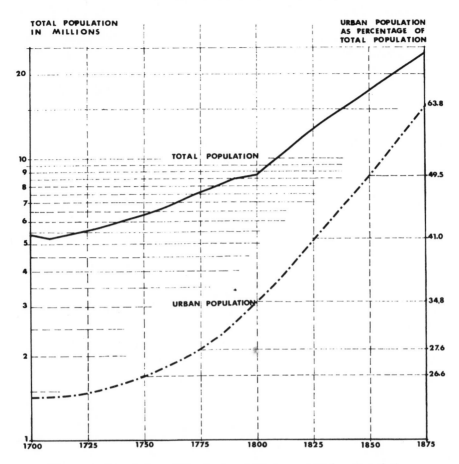

Figure 2. Population of England and Wales and Urban Population

scale industries and new manufacturing concerns. The second cycle, starting about 1821, was largely a period of consolidation and expansion of selected urban areas. The specialized functions of the larger industrial complexes allowed them to grow considerably faster than other cities and to emerge as dominant centers of economic activity. While the median size of cities remained between 2000 and 5000, industrial cities, long-distance seaports, and cities performing more than one economic function had median popula-

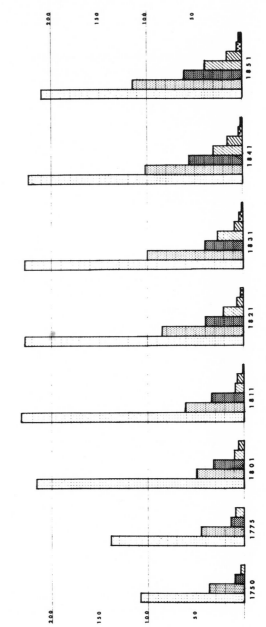

Figure 3. Rank Order of English Urban Areas

tions of 10,000–20,000 by 1811 and 20,000–50,000 by 1841 (see Figure 4). In other words, only cities that were particularly favored in terms of location or productive potential tended to take advantage of the new technology in transportation and manufacturing. The more traditional subregional market towns or even the larger county towns were not affected by these new economies of scale, unless they started performing a productive function above and beyond their former role.

In addition to these general trends—an accelerated rate of population growth, the shift from a predominantly rural to a more urban population, the absolute increase in number of urban areas, and the emergence of larger, specialized cities—there began to appear clusters of towns dependent upon, and developing in concert with, a larger central place. The phenomenon, akin to the modern metropolitan area, can be observed in a limited way as early as 1750. However, eighteenth- and early nineteenth-century interaction, either between the satellites and the central place or among the elements of the cluster, differs from the contemporary pattern. Rather than the specialized areal distribution of employment and housing linked by commutation patterns that is characteristic of the present day, one sees only a system of economic interchanges among partially specialized local productive centers and their common marketplace. For example, Manchester, long the heart of the Lancashire cotton trade, did not have a significant cotton-spinning industry of its own until the beginning of the nineteenth century; the mills were distributed on the town's periphery according to the availability of streams to drive their waterwheels.[16] Yet, in 1775, Manchester was clearly the commercial center for a cluster of twelve industrial towns, half of them former villages, whose goods were marketed through its cotton dealers. Other industries showed the same dependence upon natural power sources, which explains the prevalence of industrial centers composed of clusters of new towns dependent upon an older marketing center.

The need for more efficient transportation arose concurrently with the introduction of improved manufacturing methods. The

---

[16] There were no cotton mills in Manchester until 1789; by 1831, as a result of the introduction of steam power, there were sixty-six. A detailed description of the localization of the cotton industry within the Manchester cluster will be found in Chapter 5.

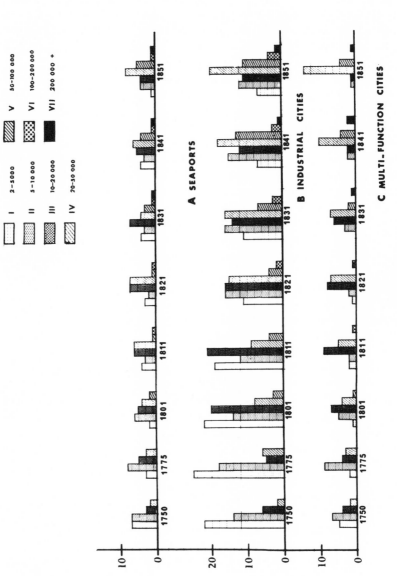

Figure 4. Rank Distribution of English Cities by Major Function

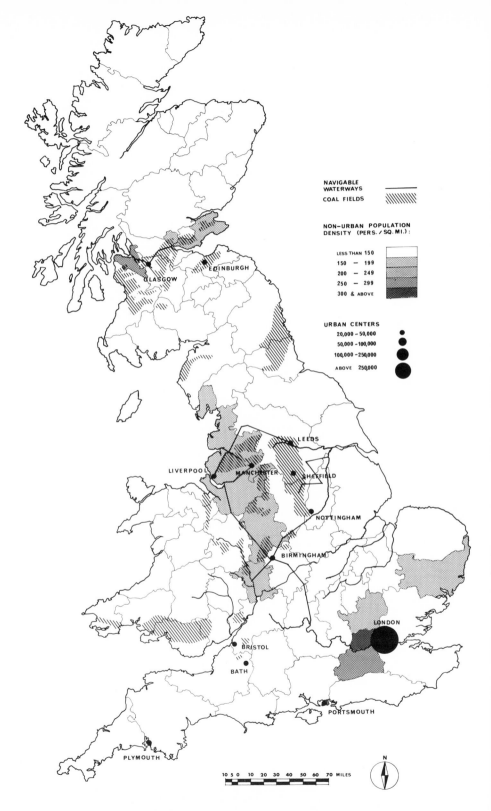

Figure 5. Population Distribution in Great Britain—1775

growth of selected urban areas and the interdependence of groups of towns within urban clusters were both determined by new transportation techniques. It is no accident that the first long-distance canal, completed in 1767, was constructed to link the cotton industry around Manchester with the growing port of Liverpool. By the end of the eighteenth century, most of the northern industrial centers were internally connected, and access between London, the industrial Midlands, and the North was provided by the Grand Trunk and the Grand Junction canals. The economic impact of the canals was enormous: the average cost of transport over medium distances (up to about fifty miles) was halved, from 1s./ton-mile to 6d./ton-mile.[17] This was particularly dramatic in the case of low-value, high-bulk raw materials such as coal, which growing factories and cities were coming to depend on. Industrial centers like Manchester "could now be supplied regularly and cheaply with coal."[18] The presence of a canal in its immediate vicinity allowed a town to expand its markets and provided it with the incentive to modernize its manufacturing facilities. Conversely, the adverse routing of a canal could spell the demise of an established industry that found itself unable to compete because of the higher transportation costs entailed by a less accessible location. "It was the canals, the arteries of commerce in the closing decades of the eighteenth century, rather than the railways, which came later, that were so influential in determining the subsequent location of British industry."[19]

The time and cost savings in moving bulk goods over medium distances determined not only industrial location but the human settlement pattern as well. A comparison of the population distribution in 1775 and 1821 (Figures 5 and 6), at the beginning and at the end of the "age of the canals," clearly illustrates the repercussions of the new mode of transportation and the growing relationship between industrialization and urbanization. In 1775, within eight years of the construction of the first canal, all the cities with populations greater than twenty thousand were located on or near navigable waterways; in addition, there were already signs of the development of two districts containing populations engaged in in-

[17] Moffit, *England on the Eve of the Industrial Revolution*, pp. 136, 138.
[18] Savage, *An Economic History of Transport*, p. 19.
[19] Ibid., p. 20.

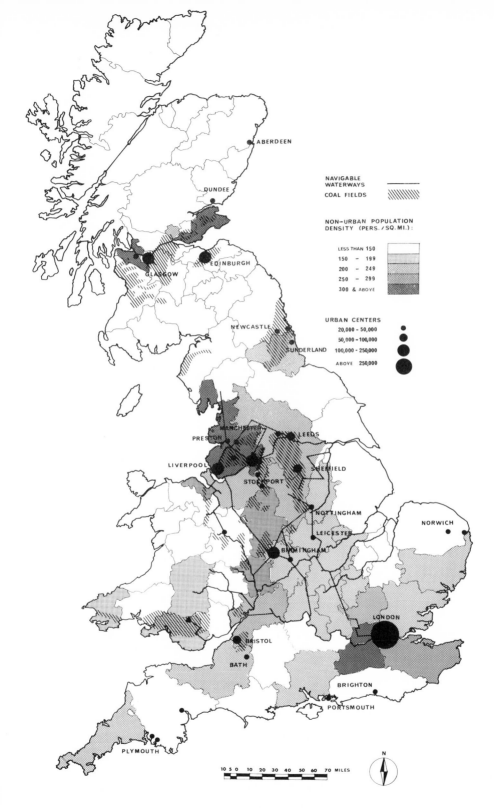

Figure 6. Population Distribution in Great Britain—1821

dustry, between Birmingham and Manchester and between Glasgow and Edinburgh, which were beginning to rival the traditional dominance of London and the Home Counties. By 1821, the industrial Midlands and the North contained the most intense population densities and the greatest concentration of large cities, all of them interconnected by canals. During this period, the rate of growth of the towns first served by the canals was almost 40 percent higher than the average annual rate for all towns.

The dramatic response to improvements in transportation illustrates how isolated the urban areas had been before the construction of the first canals. Overland communications were not only expensive but abysmally slow. Public interest in highway improvements, for example, was given its first impetus by the Jacobite Rebellion of 1745, when the Pretender marched unopposed from Edinburgh to Derby: the poor condition of the roads and the slowness of internal communications allowed him to arrive within seventy miles of London before the Royal Army could be mustered to stop him. But public interest stopped short of public expenditures. The turnpike trusts that proliferated during the second half of the eighteenth century were financed by private entrepreneurs. Invested with broad powers under various acts of Parliament, private companies were relatively free of supervision, particularly in the choice of routes, which were determined on the basis of their profit potential rather than as part of a highway system to serve the country. Similarly, the trusts were allowed considerable latitude in establishing toll rates and were not adverse to tendering preferential rates to private individuals and "farming," or subletting, tollgates for a fixed yearly rental. In the latter case, the profit expectations of the lessee became paramount in establishing the rate for a particular gate.

The contribution of the turnpikes to improved communications varied greatly from place to place, according to the competence and honesty of the trustees.[20] Generally speaking, the best roads were constructed within and among the growing industrial clusters

[20] "Even after Parliament had attempted, in the General Turnpike Act of 1773, to tidy up the complex legislation affecting turnpikes, there were no effective checks on extravagance by the Trustees, no audits of their accounts, no limits imposed on their borrowing powers, and no check on their power to divert and alter existing highways at will. . . . It is not surprising that the Trusts were unpopular." Ibid., p. 25.

of the Midlands, Lancashire, and the West Riding of Yorkshire, where twenty-five turnpike trusts were created between 1750 and 1780, as compared to eight between 1724 and 1750.[21] It is necessary to wait until the first decades of the nineteenth century (and particularly for John Loudon McAdam's new technique of roadbuilding) for the development of hard-surfaced, long-distance highways connecting the principal cities. Even then, their high cost limited their utilization to the movement of goods over very short distances (among the towns of a cluster, for example) or the carrying of the Royal Mail and a few rich passengers between the principal cities of the country. Unlike the canals, the construction of the turnpikes had little effect upon the national urbanization pattern.

The vast restructuring of the British economy whose repercussions upon two cities will be examined in detail took place principally through individual enterprise. Contemporary experience has shown the necessity of a direct correlation between the functional complexity of a society and the increasing role of government as an arbiter among conflicting interests; we have become accustomed to seeing the regulatory role of government reflect structural innovations—technological, economic, or social. The approach of eighteenth-century England, or at least its politicians, was different. Although the country was being rapidly transformed from a parochial, agricultural society into an industrial, "universalistic" nation, few changes, if any, were thought necessary in the role of government, in spite of the mounting evidence of social and economic stress. Reform-minded Whigs, as well as anti-Jacobin Tories, supported the practice of laissez-faire.[22] Most of the energy of public men was spent first on the struggle for power between the Crown and an oligarchic Parliament and later on the conduct of the Continental Wars. Economic benefits accruing from the industrial revolution were considered the rightful rewards of the entrepreneurial wisdom of factory owners. Government made no effort to

[21] Moffit, *England on the Eve of the Industrial Revolution*, p. 290.

[22] Trevelyan gives the following synopsis of the pervasive attitudes of the time: "The political spirit of the English eighteenth century—aristocratic power tempered by Parliamentary control and individual rights—had little in common either with continental despotism or with the bureaucratic democracy of our own time. When the Reformers . . . took in hand the problem of the relation of this old governmental system to the new facts of the Industrial Revolution, their first belief was that the remedy lay in reduced taxation and less State interference." *History of England*, p. 614.

achieve a better distribution of the national wealth, since it viewed the new economic structure of the country as something to be expanded through protection of a rising middle class, not only for its own sake but as a timely source of additional public revenues to support England's involvements on the Continent.[23]

Government interference in the economy had traditionally been limited to statutes pertaining to the quality of various products and the places where they could be manufactured,[24] wages, and the regulation of the import and export of cereals. These early statutes, which were intended to stabilize the cost of living, were of questionable effectiveness, although the wide local fluctuations in costs throughout the eighteenth century can be attributed as much to the accessibility of a particular town to its hinterland as to the inadequacy of its magistrates' regulatory measures. In fact, the eighteenth-century Corn Laws were more intent on ensuring an "adequate" profit to native wheat growers (who were well represented in Parliament) than on stabilizing the price of a commodity that formed the staple diet of the population. Government response to the frequent food riots took the form of temporary relief: public purchase and distribution of food by municipal authorities, attempts to prevent hoarding by middlemen or retailers, embargoes on wheat-carrying vessels in British ports, and control of bread prices through local assizes.[25]

----

[23] "The prosperity brought about by the revolutionary changes in the technique of textile and iron production enabled Pitt to raise the taxes necessary for carrying on the war. At the same time, government purchases contributed to the boom in industry and trade." Schumpeter, "English Prices and Public Finance, 1660–1822," p. 29.

[24] For example, the first comprehensive statute relating to the manufacture of cotton goods dates back to 1551 (5 & 6 Edw. 6, cap. 6). The length, width, and unit weight of cloth were prescribed, as well as the amount of stretching. Similar regulations for the woolen trade are even older. The Weavers' Act of 1555 (2 & 3 Phil. & M., cap. 11) concentrated the cloth industry within corporate towns and specified the apprenticeship for weavers. See George W. Daniels, *The Early English Cotton Industry* (London: Longmans, Green, 1920), Chapter 1, for a summary of the development of the cotton trade.

[25] All of these techniques had been used since antiquity to forestall periodic food shortages in urban areas. Greek and Hellenistic cities used public funds to regulate the cereal market, as did Rome; the Hanseatic League cities had compulsory purchase of part of the wheat cargo of every ship that entered their ports, the percentage varying with local supply conditions; most medieval towns imposed restrictions on wholesale purchases and storage of

The destitute condition of the early industrial worker can be attributed largely to the differential ability of government to interfere in the economic life of the country: ineffective in controlling rising prices, government was extraordinarily effective in keeping wages at a low level. The Elizabethan statutes of 1563 (5 Eliz. 1, cap. 4), which established daily wages at 1s. 6d. for artisans and 1s. for laborers, were still in force during most of the eighteenth century. Even when these statutes started to break down under the combined pressures of rising prices and labor unrest in the new industrial centers, the principle of a negotiable wage rate was rarely either accepted by employers or supported by Parliament. Wage increases were granted from time to time, but they were still established by the justices at quarter sessions and allowed to fluctuate as a function of the profit expectations of the factory owners rather than as a function of the cost of living. The effectiveness of the factory owners in convincing the justices of their perilous economic position can easily be understood when one remembers that most of the justices were drawn from their own ranks. The attitude of the factory owners toward wages and prices was that even a modicum of prosperity for the workers would only goad them to laziness and intemperance:

In general, [manufacturers] find that their best friend is the high price of provisions. I was particular in my enquiries on this head, and found the sentiment universal. . . . [When prices are low, the spinners and weavers] never worked six days in a week; . . . not five, nor even four. [Their] idle time [is] spent at ale-houses, or at receptacles of low diversion. . . .

The master manufacturers of Manchester wish that prices might always be high enough to enforce a general industry; to keep the hands employed six days for a week's work; as they find that even one idle day, in the chance of its being a drunken one, damages all the other

---

cereals in an attempt to prevent the creation of artificial shortages based on speculation. There are numerous examples in antiquity of various forms of price controls, and the free distribution of grain was one of the characteristics of Imperial Rome.

Although these techniques were never fully effective, they were nevertheless more appropriate in periods when urban populations were small and relatively stable, and urban dependence upon locally grown supplies was still great. With industrialization and the rapid growth of urban population, it became essential to develop means of ensuring an adequate level of supplies at stable prices. None of the traditional techniques was able to achieve this in eighteenth-century England.

five, or, rather, the work of them. But at the same time they are sensible, that [prices] may be too high, and that the poor may suffer in spite of the utmost industry; . . .

The line of separation is too delicate to attempt the drawing; but it is well known by every master manufacturer at Manchester, that the workmen who are industrious, rather more so than the common run of their brethren, have never been in want in the highest of the late high prices. Large families in this place are no incumbrance; all are set to work.[26]

Although some concern with social welfare might be read in Gilbert's Act of 1782 (22 Geo. 3, cap. 83), which introduced a supplementary allowance for "able-bodied" workers, proportionate to the number of children they had or to their general family responsibilities, the manufacturers were quick to realize that women and children were not covered by the act and were, therefore, an attractive substitute source of cheap labor for their factories.[27]

The principle of statutory wage controls was a two-edged sword from the point of view of the workers. If, in a boom period, they were sometimes successful in convincing the manufacturers and their friends the justices to consent to a wage increase, they were in an exceedingly vulnerable position during one of the frequent recessions that affected the new industries during the first century or so of their existence. These cycles, caused by overproduction, shifts in the relative distribution of various cost components, and competition and inadequate marketing techniques, resulted in a generally narrowing margin of profit. For example, the margin on a pound of spun cotton yarn was 8s. 11d. in 1784; in 1812, it had fallen to 1s., and in 1832 to 4d.[28] Although the drop in profit per unit of production was usually offset by increased production, the downward trend was still impressive enough to be worrisome to the manufacturers. Since the only relatively flexible component of costs was wages, it is not surprising that every effort was made not only

[26] Arthur Young, *A Six Months Tour through the North of England* 4 vols. (London: W. Strahan, 1770), 3:193–194.

[27] Rogers, in his description of the purposes of the act, suggests that such a shift in the composition of the labor supply might well have been within the intentions of Parliament: "By this means, they would be able to prevent a general increase of wages, to fix the wages of the single and the childless at a low amount, and compel all occupiers to contribute towards the cost of agricultural operations." *Six Centuries of Work and Wages*, p. 437.

[28] Thomas Ellison, *The Cotton Trade of Great Britain* (London: E. Wilson, 1886), p. 61.

to keep them stable but to lower them, at least in industries affected by mechanization. The average weekly wage of Bolton weavers, for example, fell from 33s. in 1795 to 14s. in 1815 and to 5s. 6d. in the early 1830s.[29]

No sustained attempt to regulate working conditions accompanied government concern with "stable" wages. Rather, the bulk of eighteenth-century legislation was aimed at forestalling any concerted action by labor to improve its working and living conditions. The harsh deliberateness of Pitt's legislation is in striking contrast to the lack of organization among the working class and the limited objectives of the trade unions and clubs of the time. Still influenced by their medieval and Renaissance traditions, their main concern was twofold: mutual help among members, particularly during periods of seasonal unemployment,[30] and protection of the craft and its standards. Faced with a rapid decrease in importance, owing to the technical obsolescence of many of their activities, the unions and societies made futile and erratic attempts to protect themselves. Their political efforts were usually limited to petitioning Parliament to enforce the Elizabethan statutes on wages and apprenticeship, which had begun to fall into disuse because of the displacement of skilled workers by machines operated by women and children. Instead of attempting to speak for the new working class and to represent its interests, which were also their own, labor leaders tended to be more conservative than the ruling class itself, inasmuch as they were trying to preserve an established order, while Parliament and the new industrialists were willing to take advantage of changing conditions.[31]

[29] Edward Baines, *History of the Cotton Manufacture in Great Britain* (London: Fisher, Fisher, and Jackson, 1835), p. 489.

[30] One of the characteristics of the early English labor unions was the existence of the "tramping" member. A union member who wished to migrate obtained a "clearance" or "document" that showed him to be a member in good standing of his society. This entitled him to one night's lodging, a free meal, and a "tramp allowance" from local branches of his society. If work was available in the town, it was listed in the branch's "call book"; if there was none, the member tramped on. Unlike the European custom of acquiring experience and stature in one's trade by becoming a journeyman, the "British tramping system seems to have been a device for meeting seasonal or irregular employment." E. J. Hobsbawm, "The Tramping Artisan," *Economic History Review* 3, no. 3 (1951):301.

[31] Cole points out that, until well into the nineteenth century, labor organizations were led by older, established craftsmen, "whose statutes and

Despite the lack of any organized effort by the working class to better its conditions, severe regulatory measures were introduced in the 1790s, partly to prohibit the spread of revolutionary ideas from France. In the absence of a permanent police force, troops were used to deal with unrest, habeas corpus was suspended, and trade unionism suppressed.[32] The Combination Acts of 1799 (39 Geo. 3, cap. 81) established a procedure whereby the traditional protection of the law was withheld from the workingman: he could be brought in front of a single magistrate and sentenced to jail for three months, or to hard labor for two, if it could be shown that "by any Means whatsoever, directly or indirectly," he had attempted to "decoy, persuade, solicit, intimidate, influence or prevail or attempt or endeavour to prevail" upon any other workingman to combine with him to obtain an increase in wages, refuse to work, or attend a meeting intended to promote such purposes. Furthermore, both parties and witnesses brought before a magistrate under this statute were forced to give evidence under oath, even though such evidence might be self-incriminating. Appeal to higher courts was almost impossible since the appellant had to provide two sureties of £20 each, a sum almost no workingman could be expected to possess, particularly when outside contributions were forbidden and punishable by a heavy fine. The high courts were in fact powerless to act, since overturning the magistrate's verdict by certiorari was expressly forbidden by the statute.

Although the harshness and doubtful constitutionality of the Combination Acts did arouse some opposition among the more liberal members of Parliament, the amendment introduced the following year (39 & 40 Geo. 3, cap. 106) afforded only marginal relief. Two magistrates, neither of whom could be a master in the trade affected, were required to sit instead of one, and there was some tightening of the section dealing with motive, "wilfully and maliciously" being substituted for "directly and indirectly." In

---

standards were menaced" by the industrial revolution. G. D. H. Cole, *A Short History of the British Working Class Movement, 1789–1947* (London: Allen & Unwin, 1948), p. 37.

[32] "Pitt abolished the old practice of billeting troops in the homes of the people, where they might easily become contaminated with Radical doctrines. Instead, he built barracks at strategic points throughout the country and used his concentrated military force to overawe the people." Ibid., p. 38.

addition, a new arbitration clause was introduced: in case of disputes over wages or hours, each party could appoint an arbitrator to represent it. Should the two arbitrators fail to agree, either party could request them to submit the points of contention to a justice of the peace, whose decision was final.

It should be pointed out that, at least in principle, combinations of factory owners to fix wages and hours were just as illegal as labor's attempts to organize in order to obtain better treatment at the hands of employers. But there was never any attempt to enforce the Combination Acts against the masters. They, as well as members of Parliament, believed that the primary purpose of the acts was to forestall the spread of radicalism from across the Channel. The good of the country was equated with the interests of the property owners, and the role of government was to ensure an adequate supply of cheap labor, regardless of the means employed or the hardships caused.[33] Unlike the concept of laissez-faire, which implied governmental neutrality in the struggle between labor and capital, or at most the enforcement of the "rules of the game," the harsh effects of eighteenth-century regulatory practices are nowhere more evident than in the willingness of public authorities to assume the role of suppliers of labor to the factories. In spite of their pious-sounding statements regarding the need to give a moral upbringing to children under public guardianship and teach them a trade, the parish commissioners, particularly in London, were eager to consign their charges to the factory owners from an early age. Working between twelve and fifteen hours a day in wretched conditions, often mistreated, given a trifling wage that varied from food and lodging alone to a fraction of an adult's wage, they pro-

[33] "The Combination Acts lasted for a quarter of a century, and during that time the work people were at the mercy of their masters . . . . Under cover of these laws, magistrates had threatened workmen with imprisonment or service in the fleet as alternatives to accepting the wages their masters chose to offer them. . . .

"The Combination Acts forbade combinations among masters as well as among men, but in this respect they were a dead letter. The masters were not obliged, like their men, to give evidence against each other. . . . Some of the masters were not aware they came under the laws at all, and the magistrates turned a blind eye on the most public and overt acts of employers. There was indeed no concealment of the truth that the masters acted habitually and openly as if the laws had placed no restraint on their freedom for reducing wages." John L. and Barbara Hammond, *The Town Labourer* (London: Longmans, Green, 1917), pp. 129 ff.

vided both a welcome source of labor for the factories and a means for the parishes to reduce their expenses.[34]

Even the early legislation supposedly intended to protect apprentices is another glaring example of governmental noninterference in a situation that presented obvious economic advantages to the factory owners.[35] The only protection afforded under the Act of 1747 (20 Geo. 2, cap. 19), for instance, was the provision that an apprentice could appeal to the local magistrate against his master's ill-treatment and, if he could prove his case, obtain a discharge. The amendment of 1792 to this act (32 Geo. 3, cap. 57) stipulated that a successful complaint might entail a fine of £10 against the master. Although it is not known how many apprentices availed themselves of this recourse, the number must not have been very large, considering that local magistrates were masters on their own or had similar vested interests.

It is necessary to wait until the 1784 epidemic of "putrid fever" in the Radcliffe mills, near Manchester, to find an awakening of conscience on the part of some officials. The Manchester magistrates, for example, resolved that they would not sanction the indenture of parish apprentices to cotton mills that worked them over ten hours a day, and this example was followed by other North Counties magistrates. London, where no such resolution was passed, remained the main supplier of child labor. Public interest in the

---

[34] "The manufacturers were anxious [to obtain child labor], and in one case, at least, a Lancashire millowner agreed with a London parish to take one idiot with every twenty sound children supplied. The [public] guardians had thus found a system of transportation for poor children which was cheaper and more effective than the transportation system to the colonies that had brought relief to the London prisons." Ibid., p. 145.

Mantoux points out that "for certain processes the small size of the children made them the best aid to the machines. They were preferred, too, for other and more conclusive reasons. Their weakness made them docile, and they were more easily reduced to a state of passive obedience than grown men." *Industrial Revolution*, p. 420.

[35] The development of many of the early textile mills, dependent for their location upon the availability of waterpower, may not have been possible without the transportation of children in large numbers from urban parishes. "Especially during the first period of machine industry, when factories were built outside and often far from the towns, manufacturers would have found it impossible to recruit the labour they needed from the immediate neighborhood. . . . Lots of fifty, eighty, or a hundred children were supplied [by the Poor Law authorities] and sent like cattle to the factory, where they remained imprisoned for many years." Mantoux, *Industrial Revolution*, p. 420.

welfare of working children was largely local and sporadic until the turn of the century.

The Health and Morals of Apprentices Act of 1802 (42 Geo. 3, cap. 73) was introduced by Sir Robert Peel, himself an important Lancashire factory owner who had employed over a thousand children at one time in his own workshops. The main features of the act, which applied only to parish apprentices, were that children should not work more than twelve hours a day or before six A.M. or after nine P.M.; that the locales should be kept "clean and airy"; and that part of the working day should be given to basic schooling and religious instruction. In addition, certain minimum standards were prescribed for living quarters: boys and girls were to sleep in separate rooms and no more than two to a bed. Enforcement of these clauses was entrusted to two "visitors," a justice and a clergyman, to be appointed at quarter sessions.

Although this first factory act did not apply to the thousands of "free labor" children, the sons and daughters of the laboring classes, it evoked angry responses from the masters:

From Manchester, Glasgow, Preston, Leeds, Keighley, Tutbury, and Holywell came protests from mill owners, declaring the Act to be "prejudicial to the Cotton Trade," and also "impracticable." . . . They pointed out that the cotton trade cannot go on unless about one-sixth of the apprentices can be worked at night. "Free labourers cannot be obtained to perform the night work, but upon very disadvantageous terms to the manufacturers." . . . "No doubt education is desirable" . . . but to take an hour or two from the twelve working hours "would amount to a surrender of all the profits of the establishment."[36]

The government's interference with labor and its vigorous support of the factory owners' efforts to keep costs down were matched by its willingness to lend public powers for private speculation, particularly in the construction of new transportation routes. The eighteenth-century "boom" in canals and turnpikes, whose effects on urbanization I mentioned earlier, required the support of government. Canals and turnpikes were usually initiated and financed by joint-stock companies composed of local businessmen who recognized the opportunities for profit they offered. However, each such venture had to be authorized by an act of Parliament, which was

[36] J. L. and B. Hammond, *The Town Labourer*, pp. 152–153. Their quotes are from testimonies of the mill owners during the parliamentary debate on the act (February 11, 14, 22, 25, 1803).

necessary not only to form a joint-stock company but to obtain the power of eminent domain to acquire land for the proposed route. The intentions of Parliament were clearly to encourage private investment in order to give the country an adequate communications network at little or no cost to the public purse. Privately owned canals and turnpikes were treated alike: they were open to all upon payment of tolls, which were to be commensurate with the costs of construction and maintenance and ensure an "equitable" profit. In order to prevent a monopolistic differential in carrying charges, canal companies were forbidden to act as public carriers themselves. The toll rates were authorized by Parliament after an inquiry into the economics of the project.

It is not surprising that this piecemeal approach to the transportation problems of a rapidly developing nation was less than satisfactory. The adequacy of canals and highways became dependent upon the foresight and profit expectations of investors; advantageous routes in the North and the Midlands were fought over and duplicate facilities provided, while large sections of the country were badly served. As in the cases of wages, prices, and working conditions, government was unwilling to interfere with vested interests, and canal and turnpike companies were quickly able to establish preferential toll rates, escape audit, and extend their activities beyond their statutory limitations. Routes were closed and opened almost at will, with total disregard for local needs or, indeed, for any purpose other than the profits of the companies themselves.[37] Although government support contributed immensely to the development of early industries and the localization of particular industrial activities, the absence of adequate public supervision al-

---

[37] "Complaints were made about the delays and difficulties of transshipment from one canal system to another. There were criticisms of the uncertainty, partiality and inconsistency of carrier's charges. There were no published lists of rates or classes of goods and detailed information about rates and charges was difficult to obtain. Collusion among carriers over rates was far from uncommon and the monopolistic position of some undertakings was a source of public resentment. A letter published in 1825 accused the Bridgewater Canal trustees of charging double the amount of the authorized tolls and of having acquired all the available land and warehouses along the canal banks at Manchester, thus creating 'the most odious and unjust monopoly known to the trade of this country.' . . . The high dividends of some canal undertakings were almost certainly due to monopolistic exploitation and to inadequate public supervision of rates and charge." Savage, *An Economic History of Transport*, pp. 23–24.

lowed local fluctuations in the supply and cost of goods to continue uncontrolled.

The lack of a comprehensive public approach to the regulation and channeling of the new forces brought about by industrialization was symptomatic of all government activities of the time, whether at the national or local level. Where specific policies were formulated to cope with particular problems—transportation companies, the relief of the poor, the control of labor, rising prices—they were not inspired by governmental concern for the common welfare but were the result of demands made by pressure groups for specific powers under a local act. The failure of the national government to legislate in the face of a rapidly evolving situation was due not to its inability to act but to the fact that its members were of a rich landowning minority, largely unconcerned with the problems of industrialization. The absence of adequate channels of communication between the people at large and the oligarchical elite sitting in Parliament insulated government from the pressures of urbanization and made it slow to take appropriate action with regard to the exploitation of the laboring class by the factory owners, child labor, and the wretched conditions in the new factory districts. The following chapters on Liverpool and Manchester will show that a similar narrowness of representation was largely the cause of public indifference to the living conditions of the majority of the population in these two cities.

CHAPTER THREE

The Municipal Borough of Liverpool

THE RISE OF THE PORT

Located at the mouth of the River Mersey, the boundary between Cheshire and Lancashire, Liverpool was created a royal borough by letters patent given by King John on August 28, 1207. During the Middle Ages, Liverpool was engaged predominately in the Irish trade; it also served as a troop assembly and supply port for the Welsh and Scottish campaigns of Edward I and for the French and Irish wars of Edward III. But it was still a town of little importance, even by the standards of the time: Liverpool's medieval population was in the hundreds and did not reach a thousand until late in the seventeenth century,[1] because its port was exposed to northwesterly gales and was, therefore, a less favorable anchorage than Chester, some twenty miles away at the head of the River Dee.

It was not until deep-sea ships greatly increased in draught and, although this was a negative rather than a positive factor, not until the natural difficulty of the Dee to flush its estuary on the ebb tide caused silting beyond the limits of tolerance, that Liverpool became the first port of the Lancashire-Cheshire Plain.[2]

The Tudor economic revival saw the establishment of close links between Liverpool and the developing North Counties industries. Coal, iron, copper, Manchester "mixed fabrics," and York-

---

[1] Richard Lawton, "Genesis of Population," in *A Scientific Survey of Merseyside,* ed. Wilfred Smith (Liverpool: Liverpool University Press, 1953), p. 120.

[2] Wilfred Smith, "Merseyside and the Merseyside District," in ibid., p. 11.

shire woolens were exported to Ireland in exchange for Irish linen, leather and skins, salt herring, and salt beef. Spices and other foreign luxuries shipped to Liverpool were reexported to other English ports as well as abroad. Although small handicraft industries (mainly tailoring and weaving) were well established in Liverpool by the end of the reign of Elizabeth I, agriculture rather than commerce was still the dominant activity in western Lancashire. Following the Stuart Restoration, Liverpool became a center of colonial trade, mainly as a result of the growth of French naval power, which threatened England's large southern ports. Of particular importance were the tobacco trade with Virginia and the sugar trade with the West Indies, which, together with the export of salt, accounted for much of Liverpool's prosperity in the eighteenth century. By 1700, the customs collections of the port amounted to over £50,000, or one-third of the country's total customs revenue.[3] By 1702, Liverpool was England's third port in terms of tonnage handled and number of seamen.[4]

By the middle of the eighteenth century, Liverpool had transformed itself from a slumbering provincial town into one of England's most prosperous cities. Construction of a new dock, an enclosed basin with 652 yards of quay at the junction of the Old Pool and the river, was authorized in 1709 (8 Ann, cap. 12). Completed in 1715, it was the first English "wet dock" reclaimed from the sea, equipped with floodgates to keep the ships afloat at low tide; it was considered "among the most useful works, and the principal object of curiosity in the town."[5] A drydock was started the following year, and an additional one, to the south, was authorized in 1738 (11 Geo. 2, cap. 32) and completed in 1753, giving the port 1600 yards of quay. This allowed the simultaneous handling of about 12,000 tons of shipping, "all with their broad sides to the quay at one time, besides sufficient space in the middle of the Docks for ships unemployed."[6]

[3] Frederick James Routledge, "History of Liverpool to 1700," in ibid., p. 106.

[4] London: 84,000 tons and 10,065 seamen. Bristol: 17,325 tons and 2359 seamen. Liverpool: 8619 tons and 1101 seamen. Thomas Baines, *History of the Commerce and Town of Liverpool* (London: Longman, Brown, Green and Longmans, 1852), p. 395.

[5] William Enfield, *An Essay towards the History of Liverpool* (London: J. Johnson, 1774), p. 59.

[6] Ibid., p. 60.

The improvement of port facilities was accompanied by the improvement of communications with the hinterland, particularly the growing industrial area around Manchester. No fewer than seven acts were passed between 1720 and 1750 to deepen existing watercourses and to construct roads.[7] Yet, even after this extensive effort to improve overland communications, Liverpool, like many other provincial towns, was still isolated to an extent that is hard to grasp today. Travel was rare, difficult and costly: there were no scheduled stagecoaches connecting Liverpool to other towns, the usual mode of travel was horseback for gentlemen and hired carriages for ladies, and the dangers of highwaymen made it common to travel in caravans. The journey from London to Liverpool took four days, and the shipment of goods by wagon was considerably slower, taking ten days in summer and eleven in winter. The semi-weekly Warrington Flying Stage Coach was the first scheduled passenger service and took three days to carry passengers to London in 1757.[8]

Figure 7 illustrates the rapid and continuous rise of Liverpool as a major port during the eighteenth century. The tonnage of vessels trading out of Liverpool doubled between 1710 and 1750 and at intervals of approximately twenty years between 1750 and 1810. This increase took place in the midst of a series of wars, including Napoleon's Continental Blockade, which, although it did not succeed in crippling England's economy, did force a marked reorientation of her export trade to the Mediterranean, South America, and to her growing colonial empire. The increase in Liverpool's population paralleled its growth as a port: between 1710 and 1750

---

[7] The Douglas Navigation Act (6 Geo. 1, cap. 28, 1720) made the river Douglas navigable from the Wigan coalfields to the river Ribble and the sea, twenty-five miles north of Liverpool. The Weaver Navigation Act (7 Geo. 1, cap. 10, 1720) made the river navigable from the Mersey to Northwich, opening the Cheshire salt mines to water transportation. The Mersey and Irwell Navigation Act (7 Geo. 1, cap. 15, 1720) allowed barges to go as far as Manchester. The Road from Liverpool to Prescot Act (12 Geo. 1, cap. 21, 1725) joined Liverpool to Warrington and the principal north-south coach route. The Second Weaver Navigation Act (7 Geo. 2, cap. 28, 1734) extended navigable waters to Nantwich. The Worsley-Brook Extension Act (10 Geo. 2, cap. 9, 1737) further improved water communications to Nantwich. The Road from Liverpool to Prescot and St. Helens Act (19 Geo. 2, cap. 19, 1746) completed the first period of road building within Liverpool's immediate zone of influence.

[8] T. Baines, *Liverpool*, pp. 418 ff.

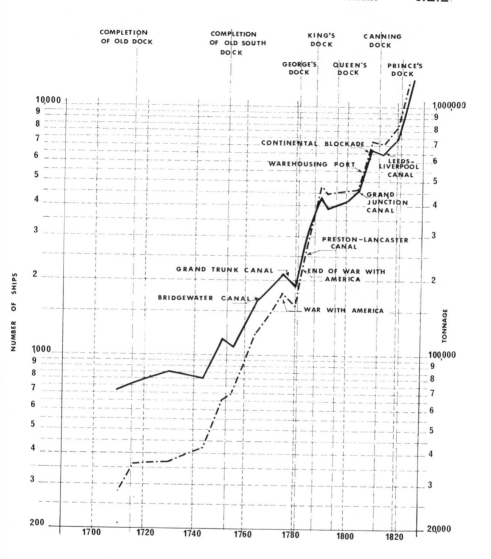

Figure 7. Number of Vessels Entering or Leaving the Port of Liverpool and Tonnage

it increased at least threefold; from then on and throughout the nineteenth century, it doubled every thirty years or so (see Figure 8).[9]

The commercial growth of Liverpool was the result of a far-sighted policy by its municipal government. Faced with the practical difficulties of beaching the larger ships that were coming into use both in coastal and in long-distance shipping and with the rising costs of unloading them by lighters, the town council was prompted by shipping interests to take direct action to protect Liverpool's trading position. Thomas Johnson and Richard Norris, the two members of Parliament for Liverpool, were instructed as early as 1709 to obtain the necessary legislation. The act, passed at the following session, created a special-purpose authority—the dock estate, composed of members of the corporation—to construct port facilities on municipal land and collect duties of 4d. per ton on all merchandise for twenty-one years. The corporation was authorized to borrow £6000 for this purpose.

When these terms proved insufficient, additional money was borrowed under an amending act (3 Geo. 1, cap. 1, 1717), which also extended the period of authorized rates to thirty-five years. The docking facilities were completed in 1720 and the approach works (buoys and landmarks) in 1736. The success of these first efforts, initially in terms of convenience and lower insurance rates and later in terms of increased activity,[10] prompted a succession of major port-improvement works. The institutionalization of the role of local government in ensuring the construction and maintenance of adequate port facilities took place in 1737. The Act of 11 Geo. 2,

[9] This phenomenal increase is true regardless of whether a "low" or a "high" estimate is taken of the eighteenth-century population. My own estimate, based upon local birth and death rates, may be somewhat on the high side, particularly when one attempts a reconciliation with Enfield's estimate for 1750. But other figures, which show peculiar decennial variations in the rate of growth, seem to indicate underestimates. Moreover, the population "take-off" would not have occurred until 1775 or later, according to Enfield, which leaves a quarter-century gap—obviously too wide—between the rapid increase in Liverpool's economic importance and its accompanying population growth.

[10] The average tonnage of vessels handled in the port of Liverpool went from 45.5 tons in 1720 to 50.1 tons in 1740 and 75 tons in 1760. By 1780, the end of the first construction phase, the average tonnage was 83 tons; by 1820, the end of the second phase, it had gone up to 110 tons. The relation between the ability of Liverpool to handle larger vessels and the port-development works undertaken by its corporation is shown in Figure 7.

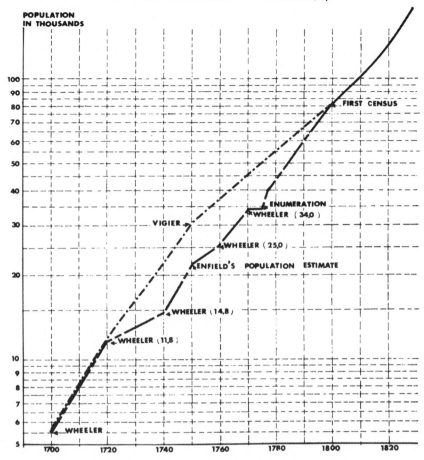

Figure 8. Estimate of Population of Liverpool

cap. 32, in addition to confirming the original dock rates and granting permission to expand current port facilities, established a board
of twelve commissioners to supervise the operations and finances
of the municipal dock estate. Four of the twelve commissioners
were appointed by "the Mayor, Aldermen, Bailiffs, and Common
Council of the said Borough," and the remaining eight by the shipping
interests of the town. Membership on this board was renewed
yearly. By 1760 the dock estates represented an investment on the
order of £ 100,000, inclusive of the works themselves and the land

donated by the corporation.[11] The revenues of the dock estate for that year were £2383.

The creation of a publicly owned, special-purpose authority such as the Liverpool dock estate to administer an enterprise in the general interest requires some explanation, since it seems a surprisingly modern concept for the time, akin to our own port, bridge, and turnpike authorities. In their exhaustive study of the development of English local government, Sidney and Beatrice Webb point out that the eighteenth century was a period of rising local independence, the revolution of 1688 having resulted in an explicit policy of nonintervention in local affairs on the part of the central government. A proliferation of small oligarchies had therefore become responsible for administering and maintaining the local customs, which were as much a part of the law of the land as were the King's laws. Each parish (the basic unit of local government) was governed by its own system of interrelationships inherited almost unchanged from the medieval "obligation to serve"; the relations among parishes, between parish and county, and between parish or county and the Crown were regulated by a complicated set of charters and uncodified agreements based upon custom. Interference by the central government manifested itself only through occasional and inconsistent parliamentary statutes.

The conservative climate engendered by this fragmented hierarchy of authority and responsibility was becoming increasingly inadequate in the face of the changes brought by industrialization. The obligation to serve had been devised primarily to maintain existing facilities—roads, common fields, drainage, and navigation ways—to enforce the King's peace, and to administer the Poor Laws, rather than to develop ways to deal with new conditions. The organizational structure itself was ill-suited to generating an imaginative interpretation of public responsibility. Parish offices were usually rotated yearly among members of the middle class; such work was unpaid and usually proved unpopular, since it took time away from private business pursuits. As a rule, the educated gentry or the wealthier merchants did their utmost to avoid public

11 The construction of the dock facilities themselves amounted to £20,000 for the Old Dock, the Dry Pier, and the Salthouse Dock. Henry Smithers, *Liverpool, Its Commerce, Statistics, and Institutions* . . . (Liverpool: Thomas Kaye, 1825), p. 174.

office, preferring to pay the fines levied for refusing to serve to giving local government the benefit of their theoretically more enlightened and comprehensive view of the world. Opportunity for illicit gains and neglect of public office, combined with honest but unenlightened performance by a tradition-oriented middle class, became characteristic of local government.

When it is remembered that . . . the public business of the Parish was becoming every day more complicated and difficult; that the mere number of the paupers was becoming overwhelming; that new buildings of diverse kinds were springing up on all sides; that paving, cleansing, lighting and watching were alike wanting; that the crowding together of tens of thousands of poverty-stricken persons was creating unspeakable nuisances; and that the amount of the rates levied on the inhabitants was at the time doubling and trebling, it will be easily understood why, in one district after another, the situation became intolerable.[12]

The remedy devised for this situation was the granting of special powers to existing public bodies or the creation of semi-independent, special-purpose authorities like the turnpike trusts and the navigation companies, which were empowered to deal with a specific aspect of the problem at hand. Since parliamentary approval was required, and the central government maintained its nonintervention policy in local affairs, the introduction of the necessary legislation was left to local initiative. The proliferation of "private" acts establishing statutory, special-purpose authorities can be explained, in part, by the dearth of educated, farsighted local officials. It became incumbent upon an aggressive, self-protecting middle class or upon enterprising noblemen, such as the Duke of Bridgewater, to take advantage of the opportunities that lay in providing badly needed public services through private companies duly authorized by act of Parliament. The Liverpool dock estate was unusual not because of its organizational structure as a special-purpose authority, nor because it was publicly rather than privately owned (since the Liverpool corporation was perhaps more representative of a private than a public body in its interest structure), but because it quickly became a self-perpetuating body, continually enlarging and diversifying the scope of its activity in response to changing conditions. In this sense, it was unlike the narrow-minded

[12] Sidney and Beatrice Webb, *Statutory Authorities for Special Purposes* (Hamden, Conn.: Archon Books, 1963), pp. 363–364.

statutory authorities, whether public or private, whose primary goal was short-term profit, which were initiated without due regard to larger public interests and needs.[13]

In order to understand the eighteenth-century reliance upon local initiative to generate the administrative mechanisms demanded by the new forces of the time, it must be remembered that the relative isolation of even the larger provincial towns tended to perpetuate both their functional autonomy and their medieval rivalry. A case in point is the century-long struggle between the City of London and the Liverpool corporation over the latter's insistence upon collecting town dues from London freemen. The town dues, an excise tax collected on all goods imported to, or exported from, a town by nonfreemen, formed an important part of municipal revenues. They comprised about 20 percent of Liverpool's revenues in 1704, 25 percent in 1720, 22 percent in 1760, 34 percent in 1775, and 24 percent in 1800. It can readily be understood that the Liverpool corporation was anxious to retain its prerogative to tax, even when faced with increasing opposition from other boroughs, which rightly argued that the prevalence of a multiple tax system, particularly on goods in transshipment, was an impediment to the development of trade. As early as 1690, the Cheesemongers' Company of London questioned Liverpool's excise privileges and brought the case before the Court of Exchequer, which ruled against Liverpool in 1700. London immediately claimed that all its freemen were entitled to benefit from this exemption. In practice, they and other freemen did continue to pay dues, most of the merchants being "either ignorant of their rights or unwilling to put themselves to the trouble of enforcing them for the sake of saving very moderate payments; and throughout the greater part of the century the dues

---

[13] "When, in the course of the eighteenth century, it became necessary or convenient to invoke Parliamentary authority for the enforcement of new regulations, or the levying of new imposts, this usually took the form, not of a statute of general application, but of literally thousands of separate Local Acts. [They] were spontaneously initiated and contrived by little groups of the principal inhabitants of particular areas; they were debated and amended in the House of Commons, not by committees of impartial persons, but mainly by the representatives of the Boroughs and counties concerned; it was not until the very end of the eighteenth century that the 'Lords' Chairman' began to insist on inserting clauses safeguarding what he considered to be in the interest of the public at large." Ibid., pp. 352–353.

were paid without question."[14] Finally, in 1799, the matter was again brought before the Exchequer; this time the court's decision was in favor of Liverpool, thereby ensuring the continuance of an important source of revenue.

The parochial and egotistic self-reliance that governed inter-town relations during the eighteenth century was paralleled by the proliferation of interest groups within the towns themselves. Prior to the population explosion caused by the rural in-migration that started during the second quarter of the century, the population of a town such as Liverpool was divided into two fairly homogeneous groups: freemen and nonfreemen. This division still carried most of the medieval privileges that one would normally associate with it: only freemen could participate in urban government (electing the mayor and bailiffs), and they enjoyed a virtual monopoly on trade and artifacts. But the freedom of the town was liberally granted to "foreigners" upon the payment of a fee, and a majority of Liverpool's adult males were freemen at the beginning of the eighteenth century. The influx of new residents, some of whom were eager to engage in commerce and industry, made it increasingly impractical to restrict trading to freemen, since the consequences of this policy were either an undesirable increase in freemen, should the freedom of the town continue to be granted liberally, or an artificial and equally undesirable curtailment of the town's economic life. The choice between giving up the traditional oligarchic pattern of government and furthering economic growth was resolved at first by the institution of "quarterage," an annual payment for permission to reside in the town and to carry on a trade, and later by granting a freedom for life that conveyed the commercial but not the political rights of freemen.

The increasing importance of this new class of "townsmen," both in terms of numbers and in terms of their contribution to the economic and intellectual life of Liverpool, was not recognized officially until passage of the Municipal Reform Act of 1835. Earlier, such townsmen had been devoid of any political influence at the local level:

[This] was the case of a large proportion of the merchants and ship-owners who were making the prosperity of the town, while among the

14 J. Ramsay Muir and Edith M. Platt, *A History of Municipal Government in Liverpool* (Liverpool: Liverpool University Press, 1906), p. 124.

freemen admitted by birth or apprenticeship were included many of the riff-raff of the town, whose votes were so openly purchasable at elections that even the unreformed Parliament in 1831 was on the point of disfranchising the borough for gross corruption.[15]

Much of the political struggle that took place in the second half of the eighteenth century, and in the nineteenth until the time of the Municipal Reform Bill, was not only between the townsmen, intent on obtaining political recognition, and the council, equally intent on defending the privileges and franchise of freemen, but also between the freemen and the council. Under the Charter of 1695, the powers of the assembly of freemen were vested in a common council of forty-one "honest and discreet men of the Burgesses," elected for life, from whose numbers a mayor and two bailiffs were chosen annually on St. Luke's Day. Although elected by the assembly of freemen, and thus presumably responsive to their wishes, the mayor and bailiffs were little more than the instruments of the council, in which all the governing powers of the borough were vested. Upon numerous occasions the freemen and the mayor attempted to bypass the authority of the council by taking advantage of a clause of the charter specifying that no legitimate meeting of the council could take place without the mayor and one bailiff. The ambiguous wording of clause 39 of the charter[16] provided the legal basis for several short-lived attempts to restore the authority of the freemen.

A small group of traditional vested interests determined to monopolize power was the normal pattern of urban government in eighteenth-century England, and the closed, self-perpetuating oligarchy of the Liverpool common council was fraught with the dangers of extreme conservatism and corruption. But unlike their counterparts in rural parishes, whether these remained agricultural or were slowly transformed by industrialization, the urban corporate oligarchies did represent a relatively broad pattern of interests and values that partially justified their insistence on governing

---

15 Ibid., pp. 121–122.

16 Clause 39 empowered the mayor, one of the bailiffs, and any twenty-five freemen to act as a common council. It is to be presumed that the intention of this clause was to provide an emergency mechanism in case the common council was unable to meet, although no specified mention is made of the particular circumstances that would bring this clause into effect. Conversely, there is no mention that it could not be invoked against the common council.

unchallenged. The merchants, from whose ranks councilmen, bailiffs, and mayors were elected, were interested not only in preserving their privileges but also in ensuring the enlargement of their mercantile activities in an increasingly competitive situation. Circumstances forced them to broaden their outlook as they became dependent upon long-distance commerce for their livelihood. Thus, the traditional competition between Chester and Liverpool for the Irish market was substantially responsible for the determined efforts of the Liverpool corporation to improve its port facilities; similarly, the Act of 1732 "to recover and preserve the navigation of the River Dee," presented by Chester in an effort to regain its former commercial prominence, provided Liverpool with the incentive for buoying and lighting the Mersey estuary and finally eliminating Chester as a serious competitor.

The immediate financial benefits derived from its first ventures into fields that had hitherto been considered outside normal "public" interference encouraged the Liverpool corporation to extend its activities even further. Its forty-one aldermen, recruited by co-option from within the old mercantile middle class, became concerned not only with improvements directly beneficial to their own commercial aspirations but with more general and costly improvements of an aesthetic nature as well. It is this spirit of concern for the public good that prompted the Webbs, usually so rightly critical of the performance of eighteenth-century local governments, to say that

the greatest of all provincial municipalities, that of Liverpool, whilst maintaining its rigidly exclusive oligarchy, showed itself, generation after generation, markedly superior in energy, dignity, integrity and public spirit to any other Municipal Corporation in the land, not excluding the "ratepayers" democracy of the city of London itself.[17]

COMMERCIAL GROWTH AND THE NEED FOR URBAN SERVICES

A contemporary account gives the following description of Liverpool in 1760:

[The town] seems to be nearly as broad as it is long. The streets are narrow, but tolerably well built; the place is populous, though inferior in that respect to Bristol. Some of the houses are faced with stone and

[17] S. and B. Webb, *Statutory Authorities for Special Purposes*, p. 378.

elegantly finished. The Exchange is a handsome structure of gray stone, supported by arches, and built at great expense under the inspection of Messrs. Wood, the father and son, to whose correct taste and great genius Bath owes some of her finest ornaments and most useful improvements. In the upper part of the Exchange are noble apartments wherein the Corporation transacts public business.[18]

After describing the new port facilities and the surrounding countryside and lamenting the poor state of the roads, the observer turned his attention to the economic and social life of the town:

Though few of the merchants have more education than befits a counting-house, they are genteel in their address. They are hospitable, very friendly to strangers, even those of whom they have the least knowledge. Their tables are plenteously furnished, and their viands well served up; their rum is excellent, of which they consume large quantities in punch made when the West India fleet come in mostly with lime, which are very cooling, and afford a delicious flavour. I need not inform your lordship that the principal exports of Liverpool are all kinds of woollen and worsted goods, with other manufactures of Manchester, and Sheffield, and Birmingham wares, etc. These they barter on the Coast of Guinea, for slaves, gold-dust, and elephants' teeth. The slaves they dispose of at Jamaica, Barbadoes, and the other West Indian islands, for rum and sugar, for which they are sure of a quick sale at home. This port is admirably well situated for trade, being almost central in the channel so that, in war-time, by coming north-about, their ships have a good chance for escaping the many privateers belonging to the enemy which cruize to the southward. Thus, their neighbours; and since I have been here, I have seen enter the port, in one morning, seven West India ships, whereof five were not insured.[19]

This image of a prosperous provincial society is substantiated by an investigation of the town's physical growth. Two principal characteristics are particularly worth mentioning: the marked increase in the urbanized area and the shift in the town's center of gravity from its medieval location to the area surrounding the new port facilities to the south. The combination of these two factors made the locational specialization of functions that is characteristic of the industrial city increasingly perceptible. Figure 9 summarizes the expansion of Liverpool between 1715 and 1820. Figure 10 is a generalization of the functional character of streets by major

[18] Letter from Samuel Derrick, Esq., to the Earl of Cork. Quoted in T. Baines, *History of Liverpool*, pp. 425 ff.

[19] Ibid.

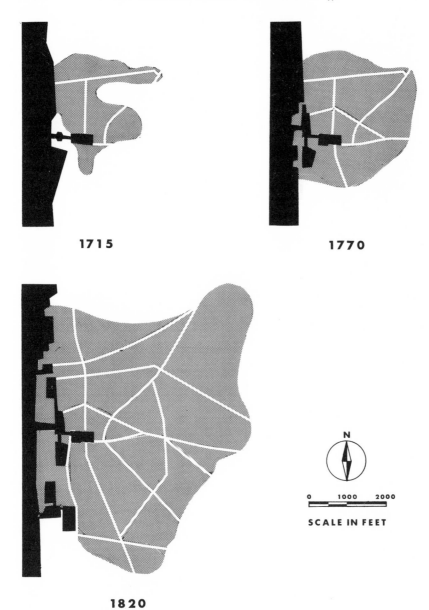

1715

1770

1820

N

0   1000   2000
SCALE IN FEET

Figure 9. Expansion of Liverpool, 1715–1820

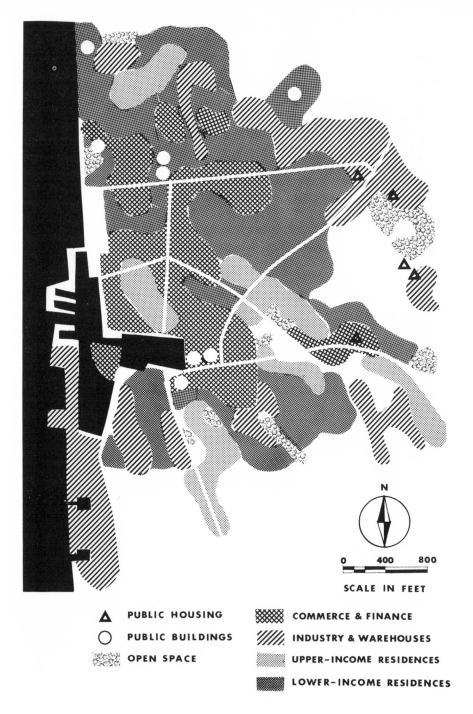

N

| 0 | 400 | 800 |

SCALE IN FEET

▲ PUBLIC HOUSING   ░░░ COMMERCE & FINANCE

◯ PUBLIC BUILDINGS   ▨ INDUSTRY & WAREHOUSES

░ OPEN SPACE   ░ UPPER-INCOME RESIDENCES

                    ▉ LOWER-INCOME RESIDENCES

Figure 10. Land-Use Structure of Liverpool in the 1770s

economic activity; it also shows the location of upper-income housing. It can readily be seen that the impact of the publicly financed port improvements was reflected not only in commercial growth, shown by the increase in tonnage of vessels and in town dues mentioned earlier, but in the proliferation of establishments concerned with the manufacturing, storing, and wholesaling of goods, as well as in the development of new upper-income residential quarters and of public and semipublic institutions. With a population between 30,000 and 35,000, the Liverpool of the 1760s had almost doubled its built-up area in forty years.

Prior to the southward and eastward expansion of the town, which resulted from the transformation of the Old Pool into a wet dock, the town center was located on Castle Street: most of the town's administrative and commercial functions were concentrated within less than three hundred yards, interspersed by the homes of the burgesses. Houses, shops, workshops, warehouses, and three churches occupied the approximately forty-acre area that was Liverpool proper, between the river and John Street. Beyond, and within a few minutes' walk from City Hall, were gardens, open fields, ropewalks for the shipbuilding industry, and a few glass and pottery works. The opening of the Old Dock in 1715 generated the beginning of the southward expansion. A new customs house was constructed on the east side of the dock, the other two sides being occupied principally with wholesale establishments, warehouses, and some retail shops. The expansion of the docks in the fifties prompted a further concentration of activities concerned with shipping (shipbuilding yards, sugar refineries, and warehouses) along the shores, to the north and south of the docks. Other new industries located on the periphery of the preindustrial town:

Half-a-score of whirling windmills busily at work gave a picturesque aspect to the rising town . . . . Rope-making was very actively carried on in long rope yards . . . . There were one or two iron foundries. Liverpool had come to be known for the excellence of her watches . . . . The principal potteries were in Dale Street and Shaw's Brow and later in Islington and other places.[20]

The commercial and business center remained clustered around the Town Hall in the old town. Water Street, Castle and High

[20] J. Ramsay Muir, *A History of Liverpool* (London: Williams and Norgate, 1907), pp. 180–181.

Streets, and the bottom half of Dale Street were lined with shops and professional offices; four semiweekly markets were held in the old town, a general market at Castle Ditch, fish markets in Pool Lane and at the old Fish House in Chapel Street, and a butchers' and general market in High Street. That the north end of Castle Street, near the Town Hall, was still used to exhibit samples of wheat to be sold at wholesale illustrates further the high incidence of the use of streets for commercial activities, a remnant of medieval town life. The area was also used as a meeting place for merchants.[21] Indeed, the appearance of Liverpool until the end of the eighteenth century must have presented a series of striking contrasts: the expanding port at the south end of the town; the peripheral industries growing in the midst of suburban gardens; and the congested old town with its "narrow, irregular, and ill-built streets," its buildings "of dingy brick," presenting to the eye "little or nothing calculated to excite admiration or interest."[22] It can be presumed that these conditions were more than incidental to the development of new high-income residential districts on the southeastern fringes of the town, along the road to Toxteth Park, in Cliveland's Square and Pitt Street, at the eastern end of Ranelagh Street, and in Williamson Square. But the more conservative merchants were still willing to live above their shops and warehouses, undisturbed by close proximity to the lower classes, many of whose pleasures they did not disdain to share. Cultural opportunities were few. The Old Theatre in Drury Lane (replaced in 1772 by a new building on Williamson Square), occasional concerts and fireworks displays in the Ranelagh Gardens, the dinners and dances offered by the mayor and the corporation in the Town Hall: these were the

---

21 "[The Town Hall] was, in fact, to have been the public exchange, but it was never used for that purpose, and [the merchants] were accustomed to meet on High Change, at the North End of Castle Street, opposite Mr. Gore's shop." Richard Brooke, *Liverpool . . . , 1775–1800* (Liverpool: J. R. Smith, 1853), p. 73.

22 Ibid., p. 118. "When Samuel Curwen, an American loyalist exile, visited Liverpool in 1780, he found the 'streets long, narrow, crooked, and dirty. . . . We scarcely saw a well-dressed person. . . . The whole complexion of the place was nautical, and so infinitely below all our expectations that naught but the thoughts of the few hours we had to pass here rendered it tolerable.' The principal streets before 1786 were not more than six yards wide, and the paving was exceedingly rough, 'the remark of all strangers.'" Muir, *A History of Liverpool*, pp. 270–271.

Custom House and Old Dock
Courtesy of Henry Young and Sons, Liverpool

Water Street
Courtesy of Henry Young and Sons, Liverpool

Dale Street
Courtesy of Henry Young and Sons, Liverpool

High Street
Courtesy of Henry Young and Sons, Liverpool

Shaw's Brow

Courtesy of Henry Young and Sons, Liverpool

sum of Liverpool's social life. Bowling, dogfights, cockfights, and bull baiting were favorite sports among rich and poor alike, and the public houses provided unrivaled opportunities for social inter-course among all classes of society at a time when "the habits of the age sanctioned persons of respectability in frequently passing their evenings in coffee-houses and taverns."[23]

The industrial city, with its concomitant crowding of the poor into squalid quarters, was acquiring a unique reputation as a place where drunkenness and licentiousness were not only tolerated but allowed to thrive unchecked. Whether out of greed for the licens-ing fees or simply from slackness, the Liverpool magistrates seemed quite willing to allow the existence of an extraordinary number of barrooms and ginshops, which found eager patrons among the poor seeking momentary solace from the harshness of their lives.

In 1795, a cynical observer, who has left us an invaluable picture of the Liverpool of his day, calculated that every seventh house in the town was open for the sale of liquor: "the devotion of the lower order of the people . . . to their Bacchanalian orgies is such as to give employment to thirty-seven large and extensive ale breweries," while rum was brought very cheaply and in large quantities from the West Indies. So serious was the licensing problem that even the Town Council, not usu-ally, a reforming body, thought it necessary in 1772 to pass a resolution urging the magistrates to reduce the number of public houses, especially round the docks, and pointing out "the wickedness and licentiousness which were due to them."[24]

In fact, there was little attempt to regulate or control any aspect of the town's daily life. No bylaws existed to ensure minimum en-vironmental or construction standards for the new housing that was being erected for the growing urban population. Streets were poorly paved and refuse collected infrequently. Police protection was nonexistent by day and restricted at night to a corps of one hundred and twenty watchmen. Taking into account the crowded condition of the town, it is no surprise that "the streets of Liverpool were constantly the scenes of riots and open fights, especially in the days of the press-gang; at night they were very unsafe."[25]

The apparent lack of concern for urban conditions originated in the structure of municipal government. The succession of royal

[23] Brooke, *Liverpool . . . , 1775–1800*, p. 164.
[24] Muir, *A History of Liverpool*, p. 273.
[25] Ibid.

charters and letters patent that added to, institutionalized, or abrogated parts of the body of local custom that forms English common law never attempted to define the responsibilities of local
government. They dealt instead with specific grievances, in response to petitions from the inhabitants. In particular, municipal
charters tended to transfer the medieval manorial prerogatives to
municipal corporations, which claimed the right to amend their own
constitutions without reference to Parliament. Although the seventeenth- and eighteenth-century charters granted to Liverpool
repeatedly refer to "public welfare," "better government," "peace
and tranquility," and local "franchises and liberties," the town
council itself never described its function as other than "the management of the corporate estate" on behalf of its fellow townsmen.[26]
This concept of local government as administrator and trustee of
the corporate estate, combined with its oligarchical character, could
only limit initiative in all but the few areas that were of particular
interest to the council as a group of individuals, rather than as a
corporate body. The investment of public funds in the development
of port facilities is a particularly good example of the use of public
power and resources by aldermen-merchants in an enterprise that
would benefit them first as merchants, and only second as aldermen
with a sense of civic responsibility and pride in a growing town.
However, public concern with the welfare of the poor or even public interest in the aesthetic character of the environment were
deemed somewhat beyond the responsibilities of the town council.

Common problems of maintenance were delegated to special-
purpose authorities, since the council was content to limit its activities to the protection of its vested interests and the administration
of justice. (The justices sitting on criminal cases at the quarter sessions were recruited from among the aldermen; the Court of Passage, which dealt with lesser offenses and civil actions, was
composed of the mayor and bailiffs.) With the exception of the
council's direct responsibility for the paving and sewerage of the
"ancient streets of the borough," the normal pursuits that we have
come to associate with municipal government were left to the initiative of the ratepayers of the town, or to private enterprise. For
example, when faced with the problem of ensuring an adequate

26 Brian D. White, *A History of the Corporation of Liverpool, 1835–1914*
(Liverpool: Liverpool University Press, 1951), p. 10.

water supply at a time when demand was caused not only by a growing population but by the needs of such important industries as the sugar refineries, the council restricted its intervention to lengthy negotiations with private individuals regarding the feasibility and terms of several abortive schemes to pipe water into the town. In the meantime, water continued to be brought in by carts and sold privately to householders and industry alike.[27] The removal of refuse from the streets was undertaken twice a week by a private contractor "who shall have the muck for his pains and two or three guineas a year," the inhabitants being required in accordance with the bylaws to "clean their respective streets."[28] Similarly, street lighting was a cooperative venture, with the corporation willing to provide and install street lights "for such persons as will engage to light and maintain the same at their own charge."[29] In 1748, public supervision of these *ad hoc* cooperative ventures was vested in a special body, the Commissioners of Watching, Lighting, and Cleansing, which comprised all the aldermen as *ex officio* members and eighteen householders elected by the ratepayers (21 Geo. 2, cap. 24).

It should be pointed out that shortage of funds was not the reason for the lack of municipal enterprise in maintaining and improving public facilities. It is to the council's credit that, through careful management, the corporation's accounts balanced or even showed a profit throughout the eighteenth century, in spite of substantial capital expenditures in the development of the dock facilities. Even with a growing debt, amounting to over £453,000 by the end of the century, the Liverpool corporation was never hard pressed to borrow funds in an emergency. During the panic of 1793, for example, the credit of the corporation was sufficient to enable it to borrow, at short notice, close to £100,000 on negotiable notes, in order to assist the merchants of the town. Corporate revenues depended in large part upon such traditional sources as the town dues, rents on the corporate estates, and the dock rates, which together amounted to over 80 percent of revenues. Although no

[27] In 1751, the going price for bulk delivery for industrial uses was 9d. for a cask of about one hundred imperial gallons. George Chandler, *Liverpool* (London: B. T. Batsford, 1957), p. 332.

[28] James A. Picton, *City of Liverpool: Municipal Archives and Records . . . Extract* (Liverpool: Gilbert G. Walmsley, 1886), p. 153.

[29] Ibid., p. 154.

new source of revenue was added until the Municipal Reform Act of 1835, the level of commercial activity was sufficient to ensure a rapidly growing income. Whenever additional contributions were required of the ratepayers (usually to support the activities of a new body of commissioners or to pave and maintain the streets beyond the Old Borough), it was customary to engage the Poor Law authorities to collect special rates that were earmarked for a special purpose.

Relief of the poor was vested in the parish churchwardens and in a special board of overseers elected annually by the parishioners at the Easter vestry meeting. The annual needs of the parish were established at that time and the parishioners assessed *pro rata* to pay for the upkeep of the churches, the salaries of the ministers and churchwardens, and the relief of the poor. Until 1724, the rate tended to vary from year to year, according to conditions in the town and the elected overseers' interest in the needs of the destitute.[30] But it was becoming clear that the growth of Liverpool's population was making it increasingly difficult to administer relief in this casual, traditional way. A fixed tax of 6d. on the pound was now levied on houses and quickly increased to 1s. in 1732. Part of the proceeds were used to build and operate the first of a series of workhouses where the poor could be lodged and given gainful employment, in order to reduce the burden of their support. Initially, these measures were successful, but the increase in the population during the second half of the century soon required additional levies, as the workhouse itself proved too small and "outdoor relief" (relief to those not residing in the workhouse) had to be resumed. By the mid-sixties, the rate of taxation had reached 2s. 6d. on the pound, of which less than half was attributable to the Poor Law.

The use of the Poor Law authorities to collect special taxes for purposes other than relief must have limited the parishioners' willingness to see their charitable deeds extended, although they were able to exercise more control over these activities than they could over those of the town council. For example, the fear that the over-

[30] In addition to weekly payments made to the "recognized poor belonging to Liverpool" and to foster parents, the overseers of the poor were not averse to helping deserving transients or to undertaking "unusual" expenditures, generally in the form of gifts of shoes and clothing to persons not on the relief rolls. See Chandler, *Liverpool*, pp. 389 ff.

seers of the poor might be guilty of administrative abuses led to the formation of an extralegal Select Committee, which supervised their expenditures and reported directly to the vestry, the parishioners' assembly. The delegation to the vestry of taxing powers that normally resided in the corporation was bound to increase its political influence. For while the various parliamentary acts that established special committees specified the maximum rate to be levied on their behalf, the vestry was under no obligation to levy the full rate, should it be disinclined to do so. Moreover, the abdication of municipal authority and responsibility in the important fields of maintaining adequate safety standards for the public at large and improving the town's physical facilities served to dramatize the narrow interests of the small oligarchy that held power through the town council.

The existence of the special committees and the growing importance of the vestry was in itself a sign that the closed Corporation, representing only the freemen, could no longer undertake the main functions of administration . . . . When, by restriction of the grant of freedom, the freemen had come to be in a small minority, it could no longer be pretended that their Council could justly be responsible for public order and public health, in which the non-freeman resident was equally concerned, for which he had to pay, and in the control of which he claimed to be represented. Hence, the result of the closed Corporation and freeman system had been to reduce on all sides the authority of the chief municipal body, and to begin that practice of establishing numerous and confusing separate governing bodies, each charged with distinct and small functions.[31]

The same lack of interest and inertia characterized the town council's approach to education and health. The town's only school, founded under Edward VI to provide a free education to the sons of the town's freemen, was allowed to fall into desuetude and was finally closed in 1802. Indeed, public education was of no concern to the Liverpool merchants. The provision of the most rudimentary forms of schooling had to wait until the religious revival of the 1780s, one of whose manifestations was the development of Sunday schools where children were taught reading and writing as well as the Scriptures. The costs of such education were borne by the parishioners. "The children were to go to school at one o'clock every Sunday and to be kept 'til evening comes on. They were to

[31] Muir and Platt, *Municipal Government in Liverpool*, p. 146.

be taken to church."[32] A somewhat higher level of education for the middle class of shopkeepers and artisans became available in 1789 with the founding of a private day school in Moorfields, which took in 200 boys and 120 girls for the modest fee of 1d. per week. Connected with the parish church, the school at Moorfields was the first attempt to provide an education for children whose families were not rich.[33] The sons of aldermen and other prosperous merchants were sent to public schools, which may explain their fathers' lack of interest in the local school system.

The growing willingness of individuals and groups to intervene in order to remedy the lacunae of municipal government is nowhere more evident than in the proliferation of the charitable institutions that were to become one of the redeeming features of the English industrial towns. One of the first of these was the Liverpool Blue Coat School, founded in 1708 by Bryan Blundell. A ship's captain and owner, Blundell made his fortune first by transporting the poor to the New World and later by the slave trade. Struck by the plight of homeless children wandering in the streets of the town, he bought a small building in School Lane, hired a master at £20 a year, and undertook to feed, clothe, and educate 50 children. Thanks to his efforts at raising money by private subscription (he provided one-tenth of his own annual income for support of the school), a larger building was constructed on a piece of ground donated by the corporation. By 1756, 100 children were being cared for, and his charity was well endowed, "commanding the interest and support of all that was respectable in Liverpool."[34]

In 1745, a drive to raise funds for a hospital was initiated among the leading citizens; £2248 7s. 11d. were raised, and in 1749 the

[32] Muir, *A History of Liverpool*, p. 287.

[33] "In the years which followed . . . a whole series of [private day schools] were founded. Some of them were wholly or partly endowed by individuals; most were supported by one religious denomination or another; and all the denominations strove in honourable rivalry to fill this glaring need [for education]. By 1835, when the state was awakening to the importance of encouraging and aiding these schools, Liverpool was, on the whole, tolerably well supplied, according to the standards of England at that date." Ibid.

[34] Ibid., p. 189. "The boys are taught reading, writing, and arithmetic, the elements of the English grammar, and the outlines of geometry and astronomy; those intended for the sea, navigation; the girls reading, writing, arithmetic, sewing, knitting and housewifery. The girls knit their own and the boys' stockings and make their own clothes." Brooke, *Liverpool . . . , 1775–1800*, pp. 65–66.

Liverpool Infirmary was opened on Shaw's Brow at the periphery of the town, on land donated by the corporation. The infirmary contained thirty beds supported by yearly subscriptions of close to £500. In its first year, it treated 122 in-patients and 72 out-patients. A few years later, two wings were added, housing the Seamen's Hospital "for seamen, their widows and children." But these two institutions, together with the dispensing of medicine and medical advice by the Poor Law authorities, were the only health facilities that the poor of Liverpool could count on.

These early forays into charitable practices by the Liverpool merchants revealed a certain business acumen. Since the custom of transporting the poor to the colonies had fallen into disuse and it was necessary to care for them at home, more efficient and economic means were not to be disdained. As a rule, charitable institutions were organized as a joint venture between private individuals and government. The corporation was usually amenable to providing a free piece of ground out of its vast holdings, and the corporation or the vestry might be willing to grant some financial support, especially if it could be demonstrated that the proposed charity would reduce their ordinary expenditures. For example, the Liverpool Dispensary, established in 1778 by private subscription to provide the poor with free medicine and medical advice, was given a yearly grant of £105 by the vestry, which declared that the dispensary "would be a great relief and aid to the sick and diseased poor, and in part [would] ease the Parish of the charge of providing medical and surgical attendance and assistance for such poor."[35] The parish immediately took advantage of this new voluntary service by dismissing its own apothecary. Similarly, both private charity and public welfare were preoccupied with the "deserving poor" rather than with poverty as a societal symptom of the times. The Blue Coat Charity School was organized "for the education of orphans and fatherless children, and of those who have indigent but honest parents"; old sailors and sailors' widows were the tenants of the privately endowed almshouses of the town; and the workhouse, 50 percent of whose inmates "were lunatics, idiots, sick, lame, very old or very young,"[36] was conceived of largely as a device "wherein to employ the poor of this Parish and thereby to

[35] *1780 Liverpool Vestry Books,* quoted in Chandler, *Liverpool,* p. 401.
[36] Ibid., p. 396.

ease the inhabitants of the great burthen the poor are at present."[37] Naturally enough, the preoccupation with minimizing welfare expenditures and providing employment for the poor led to the widespread use of the workhouse as a source of child labor for the mills.

The abuses that seem shocking to us—child labor, the wretched working conditions of factory workers in general, the municipal government's lack of concern for public welfare—did not receive much attention from the educated classes of the eighteenth century. Although ignorance of social conditions may have been partly to blame, the wealthy were aware of the poor primarily as a threat to their own safety, as when the prosperous residents of the new development of South Toxteth Park subscribed a few guineas a year to maintain a private patrol to protect them from a neighboring slum. A sense of social responsibility developed enough to use public resources to promote even restricted social goals was simply lacking. The very merchants who sat on the town council or who endowed private charities were eager to promote their personal fortunes by taking advantage of the Act of 1730, which opened the slave trade to all persons willing to pay a registration fee of £2. On the one hand, they considered it their duty to administer the corporate estate honestly, if conservatively, and to offer relief to the deserving poor; on the other, they felt no compunctions in vying with Bristol and London for a virtual monopoly of the slave trade. During the second half of the eighteenth century, the trade greatly aided the commercial rise of Liverpool, bringing into their coffers an average annual profit of nearly £300,000. Yet, the merchants' contribution to an improved social and physical environment increased only marginally.

It is no surprise that the men who held the reins of power but who were, first of all, merchants intent upon exploiting every new commercial opportunity were more interested in improving the competitive position of their town as a port than in bettering the social and physical conditions of the poor. That their attitude was parochial and that their actions, or rather their inaction, set the stage for the chaotic and often abominable living conditions characteristic of the industrial town was perhaps due less to a lack of

[37] Municipal Records for March 1, 1731. Picton, *Liverpool Archives and Records . . . Extract*, p. 160.

vision than to the rapidly changing conditions of the time. The slave trade that was bringing them unheard of profits was not

. . . considered to be guilty or even dubious. Until almost the end of the eighteenth century there was scarcely a man in Europe who would not have regarded such phrases . . . as the language of misguided sentimentalism. In the eyes of the Liverpool merchants, and in the eyes of all the world, the success of Liverpool was a thing to be envied, the legitimate reward of enterprise which everyone would have been delighted to share.[38]

In the same spirit, the expansion of the town, whether measured in terms of the development of trade or the growth of population, was a thing to be desired regardless of the consequences.

[38] Muir, *A History of Liverpool,* pp. 192–193.

CHAPTER FOUR

The Corporate Oligarchy of Liverpool

The fifty years that elapsed between the development of the prosperous but still provincially small seaport and the close of the Continental Wars was a period of intensive commercial and physical growth that culminated in the emergence of Liverpool as one of the major seaports and most populous cities of England. Neither the American Revolution nor the twenty years of almost uninterrupted global warfare in which England was engaged offered more than temporary setbacks to the growth of Liverpool.

The last decades of the eighteenth century were the beginning of a new technological age in transportation and manufacture. Parliamentary authorization for the first long-distance canal was obtained by Francis, Duke of Bridgewater, in 1761 (2 Geo. 3, cap. 96). Completed in 1767, the Bridgewater Canal connected Manchester to Liverpool, and the cost of carrying goods between the two towns was reduced to 6s. a ton as compared to the earlier 12s. by river and 40s. by road. Within the next thirty years, most major towns in the North Counties and the Midlands were connected by canals; the Grand Trunk, opened in 1777, joined Liverpool to Birmingham, and the Grand Junction, opened in 1805, completed the system by providing an inland water route between London and the North. For the first time,

coals, salt, iron, timber, and other heavy articles could be conveyed a hundred miles into the country for the same sum which it had formerly taken to convey them twenty-five miles; and wheat, which formerly could not be conveyed a hundred miles from corn-growing districts, to the large towns and manufacturing districts, for less than 20s. a-quarter, could be conveyed for about 5s. a-quarter.[1]

Between 1760 and the beginning of the Continental Wars, fourteen major acts were passed dealing with the construction or improvement of water transportation within the immediate vicinity of Liverpool; an additional thirteen acts were passed through 1815. Although the end of the eighteenth century saw notable developments in road transport, these did not compare to the engineering feats of the great canal builders. In spite of the proliferation of Turnpike Acts (1600 between 1751 and 1790; 2450 between 1790 and 1830)[2] and improvements in coach building, overland transportation remained expensive and uncomfortable for passengers; for goods, it was still limited to short distances.

There were parallel developments in manufacturing technology, particularly in the textile industry. In the seventies, the first truly modern factories were established in the North Counties, mainly as a result of Arkwright's water frame, which used rollers activated by waterwheels to stretch the yarn. A later improvement, Samuel Crompton's "mule" (1779), which combined the advantages of the water frame and of Hargreaves's spinning jenny, increased the output of spun yarn to such an extent that it created an acute shortage of weavers[3] until the introduction of Cartwright's power loom in 1793.[4] The introduction of Watt's stationary steam engine between 1775 and 1800, first in the coal mines, then in iron factories, and

[1] Thomas Baines, *History of the Commerce and Town of Liverpool* (London: Longman, Brown, Green and Longmans, 1852), p. 440.

[2] Charles P. Hill, *British Economic and Social History: 1700–1914* (London: L. Arnold, 1957), p. 83.

[3] "In the 1780s and 1790s there was so much yarn available that weavers could get steady employment at high rates of pay . . . . At Bolton in 1792 weavers were getting 3s. 6d. a yard, and gave themselves great airs, going about the streets with £5 notes stuck in their hatbands." Ibid., pp. 65–66.

[4] The use of Cartwright's invention became widespread only in the middle of the nineteenth century. "At the beginning of the nineteenth century the development of power loom weaving had hardly begun. Against the several million spindles already at work in the spinning mills there were in all England no more than a few hundred power looms. But the results were plainly visible. Two steam looms, looked after by a fifteen-year-old boy, could weave three and a half pieces of material, while in the same time a skilled weaver, using the fly shuttle, wove only one." Paul Mantoux, *The Industrial Revolution in the Eighteenth Century*, 2nd ed. (New York: Harcourt, Brace, 1929), p. 244.

finally in the textile industry, put a final imprimatur on the "age of the factory," freeing manufacturers from dependence upon local water resources for power. There were substantial, although perhaps less dramatic, technological improvements in industries engaged in calico printing, soap manufacturing, and pottery.

Liverpool prospered as the Midlands and North Counties increased their share of England's manufactured export goods. Between 1760 and 1775, the dock rates (levied on ships and cargo using the port facilities) increased by 125 percent, while the town dues (the tax levied on goods sold locally) increased by 300 percent. By 1792, Liverpool's share was 17 percent of all tonnage cleared through English ports, as compared to 4 percent at the beginning of the century,[5] and its trade was worldwide, with particular emphasis on Africa, the West Indies, and the American continent. By the end of the century, over 85 percent of the slave trade belonged to Liverpool, representing an average annual return of some £1.5 million.[6] The slave trade represented an important part of a profitable triangle in which manufactured goods were exported to Africa, where they were sold and used to purchase slaves. The slaves were then transported to the West Indies and the southern United States and sold, mainly for labor on cotton plantations, in return for cotton, tobacco, rum, sugar, and spices, which were in great demand at home. Each leg of the triangle yielded its share of profit. There were, understandably, strong economic arguments against the abolition of the slave trade, as shown in a Liverpool letter "addressed to the gentlemen of Manchester 'calling themselves a Committee for the Abolition of the Slave Trade' . . . ." The writer declared that the proposal of the committee was "totally inconsistent with the true interests and safety of their country," inasmuch as cutting off the supply of slaves to the West Indies ("those very islands from which manufacturers are supplied with cotton—those very islands which have cost England so much blood and treasure to gain and keep possession of") would make them change their allegiance to France, Spain, Portugal, or Holland. "In that situation, what will become of the town of Manchester and the county of Lancaster at large, when France tells you, 'Gentlemen you shall have none of our cotton for the supply of your manufac-

[5] T. Baines, *History of Liverpool*, p. 492.
[6] Hill, *British Economic and Social History*, p. 101.

tories, without paying us 1s. or 2s. a pound duty upon it.' "[7] The strength of this argument was glaringly evident: in 1790, 31 percent of England's total cotton imports came through Liverpool, whose West India trade alone accounted for 3 percent of the country's total trade.

Of course, the abolition of the slave trade in 1807 had none of the dire consequences predicted for it. The considerations brought to bear, however, were symptomatic of the city's mercantile vision: moving from a purely parochial outlook, the Liverpool merchants were becoming increasingly interested in world affairs, at least to the extent that their own interests were affected. The mounting tension in the American colonies, for example, aroused deep concern in Liverpool, and in 1775 merchants met to protest the government's measures against the colonists, on the grounds that such legislation interfered "with the friendly and commercial relations with America."[8] This concern was justified, since the American War of Independence resulted in a 12 percent drop in the tonnage handled in Liverpool between 1775 and 1800 (Figure 7). The war was generally unpopular in England but particularly so in the ports, where merchant seamen often fought pitched battles to avoid impressment into the Royal Navy. But most of all, the economic consequences of the war were deplored, as shown by this dramatic description of the situation in Liverpool:

Our once extensive trade to Africa is at a stand: all commerce with America is at an end. Peace, harmony, and mutual confidence must constitute the balm that can again restore to health the body politic. Survey our docks; count there the gallant ships laid up and useless. When will they be again refitted? What become of the sailor, the tradesman, the poor labourer, during the approaching winter?[9]

[7] T. Baines, *History of Liverpool*, pp. 476–477.

[8] Ibid., p. 449. "The whole remonstrance," says a writer in Williamson's *Liverpool Advertiser* (January 20, 1775), "was couched in decent, manly terms; and, in point of style, good sense, and precision, showed the committee appointed for drawing it up every way equal to the great trust delegated to them."

[9] Ibid., pp. 450–451. It should be noted that the effects of the American War were not only relatively minor (the level of trade in 1780 is still substantially higher than that of 1770), but also short lived. The Peace of 1783 was followed by an intensive resumption of trade with the United States, which "to Britain's surprise and gratification, continued as a major market despite their new political status. Both in relative increase and in absolute

The end of the American War coincided with the completion of a new wet dock, George's Dock, which had been authorized twenty years earlier (2 Geo. 3, cap. 86, 1761). Constructed at a cost of £21,000, it added seven hundred yards of quays and increased the handling capacity of the port by 60 percent. A few years later, large public warehouses were built, first on Goree's Causeway, and later on the western promenade of the new dock. George's Dock was the center of the West India trade, and sugar and cotton were stored in its new warehouses. The postwar trade boom prompted the dock estate to enlarge its facilities even more. In 1784, three years after the completion of George's Dock, an enabling act was passed for the construction of two additional docks (25 Geo. 3, cap. 15). The first of these, King's Dock, was completed in 1788 and the second, Queen's Dock, in 1796. Together, they again doubled the capacity of the port, at a total cost of some £70,000, including improvements in the navigational aides of the river itself. King's Dock was the center of the tobacco trade with Virginia, a large bonded warehouse holding 7000 hogsheads having been constructed by the council in 1795.

With a population of about 65,000 by 1790, Liverpool continued to expand southward and eastward. While the eastward expansion occurred along a natural line of growth formed by the major roads connecting the city with the interior, the southward expansion was due to the development of port facilities. George's Dock was the natural completion of the system that began with the Old Dock in 1709.[10] Located at the foot of Water Street, less than a thousand feet from the Town Hall, it reestablished a traditional balance with the commercial and administrative center of the town. However, the presence of King's and Queen's Docks at the southernmost extremity of the city contributed to transforming the first planned,

---

quantity the export figures to the United States are the outstanding feature of British foreign trade during [the period that lasted until 1793]." Arthur D. Gayer, Walt W. Rostow, and Anna J. Schwartz, *Growth and Fluctuation of the British Economy, 1790–1850*, 2 vols. (Oxford: Clarendon Press, 1953), 1:13.

10 "These three docks [Old Dock, South Dock, and George's Dock] have a communication with each other, so that the vessels can pass to either of the other two docks, or to the graving docks, without being subject to the inconvenience of going out into the river." *The Stranger in Liverpool*, 3rd ed. (Liverpool: Thomas Kaye, 1812), p. 61.

large-scale addition to Liverpool from a middle-class district into a slum (see Figures 9 and 11).

In 1775, the Earl of Sefton developed for housing part of his estates in Toxteth Park, a fifty-two-acre tract adjacent to the southern boundary of Liverpool. Originally intended as a new town called Harrington, the land was platted in a gridiron pattern, with the 600-foot blocks running north-south. The streets were generously laid out, and a church, St. James's, was constructed on land given by Lord Sefton with a view to attracting middle-class residents, but development was slow until the beginning of the nineteenth century, when it was finally sparked by the completion of Queen's Dock. Industries, including an iron foundry, were established at the northern end of the property along Parliament Street and in the area just south of the docks. These industries, in turn, attracted a low-income population, whose demand for cheap housing adjacent to their place of work spurred the rapid and uncontrolled development of Toxteth Park.

The interior of the blocks . . . laid out judiciously enough at right angles . . . was left to be arranged as chance or cupidity might direct. Hence arose subdivisions of mean, narrow streets, filled with close, gloomy courts, into which as many dwellings as possible were packed, irrespective of light and air. The result has been the impression of an inferior character on this quarter of the town, from which it has never been able to recover.[11]

That the pattern was set was confirmed by the first social survey of Liverpool, which estimated that over 30 percent of the city's paupers lived in Toxteth Park.[12]

The growth of pauperism in Liverpool was due to a combination of a high rate of in-migration and relatively limited employment opportunities. Liverpool, by the end of the eighteenth century, was the principal port of entry for Irish and Welsh migrants seeking work in the Lancashire industries, even though it was not yet an industrial town. Although some factories were to be found, such as watch-making, pottery, sugar refineries, breweries, and a few textile works, they were small and relatively unimportant in comparison

[11] James A. Picton, *Memorials of Liverpool*, 2 vols. (London: Longmans, Green, 1875), 2:460.
[12] Abraham Hume, *Condition of Liverpool, Religious and Social* (Liverpool: T. Brakell, 1858), pp. 21 ff.

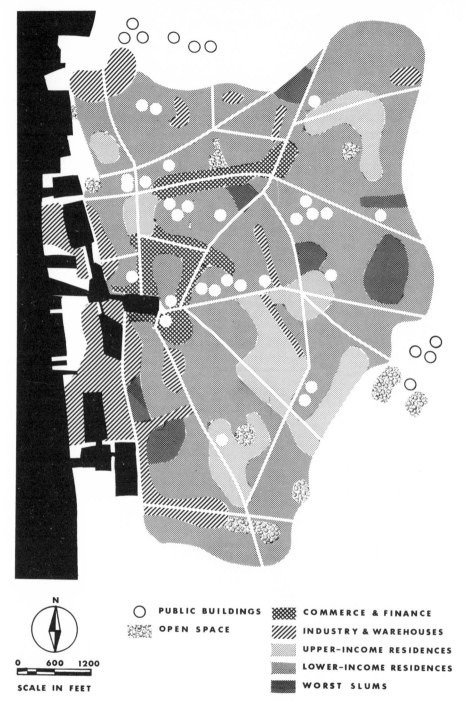

N

PUBLIC BUILDINGS   COMMERCE & FINANCE
OPEN SPACE   INDUSTRY & WAREHOUSES
    UPPER-INCOME RESIDENCES
    LOWER-INCOME RESIDENCES
    WORST SLUMS

0   600   1200
SCALE IN FEET

Figure 11. Land-Use Structure of Liverpool in the 1820s

with the port. With the exception of ship construction and refitting, which remained in the hands of a closed corporation of highly skilled craftsmen,[13] there were few local employment opportunities, particularly for the unskilled migrants from rural areas. Many of them stopping in Liverpool either temporarily or permanently found casual jobs in the port and swelled the growing mass of those dependent upon the Poor Law authorities when fluctuations in trade turned them out of their jobs.

The increasing number of people on the relief rolls, the growing poor rate, and the inability of local industries to employ the inmates of the workhouse prompted the Poor Law authorities to enlarge it "in order to include some manufacturing therein as the most likely means of gaining something towards support and maintenance [of the poor]."[14] By 1795 there were almost 1200 inmates in the Liverpool workhouse, and the total expenditures of the Poor Law authorities for indoor and outdoor relief was for that year on the order of £18,000. In 1800, £33,000 was spent on relief, and the rate reached 3s. on the pound of assessed valuation of land and building. Statistics on the number of people on relief are incomplete and scattered, but a conservative estimate would put this number at about 15,000, or 21 percent of the total population in 1795, with about 27,000, or 34 percent, in 1800.[15] Much of this increase can be attributed to the side effects of the war with France, particularly in terms of aid to the wives and children of sailors.

Although faced with the spread of slums and a high proportion of destitute persons among the population, the corporation still did

[13] "The ship-carpenters of Liverpool were a powerful body at political elections, as well as at elections of Mayors. Great numbers of them were freemen. . . ." Richard Brooke, *Liverpool* . . . , *1775–1800* (Liverpool: J. R. Smith, 1853), p. 313. "Ship building is carried on to considerable extent in the vicinity of Liverpool. There are a number of slips for building or for repairing vessels. Between the years of 1778 and 1811, twenty-one frigates and other smaller vessels of war were built for government service. . . ." Henry Smithers, *Liverpool, Its Commerce, Statistics, and Institutions* . . . (Liverpool: Thomas Kaye, 1825), p. 190.

[14] *1757 Liverpool Vestry Books*, quoted in George Chandler, *Liverpool* (London: B. T. Batsford, 1957), p. 392.

[15] The expenditures of the Poor Law authorities have been used to arrive at these approximate figures. The per capita expenditure for indoor relief was taken to be on the order of £4, which is comparable to Glasgow (Smithers, *Liverpool*, p. 300), and £1 for outdoor relief, which was more sporadic in nature.

not see fit to alter its traditional role and take measures to remedy these symptoms of a rapidly expanding city. It was content to apply to Parliament, in 1785, for an act to improve the streets of the Old Borough (26 Geo. 3, cap. 12). Some £150,000 were spent under this act, mainly to improve sewers. In addition, the main streets around the Town Hall were widened, straightened, and repaved, as were a number of other streets, and three new streets were laid out. Although the repaving of the old streets had been carried out sporadically for some years, the Act of 1785 was the first concerted attempt at a major improvement.[16] But the provision of water, for example, was still left to private carriers who brought in casks from distant springs, for the shallow wells within the city itself had become hopelessly polluted. It was not until 1799, exactly ninety years after the enabling legislation had been approved by Parliament (8 Anne, cap. 25), that a joint-stock company was formed, the Bootle Water Company, to supply piped water to Liverpool. Similarly, the corporation spent only £4400 between 1774 and 1800 on the relief of the poor, most of it as provisions resold below the market price, while it frequently granted sums of money ranging from a few pounds to several hundred to members of the council and others, to repay them for sundry public services.[17] Meanwhile, corporate

[16] Shortly before the act was passed, there was a scandal connected with a repaving contract. The contractor was dismissed summarily "on a complaint this day made by Mr. Mayor to [the] Council against George Byrom Paviour for great misbehaviour and abuse given to Mr. Mayor and other gentlemen of the Committee appointed for repaving Hanover Street." James A. Picton, *City of Liverpool: Municipal Archives and Records . . . Extract* (Liverpool: Gilbert G. Walmsley, 1886), p. 273.

[17] 1765: "Ordered that the sum of twenty guineas be repaid Mr. Mayor for so much money given by him to a poor Prince of Palestine, dispossessed of his dominions by the Grand Signiors Officers there, and recommended by his Excellency General Conway, one of his Majesty's principal Secretaries of State." 1772: "Ordered that the Corporation Treasurer do pay Messrs. Parr, Wilson and Allen for certain new Councilmen's blew [sic] gowns . . . fifty pounds and eight shillings . . . ." 1773: "Ordered that any sum not exceeding two hundred pounds be granted to be laid out in useful Plate for this Corporation, to be used by the Mayors for the time being of this borough, as complaints have been made by gentlemen who served this office, that there is not a sufficiency of useful Plate belonging to this Corporation and that they are often put to great expenses herein, and therefore is a discouragement to gentlemen to accept of said office of Mayor." 1797: "Ordered that Mr. Alderman Dunbar the late Mayor, be requested to accept the thanks of this Council for his very spirited, active, and upright conduct during his Mayoralty, and that he be paid the sum of eight hundred pounds towards the expenses of his Mayoralty by the Treasurer." Ibid., pp. 193 ff.

Custom House and Canning Dock
Courtesy of Henry Young and Sons, Liverpool

St. George's Crescent
Courtesy of Henry Young and Sons, Liverpool

Ranelagh Street

Courtesy of Henry Young and Sons, Liverpool

Bluecoat Charity School
Courtesy of Liverpool City Libraries

Chorley Court
Courtesy of Liverpool City Libraries

revenues during the same period had risen from £12,400 to £85,400 per annum, and many of these years showed a budget surplus, in spite of the extraordinary contributions made to the Crown from time to time to help defray the costs of the American and French wars.

The growing dissatisfaction with the corporation in all municipal affairs other than the development of port facilities prompted the leading citizens to attempt a reform in the winter of 1790–1791. On October 5, 1790, a petition signed by 1098 freemen, including many prominent merchants, was presented to the mayor to request him to summon a "common hall" (an assembly of freemen) to fill existing vacancies on the council and to review its past actions. The language of the petition is revealing. Although it was drafted by the council members' peers, it expresses its "disapprobation not only of the mode of election of the Councilmen, but of the persons who are frequently chosen into that body . . . . We think we are warranted in saying that the Council, in choosing their own body, do not consult the wishes or interests of the burgesses."[18] Encouraged by a liberal mayor, and over the opposition of the council, the assembly met in January and promptly resolved "that all previous decrees giving to the Council power to fill vacancies in its own body . . . should be annulled."[19] The assembly, aware that it could not hope to do away with the council, was attempting by this resolution to regain control of it. The immediate threat was slight, inasmuch as the councilmen were elected for life and there were only four vacancies, which were filled from among the members of the assembly. Nevertheless, the council's reaction was violent: at their February meeting, they refused to seat the new councilmen and passed a motion declaring the whole proceedings illegal and "contrary to the immemorial usages, customs, charters and to the very constitution of this borough and corporation."

The council's refusal to seat the new members elected by the assembly was due to two other resolutions passed by the assembly a few days earlier that were even more threatening to the exclusive prerogatives of the council. The first stated that all corporation accounts were to be audited annually by a joint committee made up of four councilmen and four freemen chosen by the assembly; the

[18] Ibid., p. 203.
[19] J. Ramsey Muir and Edith M. Platt, *History of Municipal Government in Liverpool* (Liverpool: Liverpool University Press, 1906), pp. 129–130.

second, that a committee from the assembly was to be appointed to examine existing bylaws and draft new ones as needed. This committee was duly appointed, and its first new bylaws justified the fears of the council. It decreed that there should be an annual meeting of the common hall on the second Wednesday of April and that all decrees passed by the assembly would have the force of law. To the conservative council, this smelled strongly of the Jacobinism that was raging across the Channel. But for tactical reasons, the council decided to fight over the auditing of its accounts. The treasurer was forbidden to show his accounts to the Audit Committee, and the matter went before the courts. Both the assizes and the Court of King's Bench, to which the council had appealed, ruled in favor of the freemen. The council then moved for a new trial on a technicality, and the freemen abandoned further litigation.[20]

THE WAR YEARS

England's decision to oppose France's annexation of the Low Countries put an end to the period of prosperity that had followed on the heels of the American War of Independence. The next twenty years were characterized by a series of sharp, short-term business cycles, owing to the costs of carrying on the war, the need to find new markets as traditional continental outlets were cut off, and a general increase in the price of imported commodities, resulting from the uncertainties of wartime shipping. The dependence of the English economy on foreign trade was dramatically highlighted.[21]

[20] "It became . . . evident that the Council were prepared to use every possible effort and to spend any amount of money to defeat the action of the Burgesses, and being unprepared to meet it on equal terms, the plaintiffs reluctantly abandoned the prosecution, and so the matter slept until revived in 1835." Picton, *Memorials of Liverpool*, 2:208.

[21] "Business cycles in Britain, from 1790 to 1850, were, in large measure, a function of fluctuations in the export demand for textiles . . . . In part, of course, the export demand was not independent of conditions in England. Exports were financed almost entirely on credit, and increases in exports can be traced often to long- and short-term lending from Britain. The enterprise of merchants and bankers at various times thus helped to create the export demand. The export booms centering on Hamburg (1797–1802), on South America (1805–10, 1819–25), the United States (1832–36), and India and China (1842–45) cannot be understood without reference to British lending operations." Gayer, Rostow, and Schwartz, *British Economy*, 2:533.

The initial impact of the war was an enormous increase in the price of wheat, starting with the winter of 1794–1795. The causes were a poor crop in 1794, the demands for provisions made by the army and the navy, and the general fear engendered by the possible closing off of the country's continental sources of supply.

It is not clear whether the disturbances induced in the national economy by the war were due to temporary instability or to basic structural factors. The financial crises of 1793, 1797, and 1799 were short lived. The severest of these, the suspension of cash payments by the Bank of England in 1797, when its bullion reserves had fallen to an all-time low of £0.9 million, resulted largely from domestic hoarding of gold prompted by the fear of a French landing. Within a few months, however, the new £1 and £2 notes had been accepted by the public, and in October 1797 the bank offered to resume cash payments.[22] The postponement of cash payments until "six months after the ratification of a definitive treaty of peace" was merely an expression of the conservative attitude of the government.

England was able to expand her foreign trade in spite of the Continental Blockade because of her capacity to find new markets whenever old ones were closed. Trade with Europe continued to account for 40 to 60 percent of total trade during the war years. When France and Holland became inaccessible to her ships, first Germany and Prussia and later Russia and the eastern Mediterranean ports became her principal European outlets. Within a year of the declaration of war, Germany and Prussia accounted for over 90 percent of England's European trade, while in previous years they had accounted for 35 to 45 percent. But the need to search for new markets and the neccessity to reroute shipping harassed by privateers helped to produce a sharp rise in the cost of living, which reflected the general uncertainties of the time (especially in their effect on grain imports), as well as the government's unusually high demand on manufactured goods. Schumpeter's index of consumer goods shows a rise of almost 100 percent between 1790 and 1800;[23] the

[22] "With the return of confidence and the acceptance of the newly issued £1 and £2 notes, gold came quickly out of hiding, while an increasingly favourable foreign exchange brought bullion from abroad." Ibid., 1:52. The reserves of the Bank had risen to £10.5 million by early 1799.

[23] E. B. Schumpeter, "English Prices and Public Finance, 1660–1822," *Review of Economic Statistics* 20, no. 1 (1938): 21–37.

price of colonial products trebled during the first six years of war.

Although money wages increased steadily from 1780 to the end of the war, especially in the industrial North, where there was a shortage of labor, the rise in the cost of living after 1790 caused a severe, if temporary, decline in real wages. Indeed, it is likely that most of the riots in the industrial areas were prompted by the demand for cheaper food rather than by political unrest or even by fear of the economic consequences of mechanization.[24] The situation was compounded by the general misunderstanding of the extensive labor troubles at the end of the century which culminated in the severe Combination Acts of 1799 and 1800. London regarded the unrest in industrial areas as the forerunner of a Jacobin revolt, a consideration that prompted Pitt to order the brutal use of troops and to suspend habeas corpus, but others tended to blame Britain's economic dependence upon foreign trade rather than the worsening living conditions in the industrial areas.[25]

In spite of these general difficulties, the first years of the war were prosperous ones for Liverpool: the resolute action of the corporation had proved eminently successful in averting a commercial crisis,[26] and the annexation of the French West Indies in June 1794 was a commercial boon to the city. Since Liverpool's commerce was oriented predominantly toward Africa and the Americas, it was unaffected by the necessity to find alternative European markets that plagued most other English ports. Whatever wartime fluctuations occurred were due primarily to periodic difficulties in manning ships because of the impressment of sailors into the Royal Navy. The government from time to time imposed tem-

[24] Hill mentions that the Luddite riots "reflected in part the natural hostility felt by uneducated men towards machines which were putting them out of work, and in part the unemployment caused by wartime fluctuations of trade." *British Economic and Social History*, p. 113.

[25] "The difficulties of the period from the resumption of the war to the opening of the South American markets (1803–08), when the Continental trade was intermittently harried by blockade and by the necessity for re-routing, are reflected in a number of publications urging the possibility and even the advisability of Britain's maintaining its prosperity with a lesser dependence on foreign trade; e.g. Oddy's 'European Commerce,' 'A Plan of National Improvement' (Anonymous), Spence's 'Britain Independent of Commerce.' These pamphlets reflect the kind of thinking that helped create the Orders in Council a few years later." Gayer, Rostow, and Schwartz, *British Economy*, 1:68.

[26] See pp. 52–53 of the present work.

porary embargoes on all ships until the port's quota of sailors for the navy was filled; this was in addition to the normal activities of the press-gangs.[27] But it was not until the Orders in Council of 1807, prohibiting neutral trading with the French Empire, that Liverpool felt the full impact of war. The sudden curtailment of the American trade, which accounted for almost one-third of the port's tonnage, prompted the Liverpool merchants to petition Parliament against the Orders in Council; their petition was unsuccessful.[28]

Liverpool was able to withstand the adversities of war and the attendent economic crises not only because of its commercial expansion before the start of the American Revolution but also because of the stolidity of the Liverpool merchants in the difficult times they encountered:

The commencement of the war with France was attended by a commercial panic, which prostrated upwards of five hundred mercantile houses, including in the number many provincial banks, between the beginning of February and the end of May, 1793. The only Liverpool bank (out of four) which was borne down by the storm was that of Charles Caldwell and Co. All the others stood firm; and the merchants and corporation made extraordinary efforts to restore confidence in their stability. On the 23rd March, 1793, a meeting of merchants and traders was held to consider the most probable means of restoring confidence. . . . The town council held a special meeting, at which they also appointed a committee, to communicate and act with the committee of merchants. . . . An address to the inhabitants was drawn up by the joint committee, and signed by them, and by two hundred and twenty of the principal firms in the town, in which they recommended all parties to whom bills were due to make payments as easy as possible; and pledged themselves to receive the bills of all the Liverpool banks at one or two months' date, "as has been the usual custom". . . .

[27] "During the spring of 1794 the press of seamen was very hot. In May a press-gang stopped the Warrington boat coach and the York mail, at Lowhill, to look for sailors. During the scuffle the horses of the mail took fright, galloped off, and upset the coach, seriously injuring two of the passengers." T. Baines, *History of Liverpool*, p. 496.

[28] "A powerful representation was made of the importance of the American trade to Liverpool, employing annually 123,000 tons of shipping, and producing a revenue from Liverpool alone of upwards of a million sterling per annum. The American ships visiting the port expended not less than £150,000 annually amongst the tradesmen of the town, and the charges on the cargoes were £150,000 more. The injustice and impolicy of the whole proceedings was strongly dwelt upon." Picton, *Memorials of Liverpool*, 1:286.

The town council afterwards went much further. They applied to Parliament (33 George III, cap. 31) and obtained powers to issue from £200,000 to £300,000 in promissory notes, to be loaned to the merchants of Liverpool on security of merchandise and shipping. . . .[29]

In 1799, in spite of the war, the dock trustees requested an extension of their powers in order to construct two additional docks at an estimated cost of £120,000 (39 Geo. 3, cap. 29). Moreover, in 1801 it was decided to spend £80,000 on a new exchange building that would be worthy, in the words of the *Liverpool Advertiser,* "of the spirit and opulence of this flourishing place." In 1811, the corporation constructed at its own expense a new warehouse on the west side of King's Dock, with a floor area of over 130,000 square feet. At the same time, a new Dock Act was passed (50 Geo. 3, cap. 143), which increased the dock rates, raised the statutory debt limit of the dock estate to £600,000, and provided for the construction of new facilities north of George's Dock.[30] Existing facilities were enlarged and a new dock, Princes' Dock, was opened to shipping in 1816.

THE POSTWAR PERIOD

By the end of the Continental Wars, the character of Liverpool as a "modern" city was well established. A contemporary description boasts of its

. . . numerous and splendid public structures for devotion, charity, pleasure, and business (in many of which the metropolis itself is rivalled), the immense ranges of newly erected dwelling houses, distributed into streets and squares, in the most eligible situations, and in a style of superior elegance . . . [exhibiting] at one view the effects of industry directed by genius and supported by character.[31]

In spite of this somewhat vainglorious and one-sided optimism, which ignored the living conditions of the growing mass of urban poor, the comparison between Liverpool in the 1760s and in 1815 (Table 1) is striking indeed. Not only has the population quadrupled and the built-up area more than doubled, but the distribution of the population itself reflects the beginning of a middle-class

[29] T. Baines, *History of Liverpool,* pp. 494–495.
[30] The dock debt, at the time, was just under £181,000.
[31] *Stranger in Liverpool,* p. 36.

Table 1. Characteristics of Liverpool, 1760–1815

	1760s	1815
Area (acres)	2450	8300
Population		
Borough	35,000	115,000
Suburbs (Lancashire)	—	14,000
Suburbs (Cheshire)	—	2000
Total	35,000	131,000
Corporate finances		
Revenues	£4726	£98,000
Poor rate	1s. 8d.	3s. 0d.
Physical		
Places of worship	14	46
Charitable institutions	4	15
Public buildings	4	14
Places of amusements	7	15
Markets	5	8
Public services		
Water	no	yes
Refuse collection	poor	poor
Police	night watchman	15
Schools	1	20

exodus from the central city, a sharp break with the tradition of the burgess, whether merchant or artisan, living above his store or workshop and directly concerned with the affairs of his town. The city's peripheral areas show an impressive growth; the population of the four suburban townships of Toxteth Park, Everton, West Derby, and Kirkdale increased by just over 100 percent between the censuses of 1801 and 1811, while the borough of Liverpool itself had grown by 22 percent. Although the fastest-growing of these townships was low-income Toxteth Park (up 185 percent), the two middle- and upper-middle-class towns of Everton and West Derby had an aggregate rate of growth twice that of the borough.

But growth was unguided, as has been seen in the case of Toxteth Park, and the provision of urban services was haphazard and scattered. Water was now piped in five central wards, to each of which a police constable and two assistants had also been appointed, but even in the relatively affluent Old Borough, the disposal of refuse was still hopelessly inadequate.

The streets are generally well cleaned by scavengers, who are regular and diligent in their duty; but in the execution of their business, while they remove one evil they never fail to create a greater. The soil, instead of being immediately carted away, as in London and other places, is raked into heaps. . . . These Cloacenian repositories are common in every part of the town, and remain eight or ten days, and sometimes longer before they are carted away, whereby passengers in a dark night, and often in the day, tread in them to the mid-leg, and children are sometimes nearly suffocated by falling into them. The exhalations in summer . . . have a most pungent effect on the olfactory nerves of the passengers, nor are the inhabitants of those houses which are situated near them insensible of the pernicious effects of their effluvia on their health and constitutions.[32]

In spite of the demands of a rapidly increasing population, the fifteen charitable institutions and twenty schools of the town continued to find their support either in the churches (out of the poor rate) or from private donations, the contribution of local government being limited to occasional grants of money. When £20,000 was raised in 1813 by private subscription to open the Royal Institution, a university "to promote the increase and diffusion of literature, science and the arts," corporation support was again lacking, and the school languished for many years. It was this lack of interest in matters not directly affecting the commercial prosperity of the city that prompted an embittered observer to remark that

Liverpool is the only town in England of any pre-eminence that has not one single erection or endowment for the advancement of science, the cultivation of the arts, or promotion of useful knowledge. . . . When attempts have been made to fertilize them, they have been suffered to wither and decay, and finally to be neglected and forgotten. Public buildings have been completed, and attempts made to introduce and encourage them, but they produced no other effect on the minds of the inhabitants but a torpid vacuity, which plainly demonstrates that the liberal arts are a species of merchandise in which few of the inhabitants are desirous to deal unless for exportation.[33]

The same attitude often obtained in pratical matters as well: when a company was formed in 1816 to provide gas-lighting to the town,

---

[32] Picton, *Memorials of Liverpool,* 1:255–256.
[33] Ibid., p. 254.

the corporation was "supine" and refused to participate in the undertaking.

Throughout the early years of Liverpool's development, the corporation's willingness to spend large amounts on developing port facilities contrasted sharply with its neglect of the general welfare. This situation was to continue as long as no pressure was exerted by a sufficiently broad electoral base. Supported by tradition and vast financial resources, and taking advantage of the ambiguous wording of its charter, the borough council easily defended its administration against the freemen, whose attempts to regain control of local government were scattered and poorly organized. Moreover, there is little doubt that the aldermen of Liverpool believed that their concept of local government was correct and that they governed efficiently and with the public interest in mind. The mercantile class, from whose ranks a majority of the aldermen were chosen, could hardly complain that their trading interests were not in good hands. As a natural port, Liverpool was badly located; it was the vision and public investment of the corporation that permitted the port to expand. The dissatisfaction with the established order that eventually materialized did not grow from objections to the principle of a municipal tax on trade, the proceeds of which were used to finance the operation and expansion of the port, but from the unfairness to the discriminatory nature of town dues, the tax levied on nonfreemen.[34]

The various attempts to reestablish the electoral prerogatives of the freemen and to abolish the self-perpetuating council were primarily skirmishes in a war to achieve free competition within the ranks of the middle class, as the merchants showed little inclination to redirect public policy toward the general welfare. Further, if

[34] "There seems to be a general impression upon the minds of the mercantile community that the town's duties, in their present form and bearing, operate as an unjust and oppressive impost upon merchants being non-freemen . . . [rendering] it impossible for such merchants to compete with their enfranchised neighbours.

"But they concurred in admitting that a system of town's duties, constructed upon a just and reasonable scale, and bearing equally on all members of the commercial body, would, under a salutary administration of the finances of the town, contribute greatly to its prosperity, and that to such an impost they would cheerfully submit." Commissioners on Municipal Corporations in England and Wales, *Report on the Corporation of Liverpool* (London: H.M.S.O., 1833), p. 2695.

the borough council was able to pursue its policies without interference because it had isolated itself from the electorate of freemen,
this same electorate was so small it could hardly claim to be representative of the community as a whole. Theoretically, the freemen
were a cross section of the population, but the existence of a voters'
registration fee of £2 effectively denied political participation to
many who would otherwise have been eligible. For these reasons, it
is doubtful that greater involvement by the freemen of Liverpool in
local government would have resulted in improved municipal services or in alleviation of the negative effects of rapid urbanization.

In my theoretical model of the planning process, the existence of
channels of communication between government and electorate is
not enough; the government must also isolate and identify relevant
issues for community discussion and choice. It is evident that the
corporation failed to control the early development of Liverpool
because it did not understand the forces at work in the town. Although it was able to capitalize on exogenous factors affecting the
commercial position of the town,[35] the corporation consistently
equated successful urban development with population growth, even
when the social consequences of that growth were mostly negative.

It is easy to castigate the aldermen of Liverpool for their limited
outlook and for opening the way, through inaction, to future urban
ills, but this apparent dichotomy between commercial acumen and
public myopia was symptomatic of the times. Why should the
merchants of Liverpool have shown greater concern for the physical well-being of the poor than was normally expected of them as
"Christian gentlemen," when neither Parliament nor the King's

[35] Many of these exogenous factors were actually beyond the control of
the Liverpool corporation: technological improvements in the textile industry; the industrialization of the North Counties and the Midlands; and the
orientation of Liverpool's trade toward the American continent, the West
Indies, and Africa, which made her less susceptible than other ports to the
fluctuations of trade caused by the Continental Wars.

However, there is little reason to think that the northern canal system
would have found its natural terminus in Liverpool had its construction not
been preceded by extensive development of the port facilities. Since the
growth of the city was predicated upon the expansion of trade rather than
upon home industries (industrial development in Liverpool was slow, its
extent insignificant until well into the nineteenth century), it can also be
argued that it was the original development of an artificial port that caused
Liverpool's population to increase by over 100 percent in the last quarter
of the eighteenth century.

ministers exhibited much interest in the matter? The large number of privately supported charitable institutions and the rapidity with which subscriptions "for the relief of the poor" were filled testify to the willingness of members of the mercantile middle class (at least as *private* individuals) to fulfill their traditional obligations toward the poor. Although the ineffectiveness of these methods was becoming daily more evident, there was only limited comprehension of the causal relations between industrialization, urbanization, and the spread of poverty. Reformers were becoming more numerous, yet institutions for effecting reform were not only nonexistent but considered undesirable by those in power.[36] Moreover, it must have been difficult for the prosperous merchants who were guiding the commercial destinies of Liverpool so efficiently to understand why an increasingly large segment of the population seemed unable to take advantage of the new economic opportunities of the age, as they themselves had done. This faith in the munificence of the new industrial age, combined with some disdain for those not able to share in it, was a recurrent theme, expressed by many contemporary writers. The following quotation illustrates the pervasive tendency to adopt a self-satisfied, moralizing attitude toward the poor:

Those authors who have given such exaggerated statements of the misery of the lower orders in this country at present, do not compare their conditions either to that which existed in the former periods of our own history, or to that of the lower orders in any other part of the world, but to some ideal standard which they have formed in their own minds, and which excludes the existence of indolence, ignorance, vice and misfortune in the world. . . . If brought to the test of comparison and experience, we shall find the condition of the lower class at present superior in the essentials of food, clothing, and lodging, to that of any

[36] "Before 1832 Parliament made no large-scale attempt to tackle social problems. The property-owning classes could not forget the French Revolution and Napoleon, and many of them thought that reform and revolution meant the same thing, or that reform at best was a dangerous incitement to revolution. There was little prospect of Parliament's carrying out reforms until Parliament itself was reformed; and until 1832 it was firmly under the control of the landowners. Moreover, this was the age of laissez-faire. It was widely held, especially among merchants and businessmen, that government intervention in economic matters was certain to be disastrous: there were economic laws just as there were scientific ones, and it was just as foolish to meddle with one as to defy the other." Hill, *British Economic and Social History*, p. 281.

other of the old established societies of Europe, or to that of this country at any former period.[37]

Without institutionalized contacts between government and the masses, and without a benevolent form of government, public welfare policies—including adequate urban services and minimum living standards—were absent as well. Even within the limited democracy of a corporate town like Liverpool, it became increasingly apparent that a system that permitted only freemen to vote could not survive. The urban growth at the end of the eighteenth and the beginning of the nineteenth century resulted in a growing disparity between total population and number of voters. In Liverpool, for example, 7 percent of the population were polled in 1750, 2.6 percent in 1775, and only 2.3 percent in 1812. This disparity was, in itself, sufficient to permit the aldermen to maintain the *status quo*, until the Municipal Reform Act of 1835 forced upon them a wider and more representative electorate. Up to that time, they had been free to pursue their own commercial interests, insulated from any necessity to articulate public choices, to obtain public support, or to carry out policies intended to promote the well-being of the city's inhabitants.

[37] William T. Comber, *An Inquiry into the State of National Subsistence . . .* (London: T. Cadell and W. Davies, 1808), pp. 277–278.

CHAPTER FIVE

The Free Town of Manchester

THE GROWTH OF AN INDUSTRIAL CLUSTER

Medieval Manchester was a small market town that was also an ecclesiastical and administrative center. An annual fair and a weekly market were held at Manchester, and it was "the seat of the Court Baron, with civil jurisdiction over the whole barony and criminal jurisdiction over the manor."[1] The town was granted limited home rule by the Charter of 1301: the burgesses were exempt from trading tolls, a typical medieval privilege, and free to elect a "borough-reeve," or mayor, subject to the approval of the manor. Every burgess was a member of a combined administrative and judicial body, the Portmoot, "which met four times a year to transact business relating to the town and its burgesses."[2] It was this court, chaired by the lord's steward, and its similarly organized successor, the Court Leet, that presided over the destinies of Manchester until the middle of the nineteenth century.

By the beginning of the eighteenth century, the Court Leet was fully responsible for making and administering the bylaws that regulated the daily life of the town. Its expenditures were met from the fines it levied and from the county rates, a special assessment of properties within the town; it had a body of over a hundred officers, some of whom were paid by the court. Although appointed by, or

---

[1] Arthur Redford and Ira S. Russell, *History of Local Government in Manchester*, 3 vols. (London: Longmans, Green, 1939), 1:14.
[2] Ibid., p. 26.

subject to the approval of, the manor's steward, these officers were responsible to the court for keeping the peace, policing the markets, and enforcing the bylaws. In addition to its local prerogatives, the Manchester Court Leet, because of its location in the baronial seat, claimed jurisdiction over the whole barony. It acted as an administrative, recording, and civil court, and the constables of subordinate townships were either sworn in or nominated by it. But Manchester's jurisdiction was contested hotly by Salford, whose own Court Leet for the Hundred of Salford antedated Manchester's by seventy years and claimed to be the proper hierarchical step between the local administrative unit and the Crown. The rivalry between the two towns continued well into the eighteenth century, with each court fining local constables who did not attend its sessions.[3] Before eventually relinquishing its extramunicipal claims to Salford, Manchester had asserted its administrative and judicial independence long enough to have become the commercial center of southeastern Lancashire; it was natural for the farmers and townspeople who came to plead their cases before the Manchester Court Leet to do business in the town at the same time. Far from being an industrial town, Manchester was no more than a market for the textile industry located in its vicinity. Its first cotton factory was not built until 1789.

It is generally accepted that the manufacture of cotton goods was introduced into England by refugees from the Low Countries who had been persecuted by the Spaniards for their religious beliefs. The earliest statute pertaining to the cotton industry dates back to 1551 (5 and 6 Edw. 6, cap. 6) and refers specifically to "Manchester Lancashire and Cheshire Cottones" and "all cloths called Manchester Rugges otherwise named Friezes." But it was not until the second half of the seventeenth century that Manchester and the surrounding area became a synonym for the manufacture of cotton goods and not until the end of the eighteenth century that cotton displaced wool as the chief manufacture of Lan-

[3] Manchester repeatedly claimed that the "rights of the barons" exempted it and its townships from service to the Salford Hundred Court. This was denied consistently by Salford; in the late sixteenth century, for example, it repeatedly fined the constables of Manchester "for what they owed suit to that court, and came not to serve the Queen." James Tait, *Medieval Manchester and the Beginnings of Lancashire* (Manchester: Manchester University Press, 1904), p. 92.

cashire.[4] The early cotton industry was essentially a handicraft undertaking: the yarn was cleaned, carded, and spun by the wives and children of farmers and woven on handlooms by the men. The cloth was sold either to local dealers who made the rounds of the farmhouses or at the weekly markets in nearby towns. It provided a welcome source of additional cash income in an area of small farms where the poor quality of soil and the wet climate made oats and barley the standard crops.[5] Although dramatically modified by the introduction of machinery in the closing years of the eighteenth century, this custom persisted well into the nineteenth century and was influential in the location pattern of the industry.

Until the middle of the eighteenth century, the distribution of the raw cotton and the finished goods was organized on a small scale and in a largely haphazard fashion. The import of cotton, mainly through Liverpool, London, and Hull, was a speculative enterprise carried out by general merchants. The apportionment of goods among the mixed cargoes was dependent upon market conditions at home at the time ships were dispatched and upon going prices for goods in the West Indies and America when they arrived at their destination. Because of their higher margin of profit, indigo, sugar, spices, and rum were often preferred to cotton, even when it was in brisk demand. Considering the time lag between the dispatch and return of the ships and the trading authority given to their captains, it is no surprise that the Lancashire cotton market experienced wide fluctuations, due either to a real shortage of raw materials or to artificial manipulations by speculators. Such fluctuations were not particularly conducive to the rise of large establishments with fixed demands for raw material. The sale of cotton staple or yarn and the purchase of cotton goods were thus restricted to the county fairs and the periodical local markets, until they were taken over by "riders" sent out by the larger dealers. Carrying samples of their goods to the country stores, the riders' main function was to supply

[4] Sydney J. Chapman, *The Lancashire Cotton Industry* (Manchester: Manchester University Press, 1904), pp. 1–2.

[5] "The more general size of farms is from 50 down to 20 acres, or even as much only as will keep a horse or cow." John Aikin, *A Description of the Country from Thirty to Forty Miles round Manchester* (London: John Stockdale, 1795), p. 23.

. . . a numerous order of petty chapmen, hawkers and pedlars who, when shopkeeping was little developed even in towns, sold wares at the small country fairs, and had their rounds from hamlet to hamlet and house to house over the countryside.[6]

The early capitalistic tendencies of the cotton trade were therefore commercial rather than industrial, the "manufacturers" being in fact middlemen. They provided the cottage spinners and weavers they employed with the materials needed (raw cotton, yarn, and even "reeds," "healds," and other changeable parts of the looms) and with some services (the larger manufacturers employed "gaiters" to put new work on the looms), and they purchased the finished goods from the cottages on a piecework basis. Although the evidence is fragmentary, it seems that the scale of operation of these manufacturers remained quite small until the introduction of machinery. At the production end, there are numerous instances of weavers owning several looms, which they worked with the assistance of apprentices or journeyman weavers.[7] With few exceptions, their capitalist employers were probably not engaged exclusively in financing the manufacture of cotton goods but were also traders as well, merchants for whom manufacturing was one of several investment possibilities.[8] The inevitable consequence of the growing importance of the cotton industry—the rise of specialized dealers, mostly based in Liverpool, who could market the larger amounts of raw cotton that were being imported[9]—was not met

[6] Alfred P. Wadsworth and Julia de Lacey Mann, *The Cotton Trade and Industrial Lancashire* (Manchester: Manchester University Press, 1931), p. 241.

[7] Chapman, *Lancashire Cotton Industry*, p. 23.

[8] "In 1736, two brothers employed 600 looms and 3,000 persons in the Blackburn district; a little before 1750, a Warrington sailcloth manufacturer employed 5,000 persons; in 1758, a small group of Manchester checkmakers employed a great many of the weavers of Ashton, Oldham and Royton, and one spoke of employing 500 himself." Wadsworth and Mann, *Cotton Trade*, p. 211. That these were exceptions is indicated by the first *Manchester Directory* (1772), which lists 269 cotton manufacturers in Manchester at a time when there was not a single mill within the town. Chapman states that in 1774 "as many as 30,000 people about Manchester were engaged in the cotton manufacture." (*Lancashire Cotton Industry*, p. 3.) Considering that not all of them were employed by Manchester manufacturers (nearby Bolton was an important center in its own right at the time), the average manufacturer must have employed considerably fewer than one hundred workers.

[9] 1.5 million pounds in 1730; 3.9 million pounds in 1764; 32 million pounds in 1788. George W. Daniels, *The Early English Cotton Industry* (London: Longmans, Green, 1920), p. 24. Approximately one-third of eighteenth-century imports were shipped through Liverpool.

with favor by the Manchester manufacturers, who were becoming dependent upon the dealers as the scale of their own operations increased:

The rise of the cotton dealers was looked on with some suspicion by manufacturers, and the industry was subject to panics and fears of "corners." At the end of 1711, the price of cotton in Manchester rose sharply owing, it was supposed, to the manipulations of a group of dealers. Their attempts at monopoly were said to have been checked, but two years later fustian manufacturers were complaining that the same tactics were being repeated, and that manufacturers were themselves "forwarding the very evil they mean to prevent" by "so precipitately laying in large stocks of cotton on every vague report of scarcity."[10]

The changes brought about by the introduction of machinery in the scattered and decentralized cotton industry were at first far from dramatic. The first major improvement, John Kay's "flying shuttle," was adapted to the weaving of cotton cloth around 1760. It increased the production of weavers and allowed almost total flexibility in the width of cloth that could be woven by one man, since the shuttle was activated by a central lever rather than being thrown by hand. It was later improved by the addition of a "dropbox," with which shuttles containing different-colored threads could be alternated at will. Although the improved loom was still suitable for handicraft work and was so used, it had two far-reaching consequences. First, the relative complexity of the new machinery required a larger capital outlay, which increased the weavers' dependence on the "manufacturers" who could provide them with a cash advance to purchase the equipment or with the equipment itself. Second, the higher output of the fly-shuttle increased the demand for cotton yarn, causing a chronic shortage that had to be met by effecting improvements in cleaning and spinning the raw staple in order to increase production.[11]

[10] Wadsworth and Mann, *Cotton Trade*, p. 234.
[11] Even prior to the introduction of the fly-shuttle, four spinners were required to supply one weaver. (Daniels, *Early English Cotton Industry*, p. 74.) Mantoux mentions that "there was normally an almost constant shortage of thread. As soon as the fly shuttle enabled the weaver to work much faster this shortage became still greater. Not only did the price of thread go up, but it was often impossible to obtain the necessary quantity within a limited time. From this there often resulted delays in the delivery of material, much to the detriment of the manufacturers. Weavers, who had

Hargreaves's spinning jenny, patented in 1770 but in use for several years before, mechanically reproduced the hand operations of a spinner. It allowed the simultaneous spinning of several yarns, each on its own spindle, and was simple enough to be operated by children. Although it multiplied the output of the human hand by a factor of eight to twelve, it was not able to produce thread of sufficient strength and fineness for the warp. Arkwright's introduction of spinning by rollers was a different approach to the problem insofar as the technique did not depend on the human hand as a source of power. While the jenny, like Kay's improved loom, was still a handicraft type of machine, suitable for cottage work, Arkwright's water frame (1769 and 1775) was a factory-type machine that was powered most efficiently from a relatively large, central source. The introduction of the water frame marked a decisive change in pace; from then on, all technological improvements—such as Arkwright's carding machine and Samuel Crompton's "mule," which combined the principles of the jenny and the water frame—depended for their successful utilization on the economies of scale that only factories could provide. Moreover, for the first time, a surplus of yarn was produced, and England became an exporter not only of cotton cloth but of yarn as well.[12]

The availability of an external source of power sufficient to activate the machinery was the principal locational requirement of the cotton industry. The presence of a waterfall became indispensable. The numerous streams of Lancashire offered ideal conditions, but with few exceptions, the existing towns and villages did not possess an adequate waterfall, and as a result, factories were built in the countryside, drawing their labor force from nearby villages and hamlets. When it was more convenient, the factory owners constructed new workers' housing near their plants. The pattern of new clusters that accompanied industrialization was thus the consequence (at least in the case of Lancashire and the West Riding of Yorkshire)

---

to pay the spinners, found it hard to make a living." *The Industrial Revolution in the Eighteenth Century*, 2nd ed. (New York: Harcourt, Brace, 1929), p. 213.

[12] The official value of yarn exports was as follows:

1798	£ 30,271	1801	£ 444,441	1804	£ 902,208
1799	204,602	1802	428,605	1805	914,475
1800	447,556	1803	639,404		

of the dependence of manufacturing on a natural source of power.

A dramatic example of this process is the growth of Tyldesley, which in less than fifteen years was transformed from a country estate into one of the urbanized components of the Manchester cluster. Aikin gave a description of its development:

The *Banks of Tildsley*, in the parish of Leigh, are about one mile and a half in length, and command a most beautiful prospect into seven counties. The air is pure and healthy; the springs remarkably soft and clear, and most excellently adapted to the purposes of bleaching. The land is rich, but mostly in meadow and pastures, for milk, butter, and the noted Leigh cheese. This estate had, in the year 1780, only two farm houses and eight or nine cottages, but now [1794] 162 houses, a neat chapel, and 976 inhabitants, who employ 325 looms in the cotton manufactories of Marseilles quiltings, dimities, corduroys, velvets, velveteens, thicksets, muslinets, and new stripes for furniture. Lately Mr. Johnson has erected a large factory six stories high, and a steam engine, with dye-houses and other extensive buildings for the woollen business, which consists of kerseymeers and various fancy goods in all woollen, and silk and woollen. There are two other factories upon the estate, intended to be let for the woollen business, and one very large building, newly erected, intended for the spinning of woollen and worsted. It is Mr. Johnson's intention to introduce the woollen branches into this part of the country, and it certainly appears a very eligible situation, having great plenty of coal, fine water, being in the centre of some thousand weavers, and only distant four miles from the duke of Bridgewater's canal at Worsley; and the Lancaster canal will run near the estate. Mr. Johnson has been at a considerable expense in setting up the newest and most approved machinery for willowing, scribbing, carding, roving, and spinning of fine woollen yarn, which he means to employ, not only for himself, but for the accommodation of all others who may be induced to settle upon the estate in the woollen business. There are a number of boys from twelve to sixteen years of age at the factory, who are with great care progressively instructed in the manufacture of various fancy woollen articles, with a view of establishing the fine woollen business in the neighborhood; and Manchester being the first repository of manufactures, is daily frequented by foreigners, and town and country buyers, which has already induced several capital woollen houses to settle there. Every sort of new machinery seems to be encouraged by the work people of Tildsley, and the great advantages of scribbing and shearing by stream or water, with use of the fly shuttle, will most probably be a means of establishing manufactories there.[13]

The machines used in the manufacture of Lancashire cotton goods were similar, if not identical, to those used in the Tyldesley wool

[13] *Description of Manchester*, pp. 299–300.

mills, and Mr. Johnson can be considered as typical of the gentlemen farmers whose almost visionary understanding of the technological bounties of the age allowed them to join the ranks of the
new industrialists by taking advantage of the favorable ecology of
their estates—an abundant supply of water both for power and for
processing. It was the foresight and entrepreneurial skills of such
people that were transforming the quiet English countryside into
thriving industrial towns.

The impact of the new machines was felt by the closing decades
of the century. In 1750, there were only six urban places within a
twenty-mile radius of Manchester, that is, towns of fairly dense
settlement with a population greater than 2000; in 1775, there were
twelve such towns, and in 1821 there were sixteen (see Figure 12).

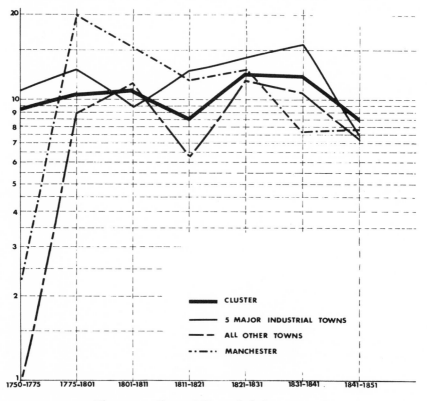

Figure 12. Rate-of-Growth Index, 1750–1851

The urbanization of the Manchester cluster occurred in phases, each reflecting the technological and economic restructuring of the area's textile trade. Prior to about 1775, Manchester's dominance was not due to manufacturing, which continued to be carried out in the countryside or in adjacent towns.[14] The growth potential of any single town within the cluster was directly related to the presence of existing manufacturing activities and hence to a combination of ecological and historical factors. This is exemplified by the high growth rate of such traditional industrial towns as Bolton, Bury, Stockport, and Oldham. The development of Manchester itself was tied to the overall level of economic activity within its cluster, since it remained the principal marketing center, largely because of its accessibility to Liverpool after the navigational improvement of the Mersey and Irwell rivers in the 1720s.[15]

The first technological innovations introduced between 1775 and 1811 led to the rapid growth of the cluster's older manufacturing towns. Simultaneously, the implantation of mills in such rural places as Tyldesley, Altrincham, and Middleton precipitated their urbanization. What emerged during this transitional stage was a complex pattern of interdependencies, which was not unusual in a period of rapid change when old economic relationships were being profoundly altered by the new manufacturing techniques. A typical example of the involved and often far-flung interests of the early textile industrialists is provided by William Radcliffe. His spinning and weaving mills at Mellor, near Stockport, provided work, in his own estimation, for "upward of 1,000 weavers," some of whom were employed at his own factories, while others "were widely spread over the borders of three counties." In addition, Radcliffe

[14] Manchester did not acquire manufacturing importance until the last decade of the eighteenth century and the introduction of the steam engine, which offset its lack of adequate streams for water power. "In 1789, the first steam engine for spinning cotton was erected in Manchester, and from that year the manufacturing prosperity of the town may date its rise." John Reilly, *The History of Manchester* (London: J. G. Bell, 1861), p. 257.

[15] Certain other towns, although dependent upon Manchester, were markets for the textile industry in their own right. For example, Bolton, most probably an older textile town than Manchester, was an important marketing center for neighboring villages, even though "its manufacturers almost universally repaired to Manchester to sell their goods on the Tuesday . . . Thursday . . . and Saturday of every week." Aikin, *Description of Manchester*, p. 263.

had warehouses in both Stockport and Manchester. His was not a unique case; the proceedings of a meeting of Stockport manufacturers in April 1800 illustrate the coexistence of the traditional handicrafts system and the new factories.

On comparing notes, we found that there was not a village within thirty miles of Manchester, on the Cheshire and Derbyshire side, in which some of us were not putting out cotton wraps, and taking in goods, employing all the weavers of woollen and linen goods who were declining those fabrics as the cotton trade increased. . . .[16]

The repercussions of industrialization can be found in the close relation between urbanization and the geographical distribution of textile mills and in the spreading network of canals and roads that were being constructed to facilitate the shipment of goods between Manchester and the surrounding region (see Figures 13 and 14). By 1800, there were about 90 mills in the immediate vicinity of Manchester alone, a remarkable progress since Britton enumerated 42 water mills for the whole county of Lancashire in 1787.[17] After 1800, when the use of the steam engine allowed greater flexibility in the location of factories,[18] Manchester industrialized quickly and started to grow faster than the combined towns of its cluster. By 1821, at which time no fewer than 66 textile factories were located within its boundaries, Manchester contained almost 50 percent of the urban population of its cluster (as opposed to 32 percent in 1775), and its economic dominance as a manufacturing and marketing center had been firmly established.

PREINDUSTRIAL MANCHESTER

The rise of Manchester from the "mere village" described by Daniel Defoe in 1727 to a thriving commercial town during the

[16] William Radcliffe, *Origin of the New System of Manufacture* (Stockport: J. Lomax, 1828), p. 12.

[17] John Britton, *A Topographical and Historical Description of the County of Lancaster* (London: Sherwood, Neely and Jones, n.d.), p. 275.

[18] "About . . . 1790, Mr. Watt's steam-engine began to be understood and introduced into this part of the kingdom, and it was applied to the turning of . . . various machines. In consequence of this, water-falls became of less value; and instead of carrying the people to the power, it was found preferable to place the power amongst the people, wherever it was most wanted." J. Kennedy, "On the Rise and Progress of the Cotton Trade," *Memoirs of the Manchester Literary and Philosophical Society*, 2nd ser. 3 (1819): 127–128.

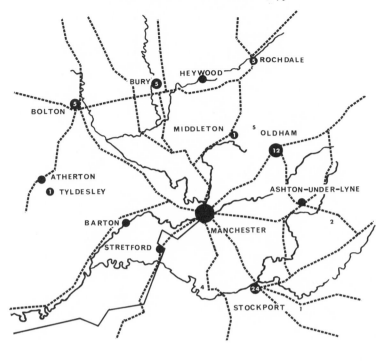

Figure 13. Manchester Cluster—1775

second half of the eighteenth century, and to one of England's
most important industrial centers and its largest city after London
in the nineteenth century, is attributable as much to the ability of
its inhabitants to adapt to changing conditions as to the ecology of
the region, which was favorable to early industrialization. But unlike
Liverpool, whose steadily accelerating rate of population growth
reflected its constantly increasing importance as one of the coun-

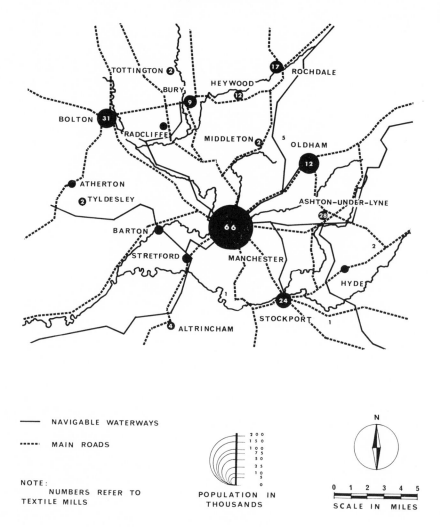

Figure 14. Manchester Cluster—1821

try's major ports, Manchester's rate of growth fluctuated, reflecting its changing regional function and its struggle for economic supremacy. Figure 15 shows a steady rate of population growth during most of the eighteenth century, owing to the city's function as a market for its industrializing hinterland. Yet during that time, Man-

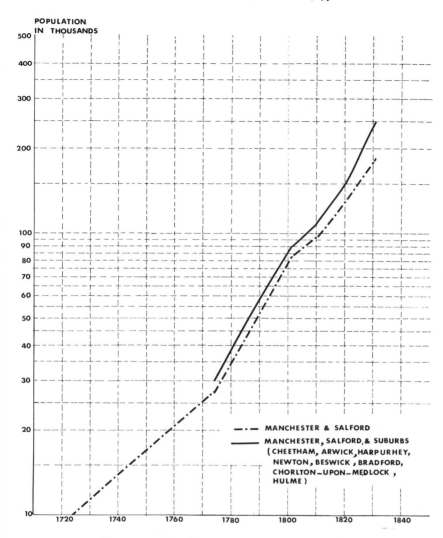

Figure 15. Population in Manchester and Salford

chester's share of the urbanized population of its cluster dropped
from 34.3 percent in 1750 to 32.2 percent in 1775, a consequence of
the rapid industrialization that was taking place in neighboring
villages and towns. In the last decade of the eighteenth century,
however, the situation changed radically: the introduction of manu-

facturing within Manchester itself, made possible by the steam engine, which was a more than adequate substitute for the natural power whose absence had retarded its industrialization, caused a sudden explosion of the population, which quadrupled in the next twenty-five years and then doubled every twenty years. Simultaneously, Manchester's rising economic dominance within its cluster is shown by the steady increase in its percentage of the urbanized population: 44.9 percent in 1801, 49.2 percent in 1821, and 47.5 percent in 1851.[19]

The developed area of mid-eighteenth-century Manchester consisted of less than a quarter of a square mile (including Salford), a rough circle with a radius of approximately twelve hundred feet. The most highly developed part of the town was between Dean's Gate, Brown Street, and the bottom of Shude Hill. The town was expanding rapidly to the south because of the docking facilities at the bottom of Kay Street, which were used by ships of up to fifty tons linking Manchester and Liverpool along the newly improved Irwell River. St. Anne's Square and the surrounding streets formed one of a number of typical residential districts for middle-class merchants, with "pleasant . . . new streets with houses of red-brick and stone, while the Square itself, a tiny remnant of the spacious Acresfield, was bordered with newly planted trees with the stately cupola of St. Ann's in the background."[20] A new exchange was being constructed on Market Place by Sir Oswald Mosley, the lord of the manor, "for the accommodation of the merchants and manufacturers of the town."[21] In fact, the whole town seems to have had the appearance of a vast construction yard, no fewer than 2000 new houses having been built between 1718 and 1738, according to a contemporary estimate.

In spite of all this activity, or perhaps because of it, eighteenth-century Manchester was lacking in most public amenities, a condition not unusual at the time, as the case of Liverpool illustrates. Aikin lamented the unpaved and unlit streets, the preempting of sidewalks by flights of stairs leading to private houses, the wretched conditions of the poor, who "are crowded in offensive, dark, damp

[19] The drop in 1851 reflects the suburbanization of adjacent areas with the introduction of commuter railroads.
[20] Redford and Russell, *Local Government in Manchester*, p. 33.
[21] Reilly, *History of Manchester*, p. 231.

and incommodious habitations, a too fertile source of disease."[22] He was also more than ready to ridicule the social mores of the new moneyed class of merchants, their lack of private carriages, and their resistance to giving up their traditional tankard of ale or homemade wine in favor of "the new-fashioned beverage of tea and coffee."

Yet the provincialism of the Manchester merchants, somewhat ridiculous to a Londoner, did not prevent them from taking full advantage of the new manufacturing processes. When the first wave of industrialization occurred in their neighborhood, increasing the local production of cotton goods, the Manchester merchants defended their town's economic dominance as a distribution center by expanding their market area to cover the whole of England and even Europe.[23] Their interest in transportation (the Irwell and Mersey Navigation Act, for example, was sponsored jointly by the merchants of Liverpool and Manchester) reflected their awareness of the struggle necessary to survive economically in a period of change. When industrialization at home became possible, thanks to James Watt's stationary steam engine, both the necessary capital and a keen awareness of the international cotton trade allowed a rapid transformation of the town from a regional market to "the Metropolis of Manufacturers." Liverpool's ascendance as a major port resulted from its oligarchical corporation's substantial public investments, particularly in the construction of docking and warehousing facilities; Manchester, devoid of any but the most rudimentary forms of local government, showed no corresponding pattern of governmental interest and effort in its economic development, but rather a collection of individual endeavors.

Surprising as it may seem to us today, the absence of local con-

[22] *Description of Manchester*, p. 192.

[23] "Whereas in the early stages of the town's commercial development [the Manchester merchant] had worked hard and frugally for a livelihood, later acquiring some capital but still living as plainly as before, by the middle of the eighteenth century he was reaching out for orders in every market town in England and acquiring for himself some of the luxuries which wealth brought . . . . With the rapid expansion of industry through the textile inventions, the merchants extended their own activities correspondingly, sending out their agents into every port in Europe, and investing their profits from these enterprises in mechanized cotton spinning." Nicholas J. Frangopulo, *Rich Inheritance* (Manchester: Manchester Education Commission, 1962), p. 41.

trols was thought to have definite advantages.[24] Foremost was the lack of regulations restricting trade to freemen of the town. While Liverpool merchants could, and did, control potential competitors by refusing them the freedom of their borough or exacting a fee for the temporary privilege of engaging in trade, Manchester was ready to welcome all comers attracted by the economic opportunities it offered, be they merchants or workmen, Englishmen or foreigners. There was a dramatic expression of this hospitable attitude in 1799, when a German merchant, Carl Brandt, was elected "boroughreeve" (mayor) of the town, an occurrence probably unique in the annals of English local government. That the advantages to be derived from this situation were recognized at the time is shown by Ogden's comment that "perhaps nothing has more contributed to the improvements in trade here, than the free admission of workmen in every branch, whereby the trade has been kept open to strangers of every description, who contribute to its improvement by their ingenuity."[25]

Although Manchester's population explosion did not take place until the closing decades of the century, by the 1770s its growth was already accompanied by many of the difficulties that became characteristic of the industrial towns and prompted nineteenth-century reformers to take action. The mercantile town was transforming itself into the finishing center for the region's cotton goods,[26] and the manufacture of laces and hats was also extensively carried out. These early manufacturing activities had started to attract

[24] Aikin (*Description of Manchester*, p. 191) mentioned that "with respect to *government*, it remains an open town, destitute (probably to its advantage) of a corporation, and unrepresented in Parliament." James Ogden stated flatly that "nothing could be more fatal to its trading interest, if it should be incorporated, and have representatives in Parliament." *Description of Manchester* (Manchester: M. Falkner, 1783), p. 93.

Strangely enough, this attitude was still shared, fifty years later, by the commissioners investigating the status of municipal corporations. "The Commissioners have generally found that those corporations which have not possessed the Parliamentary franchise, have most faithfully discharged the duties of town government, and have acquired, more than others, the confidence and good-will of the communities to which they belong." *Report of the Royal Commission on Municipal Corporations*, para. 73.

[25] *Description of Manchester*, p. 93.

[26] "Fustians were made about *Bolton, Leigh,* and the places adjacent . . . where they were bought in the grey by *Manchester* chapmen, who finished and sold them in the country." Ibid., p. 74.

workers who were crowding the existing housing and beginning to spill over into new quarters, built hastily with little or no care for the comfort or health of their inhabitants. This early form of urban sprawl led a contemporary observer to remark that "the township [i.e., the areas adjacent to the town] is indeed but of small extent; and the greatest part of it will probably, in a short time, be included in Manchester."[27]

The chronology of these migrations during the early years of the industrial revolution is somewhat nebulous, but it seems likely that Manchester was one of the first Lancashire towns to experience the successive waves of migrants from the rural areas of Lancashire, Cheshire, Wales, and Ireland that were to swell urban population in the ensuing decades.[28] The appearance of a substantial number of paupers and the problems of feeding a growing population were therefore of great concern to the Manchester Court Leet. In 1731, almost simultaneously with Liverpool, the burgesses of Manchester petitioned Parliament to establish a workhouse to employ the poor. But the project met with unexpected opposition from local Tories, who feared that they could not control this institution, since only eight of the twenty-four guardians would be appointed from their ranks, the others being selected by the Whigs and the Presbyterians. Sir Oswald Mosley also opposed the bill (which was eventually defeated in Parliament), since it could be construed as a breach of his baronial prerogatives. He built a workhouse at his own expense instead, but it was discontinued after a few years when the appointed guardians refused to pay their share of the costs.

The efforts of the Court Leet to keep the price of provisions within the means of the poorer segment of the population were

[27] Thomas Percival, *Observations on the State of Population in Manchester* (Manchester: privately printed, 1789), p. 5.

[28] The first migrants were weavers, attracted to the Manchester area by the high wages and the brisk demand for their trade when the spread of Kay's and Hargreaves's inventions led to increased production of yarn. See John L. and Barbara Hammond, *The Skilled Labourer: 1760–1832* (London: Longmans, Green, 1919), Chapter 4.

"The Irish immigration, so important in the later stages of the Industrial Revolution, had begun, and a writer in 1749, boasting of the small number of Papists in Manchester, could say 'those we have are of no note or condition being chiefly poor Irish brought here to settle by our manufacture.' By 1787 there were 5,000 Irish [in Lancashire industrial towns], and the number had at least doubled by 1804." Wadsworth and Mann, *Cotton Trade*, p. 313.

equally unsuccessful. The rapid increase in food prices, in spite of several attempts by the court to ensure an adequate supply and to control the quality and weight of produce sold within the town market,[29] brought about the first of many similar crises in 1757. On June 7,

two women cheapening some Potatoes in the Market, and the Seller asking what they thought an unreasonable Price, they without further Ceremony, overturned their Sacks, and scatter'd the Potatoes abroad, which the Boys and Women near, seized and carried away.

Encouraged by this, and joined by more Rabble, they directed their way to the Meal-House, which they entered, and began to Plunder . . . . A part of the dispersed Rioters, joined by some others near Ardwick-Green, stopped a Cart coming to Market, and plundered it of eight Loads of Meal . . . .

Flushed with their Success, and having tasted the Sweets of Plunder, they directed their Course to the Warehouse . . . situated in Toad-Lane, broke it open, and began to carry away Grain, Flower, Meal, Cheese, and here continued plundering . . . .[30]

The mob was eventually dispersed by "the Magistrates and principal Inhabitants of the Town [who] armed themselves with Stout Sticks," and by the high sheriff of the county, who came into town "attended by fifty of his Tenants, Neighbours and Friends, well armed."

This account illustrates the Manchester government's lack of means to deal with the most elementary problems of public order and its need to rely upon *ad hoc* measures with a distinctly rural flavor. Moreover, the carrying out of justice by the part-time magistrates was not always devoid of personal danger, as shown in the following contemporary account (1772) of a public whipping in nearby Stockport.

[29] Individuals were fined at almost every session of the court for selling "short of weight." At the Michaelmas session of 1756, the court decided to fine sellers of "Wheat, Barley or Beans which Load shall contain less than Twenty Pecks for every Load . . . and for every Load of Oates Exposed to Sale which shall contain less than Thirty-Six Pecks," in an effort to encourage the importation of large quantities of food. Similarly, none of these basic staples was to be sold except at a prescribed time at the weekly Saturday market, in order to ensure competitive prices and adequate quality. John P. Earwaker, ed., *The Court Leet Records of the Manor of Manchester*, 12 vols. (Manchester: H. Blacklock, 1888), vol. 8.

[30] *Manchester Mercury*, June 21, 1757.

On Friday, the 24th of July, one Benjamin Booth of Werneth, was publicly whipped, in pursuance of an Order from the Quarter Sessions, having been convicted [for the third time] for buying embezzled Yarn; but either through Fear or by a Bribe, the Punishment was inflicted in such a manner as to render it a mere Mockery, which induced the Gentlemen who had prosecuted him to order another Man to perform the remainder of the Sentence on Monday last, when he received twenty lashes; Immediately after, a Number of Persons behaved in the most brutal Manner to the principal Tradesmen, and particularly to those who have been active in prosecuting this Fellow; Several of the rioters were taken by a Warrant which our worthy Rector granted, and they are bound over to the next Quarter Sessions, and it is hoped they will meet with due Punishment.[31]

The Manchester of the 1770s (Figure 16) covered a built-up area of about 165 acres, of which 35 were in Salford, across the river. Table 2 summarizes the enumeration of 1773–1774 for the two towns and for the area immediately adjacent to Manchester. The highly urban character of both Manchester and Salford (par-

Table 2. Characteristics of the Manchester Area, 1773–1774

	Manchester	Salford	Suburbs
Population	22,481	4765	1905
Males	10,548	2248	947
Females	11,933	2517	958
Houses	3446	892	311
Inhabited houses	3402	866	311
Uninhabited houses	44	26	0
Families	5317	1099	361
Unrelated individuals (does not include members of a household)	492	31	0
Children under 15	7782	1793	763
Average size of family	4.14	4.32	5.28
Average population per house	6.61	5.50	6.13
Gross density[a]			
Houses per acre	27	23	—
Inhabitants per acre	179	122	—

Source: Percival, *Population in Manchester*, p. 2.
[a] Densities are calculated for built-up areas only.

[31] Cited in Wadsworth and Mann, *Cotton Trade*, p. 398.

▲	PUBLIC HOUSING		COMMERCE & FINANCE
○	PUBLIC BUILDING		INDUSTRY. & WAREHOUSES
▬ ▬	CANALS		UPPER-INCOME RESIDENCES
	OPEN SPACE		LOWER-INCOME RESIDENCES
			WORST SLUMS

N

0   600   1200
SCALE IN FEET

Figure 16. Land-Use Structure of Manchester in the 1770s

ticularly the former) is clearly evident: the density of the built-up part of the town is very high,[32] and the family size is smaller than in more rural areas. In addition, the growing number of unrelated individuals living in boarding and lodging houses is the first sign of the presence of a new socioeconomic group that was to increase enormously in importance over the years, changing the social characteristics of the industrial city: lone, itinerant workers, married or single, moving from town to town in search of better employment opportunities. When unable to find work or when laid off during one of the frequent economic crises, such individuals could not rely upon the assistance of other family members, and they swelled the rolls of the Poor Law authorities and of charitable organizations or joined the ranks of the urban underworld. Together with the migrants from rural areas, they epitomized the failure of the traditional welfare measures that had been devised in the more stable society of Tudor England and had now become an anachronism.

Following the dissolution of the monasteries by Henry VIII, it became necessary for government to assume the traditional function of caring for the indigent. An act was passed in 1536 entrusting to municipal and borough authorities the task of collecting alms on Sundays and holidays for a relief fund administered by the church-

---

[32] The concept of density as an index of urbanization can be misleading unless used comparatively. Harland Bartholomew found that the average *net* residential density in contemporary American cities, that is, the ratio of people to land used only or mainly for residential purposes, varied between 25.4 and 49.5 persons per acre. (*Land Uses in American Cities* [Cambridge: Harvard University Press, 1955], pp. 27–28.) The *gross* density of late medieval and Renaissance cities, that is, the ratio of population to total land area, seems to have rarely exceeded 40 to 60 persons per acre with the exception, perhaps, of some of the Dutch towns, where it may have been as high as 160 persons per acre before the seventeenth-century expansions of the city walls, at which time it fell back to about 100 persons per acre. See J. C. Russell, "Late Ancient and Medieval Population," *Transactions of the American Philosophical Society* 48, no. 3 (June 1958); H. Klompmaker, "Les villes néérlandaises au XVIIième siècle," *Recueils de la Société Jean Bodin* 7:577–601; Gerald L. Burke, *The Making of Dutch Towns* (New York: Simmons-Boardman, 1960); Pierre Lavedan, *Histoire de l'urbanisme*, 3 vols. (Paris: H. Laurens, 1941), vol. 2.

The density of settlement in Manchester and Salford at the end of the eighteenth century was therefore very high by any standard, historical or contemporary, and foreshadows all of the abominable living conditions of the lower classes that dismayed Dr. Kay some forty years later. (See pp. 134 ff. of the present work.)

wardens (27 Hen. 8, cap. 25). The Poor Law of 1601 (43 Eliz. 1, cap. 3) further institutionalized the responsibility of local authorities by creating workhouses for the poor. Parish assessors were appointed to levy a special tax, supply work for the able-bodied, give relief to the infirm and the old, and apprentice orphans and abandoned children into a suitable trade. However, when industrialization created a more mobile working class whose livelihood was affected by the vagaries of local economic fluctuations, the Poor Laws discouraged the search for better employment opportunities. In particular, the Law of Settlement of 1662 (13 and 14 Car. 2, cap. 12) was utilized to prevent the free movement of labor in order to protect economically prosperous areas from having to take on a disproportionate burden of relief. This law, "enacted for the good of the poor, for the correction of rogues and vagabonds, and for the proper employment of such as were legally chargeable to the parishes of their settlement," empowered the authorities to remove forceably to his place of origin, within forty days of his arrival, any person occupying a tenement with a rent smaller than £10 per annum. A later amendment to the act allowed migration of labor under license only, with mandatory repatriation to his parish of origin should the migrant become unemployed.[33] With some modifications, these laws remained in effect until 1835, and their enforcement, together with the administration of the proceeds of the limited funds that had been bequeathed specifically for the relief of the poor, was the sum total of the social-welfare undertakings of the Manchester Court Leet.

Until 1804, "Officers to Prevent Inmates" were appointed for each of five districts within the town to prevent the settling of poor families likely to swell the relief rolls. Their duties were

. . . to Search within their District twice a year, and to Examine Whether any ffamilies [sic] reside therein without a Certificate, that are likely to become chargeable to the Town, and to report the same to the Overseers of the poor, that such ffamilies may be Compelled to produce a Certificate from their place of Settlement, Or in Default thereof persons suffering such ffamilies to reside in their Houses are liable to a forfeiture of Ten Shillings a Month by the 31st. Eliz: Ch:7.[34]

Like many of the court's yearly appointments, the ten to twenty Officers to Prevent Inmates held somewhat anachronistic positions.

[33] 8 and 9 Will. 3, cap. 30 (1697).
[34] Earwaker, *Court Leet Records,* 9:7.

Infirmary

Hunt's Bank

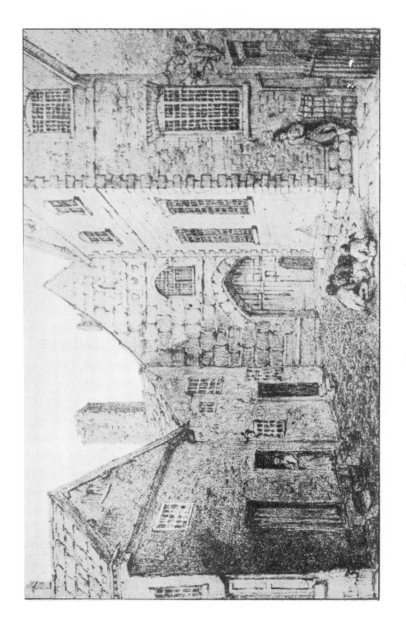

Grammar School

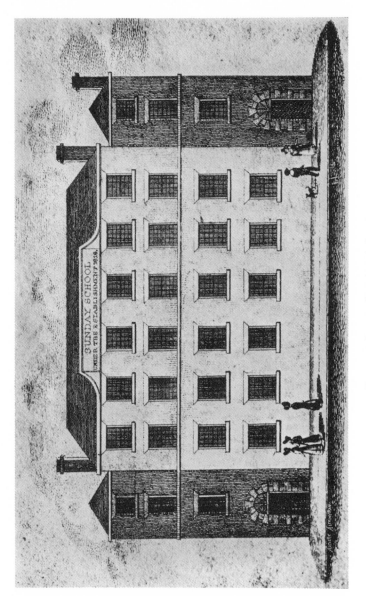

Bennett Street Sunday School

Force of habit rather than any clear understanding of changing circumstances seems to have dictated many of the court's actions. In the cases of these officers, for example, the Elizabethan statute under which they were to levy a fine of 10s. had been repealed in 1775 (15 Geo. 3, cap. 32), "but nobody at Manchester appears to have noticed the legal change for over a quarter of a century."[35]

The Court Leet's charitable expenditures consisted of trifling sums given to individuals in extraordinary circumstances ("to a poor Woman in Distress: six pence")[36] and to the supervision of the "township stock." Composed largely of bequests given to the town for the relief of the poor and the proceeds of certain fines, the township stock was administered by the churchwarden, who submitted accounts yearly for the court's approval. The court also supervised the actions of the trustees who administered various private charities, such as the Boroughreeve's Charity, which, like many others, contained strict clauses to prevent abuse.

To prevent deception, the article [to be given to an applicant] is sent to the recommender, who instructs the poor person to exhibit it to him, when it is made up into the article of dress intended; and to prevent its being pawned or sold, the cloth is marked with some permanent ink, so that pawnbrokers cannot plead ignorance of the means to secure to Poverty, the comforts which the charity of the pious founders intended for its comfort.[37]

THE NEED FOR HOME RULE

Manchester's lack of formal institutions similar to those of Liverpool was not an unmixed blessing. Legally, the Court Leet, Manchester's "local government," performed two distinct functions:

In the first place it sat as a small-debts court every three weeks and administered expensive justice to the poor. In the second place, there were two annual "great court leets," in autumn and spring, at which, presided over by the Lord's Steward, a jury of the most influential inhabitants was assembled, the manorial officers were appointed and a few cases of market offences and "common nuisances" were dealt with.[38]

[35] Redford, and Russell, *Local Government in Manchester*, 1:187.
[36] Entry for August 22, 1775. John P. Earwaker, ed., *The Constables' Accounts of the Manor of Manchester*, 3 vols. (Manchester: H. Blacklock, 1892), 3:325.
[37] *The Manchester Guide* (Manchester: Joseph Aston, 1804), p. 194.
[38] Shena D. Simon, *A Century of City Government* (London: Allen & Unwin, 1938), p. 39.

It is this second function that is of interest. The jurors' role was essentially supervisory, in that they were asked every year to approve the town's accounts and to select and appoint the court's officers, from boroughreeve to market watchers. The daily affairs of the town were vested in the boroughreeve and the two constables who were responsible for the maintenance of peace and order. The bylaws to be enforced were few and relatively simple: taxes and fees were to be gathered from Manchester and its subsidiary hamlets; the quality of goods sold in the markets was to be controlled; the public drains and water mains were to be maintained and their proper utilization supervised; the public rights-of-way were to be protected from encroachers; the removal of refuse by each householder was to be enforced; and—perhaps the most difficult and time-consuming responsibility—the saftey of Manchester's inhabitants was to be ensured.

An examination of the Court Leet's *Records* and *Accounts* for 1770 gives a fair idea of its limited ability to deal with the increasing complexities of a rapidly growing town whose population had just passed the twenty-thousand mark. Its prime concern was protective services. One hundred and forty officers were appointed at the court's Michaelmas session of October 10, 1770: 11 were tax collectors; 15 enforced the general bylaws and 52 the sanitary bylaws; 18 supervised the markets and 4 the trades; 25 enforced special bylaws; and only 2, the deputy constable and the beadle, were responsible for police protection.[39] These last two officers were the only ones who received a salary, £30 per annum for the deputy constable and £10 for the beadle; in addition, the town provided the beadle with a uniform, £12 4s. 9½d. being expended for this purpose during the fiscal year 1770–1771.[40] Table 3 shows that most of the court's expenditures were allocated to keeping the peace: maintaining the day and night watch, particularly the winter watch, which is mentioned in the minutes of each Michaelmas session, and prosecuting criminals before the Lancashire assizes. No less than 40 percent of the town's net resources were used for this purpose in 1770–1771.[41]

[39] Earwaker, *Court Leet Records*, 8:128–133.
[40] Earwaker, *Constables' Accounts*, 3:206.
[41] The actual expenditures were £291 8s. 1d. for that year, £118 7s. 2d. having been used to repay the constables for the previous year's deficit.

Table 3. Manchester Receipts and Expenditures,
Fiscal Year 1770–1771

	£	s.	d.	%
Receipts				
Taxes	306	19	8	75.2
Fines	2	2	—	.5
Miscellaneous	20	4	4	5.0
Deficit	80	9	4	19.3
Total	409	15	3	
Expenditures				
Police	116	17	6½	28.6
Construction and maintenance	13	9	3	3.3
Streets	9	18	7	2.4
Salaries	61	15	5	15.0
Fees	19	0	3	4.7
Charity	13	9	5	3.3
General administration	44	5	9½	10.6
Miscellaneous	12	11	6½	3.1
Debt repayment	118	7	2	29.0
Total	409	15	3	

Source: Earwaker, *Constables Accounts,* 3:190–207.

The court's expenditures also illustrate its administrative procedures. It paid for services rendered by individuals on a piecemeal basis, its officers, as well as outsiders hired from time to time, being reimbursed for out-of-pocket expenses, or even being paid a fee for a particular service. In the year in question, for example, Thomas Holt was paid £4 14s. "for 92 nights overlooking the watch," and Titus Note £1 19s. "for superintending the watch,"[42] in fact assisting the deputy constable and the beadle in their duties. Moreover, the unpaid officers responsible for enforcing the bylaws relied extensively upon paid informers to alert them to a breach of the law. We find numerous items such as this: "To Thomas Walker and three others attending in the Market to prevent Regrating and Forestalling . . . £2 9s. 6d."[43] Similarly, witnesses brought before

[42] Earwaker, *Constables' Accounts,* 3:195.
[43] Ibid., p. 206. Regrating and forestalling were two forms of speculation upon the price of wheat.

the court or sent by the court to the assizes to prosecute a case were paid their expenses and, in some cases, a fee.

Public investment in the town's capital plant was negligible, being restricted to maintenance of public buildings and occasional improvements carried out under a private act.[44] But of the 96 private acts pertaining to Manchester[45] that were passed during the eighteenth century, 28 were concerned with the improvement of canals and rivers, 27 with highways outside the town, 3 with churches, 1 with the relief of the poor, and only 5 with the general improvement of the town. The first of these, the Manchester and Salford Police Act of 1765 (5 Geo. 3, cap. 81), simply confirmed the constables' power to administer the cleaning of the streets and the keeping of a fire watch; the second, the first Manchester Improvement Act (16 Geo. 3, cap. 63; 1776–1777) authorized a public subscription of £10,000 to widen and improve some of the old streets around the Exchange.

The Manchester constables were not without excuse for the restricted scope of their activity. Foremost was the lack of revenue. Although the yield of the property tax did increase substantially (more than tripling between 1750 and 1775), expenditures rose even more quickly, as shown by the growing yearly deficit during this period (see Table 4). And, unlike Liverpool, Manchester did not

Table 4. Manchester Revenues and Expenditures, 1750–1776

	Revenues			Expenditures			Debt repayment			Deficit		
	£	s.	d.	£	s.	d.	£	s.	d.	£	s.	d.
1751–52	151	—	7½	90	4	1	105	9	11½	44	4	8
1754–55	169	—	3	164	2	8½	58	11	10	53	14	5½
1760–61	239	13	0	262	9	10	20	16	11	43	12	9
1763–64	473	—	8	388	2	1½	380	2	6¼	115	3	5½
1770–71	329	5	11	291	8	1	118	7	2	80	9	4
1775–76	488	11	—	463	8	7½	248	9	7	223	7	2½

Source: Earwaker, *Constables' Accounts*, vol. 3.

[44] The expenditure of £13 9s. 3d. on the construction and maintenance of public facilities seems to have been unusually high! Almost half of that sum went to repair the guardroom after a fire.

[45] See Barbara Heywood, *Acts of Parliament Relating to Manchester, 1540–1800* (Manchester: Manchester Public Libraries, 1957).

possess a large corporate estate whose revenues could be utilized to improve the town. The comparison between the two towns is striking: Liverpool's yearly revenues in the 1760s amounted to £4726, while Manchester's were only on the order of £240. Even taking into account the fact that Liverpool was a larger town (35,000 inhabitants versus Manchester's 20,000), the gap is still impressive. Moreover, the Liverpool corporation was allowed to borrow what capital it needed, the increasingly profitable operation of its dock estate ensuring the cooperation of private lenders. This was not the case in Manchester, where the yearly deficit was carried out of the pockets of its constables until the next year's revenues could be used to reimburse them. The burden upon private individuals, however rich and public-minded they might have been, was enormous, and it is not surprising that they were generally unwilling to provide the town with operating capital beyond what was needed to fulfill traditional responsibilities.

The inability of the Court Leet to broaden its activity was compounded by its lack of control over tax revenues. The Act of 1778 (18 Geo. 3, cap. 19) had transferred the defrayment of the constables' accounts to the churchwardens of the Manchester parish, who had previously been responsible solely for the administration of poor relief. The town officials' salaries, the expenses of the highway surveyors, and the wages of visiting overseers, as well as the constables' general accounts, were thus paid out of the poor rate, which was levied on real property at 1s. per pound of assessed valuation. This was not an unusual situation in England, since the Act of 1778 had simply given legal sanction to a widespread practice. In fact, the pre-1778 custom of levying a "town ley" to defray the expenses of the Manchester Court Leet seems to have been a unique procedure, most courts having to rely solely on the fines they collected.[46] But this method of assigning the collecting of revenue and its expenditure to two separate political bodies was detrimental both to the good management of the town and to poor relief.

The lack of adequate records and the fluctuating method of assessment from year to year[47] and within the six townships of the

[46] The Webbs mention that the only other town that followed the practice of a town rate was Lewes, Sussex. *The Manor and the Borough*, 2 vols. (Hamden, Conn.: Archon Books, 1963), 1:103fn.

[47] See James Wheeler, *Manchester: Its Political, Social and Commercial History* (London: Whittaker, 1836), pp. 268 ff.

parish (Manchester, Salford, Withington, Blackley, Newton, and Stretford) made it impossible to obtain a continuous series on the poor rate or to compare poor-relief expenditures to the town's population. But it seems that the yield of the poor rate during most of the eighteenth century must have been little more than £1000 yearly.[48] It is evident that this amount was grossly inadequate, considering the increase in pauperism that accompanied urbanization and the extension of the use of the poor rate to defray "ordinary" expenditures. Moreover, the lack of adequate funds was made worse by a lack of interest on the part of the unpaid churchwardens, by inefficiency, and often by downright dishonesty.[49] Although official supervision of the constables' accounts was now the prerogative of the parish vestry, no attempt seems to have been made to increase the level either of municipal services or of relief. It must be remembered that the vestry did not appoint the constables; yet the fact that they exercised far from effective control over the constables' accounts from 1778 onward indicates that their laxness in interpreting their responsibility to administer public welfare extended to their supervision of the town's affairs.

To a certain extent, the paucity of public welfare was compensated by private charities. These ranged from very small bequests in cash or land rents for "the relief of poor, aged, and impotent people, inhabiting Manchester" or for such specific purposes as the purchase of "blue frize kersey gowns, to be given to five aged men, inhabiting Manchester, on Christmas-day morning in the south porch of the collegiate church,"[50] to substantial endowments of several hundred pounds, either for general relief or for the construction of permanent facilities. By the end of the eighteenth century, the capitalized value of minor charities was on the order of £8500,

[48] In 1794, when the rate had gone up to 5s. on the pound and the town had at least doubled in size, the yield of the poor rate was £9270 14s. W. E. A. Axon, *The Annals of Manchester* (London: John Heywood, 1886), p. 121.

[49] "The unpaid parochial officers of Manchester, in the last quarter of the eighteenth century, were a slack and incompetent set of High Church Tories. If we may judge by the meagreness of their official records, a good deal of the parish business was done quite informally, perhaps at 'the veal pie feast, held monthly at the Bull's Head' which was attended by all parties in office, churchwardens, overseers, constables, town and country sidesmen, etc., a jolly clan." Redford and Russell, *Local Government in Manchester*, 1:181.

[50] *Manchester Guide*, pp. 198, 199.

yielding some £500 per annum to be distributed to the poor.[51] Although these funds must have been administered with varying efficiency, outright dishonesty in the trustees seems to have been very rare.[52] Responsibility in the administration of charitable funds was as much a part of eighteenth-century middle-class English mores as distrust of government interference in welfare and other public facilities and services.[53]

In addition to these minor charities, whose proceeds were distributed either in kind or in money, Manchester possessed four charitable institutions. The oldest, Chetham's Hospital, founded in 1651, was a boarding school for 80 poor boys, aged six to fourteen, who were taught reading and writing, as well as a trade. The town's largest library (fifteen thousand volumes) was part of this institution. The second, the almshouses in Miller's Lane, were founded in 1680 from the proceeds of several bequests and offered accommodations for 24 poor families. The Manchester Infirmary, the town's first hospital, was established in 1752 by "several worthy, and public-spirited characters."[54] It was an immediate success; in its first year, in temporary quarters in a private house, it treated 75 in-patients and 249 out-patients. A permanent building was erected in 1755 in Lever's Row on top of the town's highest hill, an airy site being considered essential both for the welfare of the patients and for prevention of the spread of contagious diseases to the town. In 1766, a lunatic hospital and asylum was added to the growing medical complex, which was becoming a teaching hospital for the training of

[51] The *Manchester Guide* (pp. 192 ff.) contains a detailed listing of these charities, their donors, the dates of their establishment, and their purposes.

[52] There is only one recorded instance of a donation having been lost (£400, given by Elizabeth Kirkham in 1762), "one of the trustees having obtained the possession of it . . . ." (Ibid., p. 203fn.)

[53] Commenting on this situation, Leon S. Marshall remarks, "The approach to the condition of the poor as a moral problem colored every effort toward social amelioration. On one hand, the rich were urged to perform their moral obligations of charity to the poor; and on the other hand, the poor were advised to be morally deserving . . . . The poor were frequently told that they themselves were morally responsible for their condition . . . . This view that the behavior of the poor created the greater part of their distress persisted into the nineteenth century and after." (*Development of Public Opinion in Manchester, 1780–1820* [Syracuse: Syracuse University Press, 1946], p. 44.) Hence, the patronizing restrictive clauses frequently included in charitable endowments.

[54] *Manchester Guide*, p. 151.

surgeons and was rapidly accumulating a good medical library. In 1781, public baths were constructed for the general use of the townsmen.

Like many other English market towns, Manchester possessed a grammar school that provided the sons of the wealthier burgesses with a classical education. Founded some time before 1520, richly endowed,[55] staffed by six masters who were well paid by the standards of the time, and housed in a new building in 1777, the Free School represented the only adequate educational facility in Manchester until well into the nineteenth century. It was restricted to the sons of the middle class, and there is no record of the school's having made any effort to bring in scholarship students. The first attempt to provide poor children with the rudiments of an education was made in 1782, when a certain Mr. Fildes, a disciple of Robert Raikes, the founder of the Sunday school movement, "opened a Sunday school in a cellar . . . . Others soon lent their support and, as a result, a second school was shortly afterwards established by them in a garret, while a third . . . was erected, at Fildes' own expense, behind a dwelling-house in the neighbourhood of London Road."[56]

Many of the churches, particularly the Methodist, followed suit and opened Sunday schools where the children were taught to read and write.[57] By 1785, a uniform curriculum had been agreed upon by the various religious sects, which had formed a joint school committee, and the use of Sunday schools as the proper means of instilling the children of the poor with basic notions of morality and learning had gained widespread acceptance. Yet the manner in which education should be carried out was the subject of much contention. In 1786 it was decided that writing should not be taught in the schoolroom, and in 1788 the Anglican church with-

[55] The endowment included land in Manchester, one wheat mill, one malt mill (the only one in Manchester), and a woolen factory. During the closing decades of the eighteenth century, the school's revenues were on the order of £1500 per annum. Ibid., pp. 215–216.

[56] Frangopulo, *Rich Inheritance*, p. 74.

[57] The Sunday school enrollment in 1788 was estimated at about 4000. (Axon, *Annals of Manchester*, p. 115.) Hence less than 50 percent of school-age children (between seven and fifteen) were receiving an education. I have estimated a school-age population of just over 10,000 children, based on the age breakdown reported in the 1773 enumeration. (See Percival, *Population in Manchester*, p. 2.)

drew from the Manchester Sunday School Committee because it could not muster a majority against the teaching of reading!

Whatever advantages may be derived from *learning to read*, it is a benefit of far higher inportance . . . to impress upon young minds a devout sense of duty toward God and their neighbours, by introducing them early to the habits of public and private worship.[58]

The continuing conflict between the liberals (largely from the dissenting churches) and the conservative Anglicans brought about a stalemate that prevented the organization of an adequate educational system in Manchester until the Parliamentary Inquiry of 1833, which led eventually to public control of education.

In the last decades of the eighteenth century, industrialization and the increased burden of taxation, largely for relief of the poor, led to demands for reform in Manchester. In 1789 the first Boulton and Watt stationary steam engine was installed in a textile mill owned by one Peter Drinkwater, and in 1790 the first power loom was installed in Mr. Grimshaw's mill, opening the way to Manchester's industrial supremacy; in 1792 the first steps were taken toward reforming the town's government, with the appointment of "commissioners for better cleaning, lighting and regulating the towns of Manchester and Salford." The first sign of public discontent with the Court Leet and, by implication, the manorial authorities was the holding of a public meeting in December 1786 for "removing certain nuisances and inquiring into the tolls levied by the lord of the manor." The purpose of the meeting was to protest what were considered excessive charges levied by the manorial officials on goods brought into Manchester, either for sale in one of its thirteen markets or for storage. A "committee for asserting the rights of Manchester" was formed to convince Sir John Parker Mosley that the Charter of 1301 specifically exempted the burgesses from such tolls. Their request was quickly denied. Prompted by this unprecedented attack upon manorial rights, Sir John attempted to strengthen the Court Leet and improve its efficiency. At the Michaelmas session of 1788, William Robert, the steward of the manor, delivered a long and energetic charge to the jurors.[59] The

[58] *Manchester Gazette*, quoted in L. S. Marshall, *Public Opinion in Manchester*, p. 76.
[59] "A Charge to the Grand Jury of the Court Leet, for the Manor of Manchester," reprinted in Earwaker, *Court Leet Records*, 9:235–253.

document is an embodiment of conservative attitudes toward local government, inadvertently pointing out all its weaknesses. After reminding the jurors that the court had existed "these thousand years, essentially in its present form," Robert stated forcefully that it could "in no way whatever violate or preserve, diminish or increase the private rights which are inherent in the Lord, or the privileges that appertain to the inhabitants of the Manor." He then berated the jurors for allowing the "legal and constitutional powers . . . of regulating the police of the town [to be] considered a mere matter of idle festivity and parade, and of useless veneration for antient [*sic*] usage." Commenting on recent progress, Robert pointed out that "a Town increasing as this is in Opulence, in Populousness, and in Importance, requires the exertion of every nerve it possesses, to combat the prevalence of Licentiousness, Irregularity, and Disorder."

Having thus justified the court's role by means of a long historical dissertation tracing the court's prerogatives to pre-Conquest days, Robert went on to enumerate its responsibilities, an extraordinary listing in that none of Manchester's problems, which were growing every day more acute, was even mentioned. The court's areas of competence were described as the punishment, by fines, of several public nuisances (allowing swine and refuse on the public ways, open cellar holes, carts blocking the street, encroachment of private buildings on the street); the task of preventing forestalling, regrating, and engrossing and of ensuring the quality of goods sold in the markets; the regulation of gaming houses and brothels and the prevention of other disturbances of the peace. Somewhat lamely, Robert concluded:

It is certain, that if the powers of the Court were once put in motion, and the Inhabitants of Manchester could see of what utility it might be, it would remain no longer in the inactive state into which it has fallen. . . . All we want, and all that are necessary, are sensible, respectable, steady, upright, active Officers. This Town is happily freed from the feuds, the riots, and the tumults of Corporation Towns—should it then be solicitous to create new sources of contention, to disturb its own tranquility?

Although this and subsequent juries seem to have been impressed by the steward's charge and were alacritous in inspecting open cellar holes and fining the culprits, the court made no attempt to deal more vigorously with the town's problems. The only notable changes were an increase in the deputy constable's salary from £20 to £150 in 1786 and the appointment of three beadles, instead of one, to assist him in the performance of his duties. Understandably enough, these minor expansions of the court's activity did little to ingratiate it with the public.

The demand for reform was moreover being aggravated by national political strife. The split between Church of England Tories and Dissenter Whigs was widened by controversy over the repeal of the Test and Corporation Acts, which prevented members of Dissenting churches from holding public office. Encouraged by the successes of the French Revolution,[60] the liberals formed the Manchester Constitutional Society to press for the reform of government along the lines formulated by Priestley and Paine. The following year, 1792, they launched their own newspaper, the *Manchester Herald.* Their efforts were short lived; the paper's offices were burned by a political mob nine months after its inception, and they found themselves the target of harsh repressive measures. The anti-Jacobin riots of that and the following year "were not merely tolerated, but even encouraged by the police officers of the Court Leet and by some of the local magistrates."[61] The house of the proliberal boroughreeve, Thomas Walker, was attacked by the mob with impunity, a glaring evidence of the ineffectiveness of the Court Leet in maintaining order.

After crushing their enemies, the Tory leaders' fear of even a friendly mob's action prompted them to extend the powers of local government by supporting the bill creating the police commissioners (32 Geo. 3, cap. 69). The commissioners consisted of the warden and fellows of Christ Church, and the Manchester and

---

[60] In November 1790, "the dissenters commemorated the revolution of 1688 with toasts and clearly indicated their desire for extensive political and economic reforms: 'May the Example of one Revolution prevent the Necessity of Another'; 'Success to the Revolution in France'; 'May complete Responsibility attach to every Public Situation'; 'the Disfranchisement of the rotten Boroughs, and a speedy, full and adequate Reform of the Representation in Parliament'; 'Freedom to Commerce and the Speedy Downfall to all Monopolies, and the East Indian in particular.'" L. S. Marshall, *Public Opinion in Manchester,* pp. 109–110.

[61] Redford and Russell, *Local Government in Manchester,* 1:198.

Salford boroughreeves and constables, all as ex officio members;[62] in addition, every person owning property with an annual rent or value in excess of £30, or occupying such premises, could become a commissioner upon taking the prescribed oath. The commissioners were described by the act as being "one Body Politick and Corporate," and in effect they preempted most of the Court Leet's responsibilities in all matters concerning the making and enforcing of bylaws for the administration of the two towns. In addition, they were given the power to levy a rate of 1s. 6d. on the pound on all properties in the towns, raising the total tax rate in Manchester to 2s. 6d. on the pound, including the Poor Rate, or 12 percent of assessed valuation—a not inconsiderable sum.

Potentially, the impact of the act was substantial, primarily because it might have furthered the democratization of local government. For the first time, the people of Manchester and Salford, or at least their middle class,[63] were given an opportunity to participate in the administration of their affairs without constant manorial supervision; more important, they were free to define the scope of their government and had sufficient financial resources to carry out needed improvements. However, there was scant popular participation, since few eligible persons became commissioners, and attendance at the commissioners' meetings was low. It was not until 1797 that the commissioners started showing an interest in fulfilling their responsibilities by establishing a night watch of fourteen men and purchasing 1100 lamps to light the streets of the town.[64] In addition, the two towns, artificially divided by a river but essentially one both economically and functionally, were united under a common government. Strangely enough, the commissioners never even at-

[62] The warden and fellows of the Collegiate Church of Christ represented the ecclesiastical government of the parish, at least as far as the "official" church was concerned. Hence, the Police Act attempted to combine, or at least to represent, all levels of local responsibility within its structure.

[63] "It is true that the property qualification for Commissioners was stiff enough to exclude all the industrial wage earners and many of the small shopkeepers; but the two towns were already wealthy as well as populous, and must have contained, even in 1792, many hundreds of persons who owned or occupied premises worth more than £30 a year." Redford and Russell, *Local Government in Manchester*, 1:204.

[64] This statement may be partially unfair, since no records of the commissioners' meetings are available before 1797. However, their first concrete act did not precede that date.

tempted to take advantage of the unification clause of the act. They quickly separated, extralegally, into two bodies, composed of the commissioners residing in Manchester and those of Salford, each body "appointing separate establishments and levying separate rates, henceforth confining their activities to their respective towns."[65]

---

[65] Sidney and Beatrice Webb, *Statutory Authorities for Special Purposes* (Hamden, Conn.: Archon Books, 1963), p. 257.

CHAPTER SIX

"The Metropolis of the Commercial System"

At the beginning of the nineteenth century, Manchester was endowed with three separate and somewhat overlapping forms of local government: the Court Leet, the parish vestry, and the police commissioners (see Figure 17). At least in theory, the Court Leet continued to be responsible for all of its traditional functions, as attested by the large number of officers it continued to appoint yearly.[1] The presence of a parallel local government that was already preempting, or about to preempt, many of its functions did not seem to have moved the court to curtail the number of its officers or to abandon any of its historical prerogatives; nor, for that matter, did it display any sense of urgency in the discharge of its duties. In actuality, only the day police and the supervision of markets (in addition to its traditional levying of fines for refusal to serve or for committing conspicuous public nuisances) were still within the scope of the court's action. Again in 1799, the lord's steward commented upon the "supine and merely formal discharge of our respective duties; in conformity to the indifference that too generally prevails toward them."[2]

The responsibilities of the parish vestry were expanding rapidly, although they were still limited by law and tradition to poor relief,

[1] 123 in 1800; 106 in 1805; 90 in 1810; and 92 in 1815. John P. Earwaker, ed., *The Court Leet Records of the Manor of Manchester* (Manchester: H. Blacklock, 1888), 9:166–169, 224–227, and 10:75–77, 137–139.

[2] "Charge to the Jury of the Court Leet by John Cross, Esq.," Ibid., 9:225.

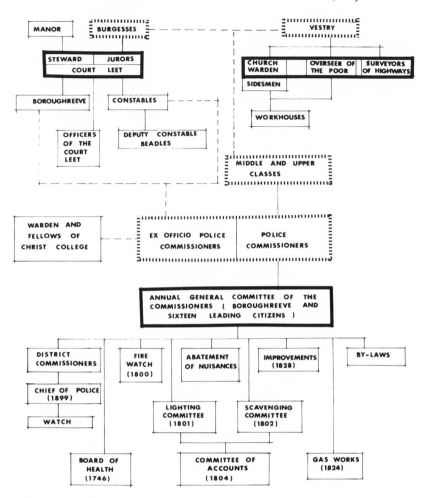

Figure 17. Municipal Government in Manchester at the Beginning of the Nineteenth Century

the upkeep of churches (and thus the supervision of what little public education there was), and the maintenance of the King's highway. The Manchester Poor House Act of 1790 (30 Geo. 3, cap. 81), "for the better relief and government of the poor of the Township," had authorized the churchwardens to concentrate their efforts on the "industrious poor," who could be sent to the poorhouse and forcibly employed "in any works, trades, manufactures and employments whatsoever," the proceeds to be used to defray the expenses of the workhouse or the poor rate in general. The churchwarden and overseers of the poor were also authorized to prosecute and punish the "idle poor." Children abandoned by their parents or found begging in the town would be sent to the workhouse "to be trained in habits of religion and industry until they were old enough to be apprenticed or put out into service."[3]

Whether through dishonesty, incompetence, or simply through force of circumstance, the vestry's increased activity proved an expensive undertaking. In the four years following the Poor House Act, the poor rate more than doubled, from £8000 to upwards of £20,000; in 1794 alone, two successive rates of 5s. on the pound had to be assessed by the churchwardens to meet their expenses and those of the Court Leet. Public pressure finally brought about an inquiry, conducted by the boroughreeve and his two constables, which revealed "an almost incredible degree of laxness and negligence . . . in all the unpaid officers, together with an audacious and long-continued venality in one or more of their salaried subordinates . . . . No cash-book, journal, or ledger was kept . . . . There was no check on the collection of the parish revenue."[4]

While the hopes of the advocates of efficient home rule lay with the police commissioners, their first decade was a time of experimentation and blundering. Attention was paid first to the internal organization of the commission: an annual general committee, composed of the boroughreeve, the constables, and sixteen leading citizens, became a more effective steering mechanism than the larger assembly of commissioners, which met rarely. The action arm of the commission was composed of forty-two district commissioners, representing the fourteen districts into which the town had been divided by the Act of 1792. By 1797, the police commission was responsible for scavenging and lighting the town as well as supervising the night watch. The latter activity was carried out under the direct responsibility of the district commissioners, while the

[3] See Arthur Redford and Ira S. Russell, *History of Local Government in Manchester*, 3 vols. (London: Longmans, Green, 1939), 2:95 ff.

[4] Sidney and Beatrice Webb, *The Parish and the County* (Hamden, Conn.: Archon Books, 1963), p. 73.

former was let out to private contractors. Both methods proved to be disastrous: the district commissioners who were supposed to supervise the watch took their duties with varying degrees of seriousness, and the performance of individual contractors was inadequate and expensive.[5] As a result, the police commissioners came under frequent and general criticism. The levying of the new police rate was resented, and in spite of the chaotic tangle of offices on the various levels of local government,[6] each level was wont to sharply criticize the activity, or lack of activity, of the others. In 1799, for example, John Cross, the court's steward, spent roughly one-third of his charge to the jury attacking the inefficiency of the police commissioners. Considering his own court's inaction, his concluding statement was rather unfair:

Thus impotent and vain are all the powers the Legislature can bestow: futile and unavailing the best system of regulations that human ingenuity can devise, alike useless and unwieldy every body politic or physical, unanimated by the voluntary exertions of those to whom are committed management and direction of their powers.[7]

To the police commissioners' vindication, they were embroiled in serious financial difficulties. Although the annual police rate of 1s. per pound of assessed value should have yielded close to £7900 a year, they were finding great obstacles to collecting even a fraction of this amount, and in spite of their modest expenditures they were already deeply in debt. One reason for their failure was the favoritism shown large property owners, particularly industrialists, who were assessed at only a fraction of real value and often granted un-

---

[5] "Both the lighting and the scavenging contracts were given to new men in 1799, and transferred again in 1800; yet there was no appreciable improvement in the work done, and the new contractors were fined [for nonperformance] almost as frequently as their predecessors." Redford and Russell, *Local Government in Manchester*, 1:210.

[6] In addition to the unpaid ex officio memberships of the boroughreeve and constables from the Court Leet and the warden from Christ Church, it was common practice for a single person to hold several of the paid offices. In 1799, the court's deputy constable was appointed to superintend the night watch, adding £75 to his sizable salary of £150; in 1796, another deputy constable, Thomas Sleck, who was also the manor's chapman and an overseer of the poor, was indicted for "having bought £100 worth of 'base and counterfeit copper coin for £40, with which . . . to pay the outdoor poor their weekly allowance.'" S. and B. Webb, *The Parish and the County*, p. 75.

[7] "Charge to the Jury . . . ," in Earwaker, *Court Leet Records*, 9:257.

explained deductions or exemptions;[8] in addition, the tax collectors, although paid at the rate of 6d. per pound collected, were lethargic in the discharge of their duties, notably in the pursuit of recalcitrant owners.

THE IMPROVEMENT OF PUBLIC SERVICES

In 1800, the commissioners started putting their house in order under the vigorous leadership of Carl Brandt, elected boroughreeve on October 14, 1799. A German cotton manufacturer who had resided in Manchester for about twenty years, Brandt had played a leading role in opposing the extension of the Cotton Arbitration Act and in the development of the Manchester Commercial Society, the predecessor of the local Chamber of Commerce organized in 1822. The commissioners' program of reform had two aims: the improvement of their financial situation and the definition of the public services they were expected to provide, as a first step toward improving the efficiency of these services. Greater control was established over the tax collectors, who were obliged to keep accurate records under penalty of prosecution for noncompliance. The tax collectors were given the full backing of the commissioners in handling recalcitrant or defaulting ratepayers, together with a new system of graduated payments to encourage them to collect the full rate.[9] These measures were eminently successful: within six months, half the outstanding debt had been paid off, and the back taxes for 1798 had been collected as fully as possible. By 1803, not only had the outstanding debt been repaid, but the treasurer's account showed a credit balance of £1000, and the commissioners made their accounts public for the first time.[10]

[8] "The Duke of Bridgewater's Manchester rates for 1797–98 and 1798–99 were still unpaid in 1800; they were then reduced, presumably in return for prompt payment." Redford and Russell, *Local Government in Manchester*, 1:212.

The churchwardens were experiencing similar difficulties created in part by a legal dispute regarding the assessability of nonresidential properties. Outright dishonesty was not infrequent; in 1804, for example, the churchwardens had "to raise a loan of more than £11,000 to make good the defalcations of a tax-collector." S. and B. Webb, *The Parish and the County*, p. 76.

[9] Instead of the flat 2½ percent they had been paid previously, the new schedule paid them 2 percent on the first third of the taxes collected, 3 percent on the second third, and 5 percent on the last.

[10] See Redford and Russell, *Local Government in Manchester*, 1:231, regarding the dispute over the chronology of the publication of the commissioners' accounts.

Turning their attention to public services, in 1800 the commissioners appointed a "special committee to abate nuisances." The number of watchmen was increased to 43 and the firemen to 22, and a paid fire chief, or "turncock or inspector of engines and conductor of firemen," was appointed for the first time.[11] The same year, growing discontent with the contract system led to the appointment of a special committee "to consider the lighting, watching and scavenging business," and in 1801 the commissioners themselves took over the task of provisioning and lighting the streetlamps. The following year, a scavenging committee was organized and assumed the responsibility of clearing the town and providing the necessary "carts, horses, land to deposit the manure upon and other requisites." To assume direct responsibility for these public services must have been frustrating as well as laborious. Previously, the commissioners could blame and fine their contractors for nonperformance; now they were liable for indictment whenever their own staff was laggard in the performance of its duties. Twice in 1804, for example, the commissioners were indicted, once for public nuisance caused by the storage of the whale oil used to light the lamps, and the second time before the Court Leet, for failing "to cleanse and remove the filth and rubbish of [Wood] Street within one Month from Notice thereof . . . and in default thereof the Court doth amerce the said Commissioners in the Sum of fifty pounds."[12]

---

[11] Factory fires were becoming a serious and costly hazard in the town. In 1800, a warehouse valued at £50,000 and a factory worth £13,000 were burned down. In 1801, 23 persons died in a factory fire, and another factory suffered damages of £2000. In 1802, a factory worth £20,000 was destroyed, and a fireman was killed at another factory fire. 1805: 4 factories destroyed, one of them valued at £20,000. 1806: £2000 worth of damages in a factory fire. A "large warehouse" was destroyed in 1809, another in 1813, and a factory in 1811. W. E. A. Axon, *The Annals of Manchester* (London: John Heywood, 1886), pp. 128, 130, 135, 137, 141, 142, 144.

[12] Earwaker, *Court Leet Records*, 9:219. Not infrequently, the court fined one of the other two levels of local government for nonperformance of duty. In October 1805, the churchwardens and surveyors of highways were presented for not repairing Jackson Row (ibid., p. 228), and again in April of the following year for not having repaired the same street and five others, at which time they were threatened with a £120 fine unless "the nuisances in the before mentioned Presentment . . . be abated before the next Michaelmas Court." Ibid., 10:6.

On at least one occasion, in 1800, the court also presented the lord of the manor for "erecting or suffering to be erected divers stalls or Butchers Shambles in a certain Public Street or Highway . . . which is a great nuisance to

The conflicts between the more democratically representative police commissioners and the Tory churchwardens and Court Leet were skirmishes rather than open warfare. Indeed, the reform initiated under Brandt's chairmanship had resulted in a fair degree of cooperation, without which even the limited success of the commissioners could not have been achieved.[13] A good example of this working relationship is the arrangement made in 1804 between the commissioners and the churchwardens to use the poor-rate books as the basis of a uniform assessment policy for both forms of local taxes. And a few years later, in 1808, an "influential committee" recommended the inclusion of the surveyors of highways in the police commission, as part of a far-reaching reform of the town government. To this end a local act, which included the purchase of the manorial rights and extensive improvements within the town, was to be obtained. Although the scheme had gained widespread support among the churchwardens, the commissioners, and the jurors, opposition of property owners led by the Tories forced its abandonment. Apparently the prospect of a new tax of 4d., although still within the scope of the original Police Act, "led to a storm of indignation . . . under the influence of which these bold projects were dropped."[14]

---

his Majesty's Subjects . . . [and] order him the said Lord of this Manor to remove the said nuisance before the next Michaelmas Court and continue the same so removed or in default or neglect thereof they do Amerce him in the Sum of One hundred pounds." Ibid., 9:162.

13 "They had greatly improved the main public services of cleansing, lighting and watching, and had extended their activities in such subsidiary branches of administration as the suppression of nuisances, the regulation of hackney coaches, and the management of the fire engines. This progress had been achieved while the town was in a most unsettled state, while prices were abnormally high and fluctuating wildly; yet the police rate had remained stabilised at one shilling in the pound throughout the period, although the Commissioners would have been legally justified in raising it to eighteenpence." Redford and Russell, *Local Government in Manchester*, 1:230.

14 Sidney and Beatrice Webb, *Statutory Authorities for Special Purposes* (Hamden, Conn.: Archon Books, 1963), p. 260. Redford and Russell (*Local Government in Manchester*, pp. 235 ff.) give a somewhat different interpretation, stating that the plan "was warmly supported by the townsmen." Leon S. Marshall (*Development of Public Opinion in Manchester, 1780–1820* [Syracuse: Syracuse University Press, 1946], p. 84) tends to support the Webbs in attributing the opposition to the scheme to "a combination of high Tories who opposed any measure of change and small-cottage owners and occupiers who objected to the imposition of higher taxes."

What is important is that local government (particularly the police commission) was showing a new interest in taking the initiative in a period of flux. Besides showing foresight in contemplating the purchase of the manorial rights,[15] the commissioners were taking other steps to extend their prerogatives and to safeguard the town's interests. In 1807, the manor's prescriptive rights to furnish water to the town had been sold to the four proprietors of a stone-pipe manufacturing concern; the following year, they presented a private bill to Parliament to incorporate themselves as the Manchester and Salford Waterworks Company. The commissioners, greatly concerned lest this or another rival scheme should fail to ensure an adequate supply of water for the town, took steps to oppose the bill. They rallied local support and, in their report to a town meeting, forcefully stated their concept of public responsibility.

Your Committee are . . . of the opinion that the supply of the town of Manchester ought to be under the direction of its own inhabitants and that it would be contrary to sound policy to entrust the furnishing and control of this important article of food and cleanliness on which the health and comfort of the inhabitants depends, to *persons whose sole object will be the promotion of their own private interests, and who are induced to the undertaking from no other motive.*[16]

In spite of the expenditure of £1760 to lobby against it, the act (49 Geo. 3, cap. 192) was passed in 1809. All that the commissioners were able to obtain was the incorporation into the act of proper safeguards against damage to streets or sewers in the course of the seventy miles or so of pipe construction to be undertaken by the company. The commissioners' fears were vindicated by the failure of the waterworks company to live up to its contract. The company went into liquidation in 1815 but was able to refinance itself, largely from local participation; it was eventually purchased in 1851 by the newly established Manchester corporation.

This first venture into "municipal socialism" had proved costly:

[15] Sir Oswald Mosley was willing to sell for £90,000, while there seems to have been a consensus within the town that no more than £70,000 should be offered. The Influential Committee's eventual recommendation to accept Sir Oswald's offer may have helped cause the public outcry that resulted in the abandonment of the scheme.

[16] Quoted in S. and B. Webb, *Statutory Authorities*, p. 261fn. (my italics). This is a particularly interesting document, since it represents the first clear articulation of a policy designed specifically to serve the public interest.

in addition to the loss of prestige suffered by the commissioners through their failure to forestall passage of the act creating the private company, they had been forced to reimburse out of their own pockets the £1760 they had spent opposing it, the Salford Hundred quarter sessions having disallowed the use of public funds for this purpose. Yet this setback did not prevent their continuing interest in the concept of publicly owned and operated services. As early as 1807, they had started experimenting in a small way with gas-lighting; in 1816 they held a special meeting to consider the suitability of extending this new technique of lighting to the whole town, where they pointed out that gas was safer than oil, as well as cheaper and more efficient.[17] They obtained unanimous support, and a resolution was passed "that it will be expedient to adopt the proposed mode of lighting the central parts of the town with gas, and for the purpose of effecting this object to raise the police rate from 15d. to 18d. in the pound."[18] Work was started immediately, and some £40,000 were spent in constructing the gas works and the conduits, and in the installation of streetlamps.[19] These expenditures were beyond what the increased police rate could provide, and the commissioners were forced to borrow heavily. But the scheme proved to be an immediate success; within seven years, half the debt had been retired through the profits from supplying private customers at the rate of 14s. per thousand cubic feet. When faced with a potential competitor in 1823, the commissioners petitioned Parliament for a monopoly on providing gas to the town. Again, they justified their stand by stating that its purpose was in the public interest:

In this great and rapidly increasing town there exists no permanent fund whatever for its general improvement, and the public, no less than the Commissioners of Police, have looked forward with great satisfaction to the acquisition of a fund applicable to that purpose; . . . the existing gas works are productive of a profit which, instead of being applied to the private advantage of individuals, is available for general objects, and may be directed either to a reduction of the public rates, or to purposes

[17] Private experiments had shown that gas-lighting of factories was possible for one-third the cost of oil or candles. Redford and Russell, *Local Government in Manchester*, 1:263.

[18] Quoted in S. and B. Webb, *Statutory Authorities*, p. 262.

[19] See Shena D. Simon, *A Century of City Government* (London: Allen & Unwin, 1938), pp. 357 ff. The Webbs seem to be in error in reporting the capital cost at £30,000 (*Statutory Authorities*, p. 263).

of public improvement, according to the varying wants and circumstances of the times as may appear best to the inhabitants at large.[20]

Largely as a result of the active lobbying of the commissioners and the discovery of fraud in the application of the rival Manchester Imperial Joint Stock Oil Gas Company, a private act was granted the commissioners in 1824,[21] and their "liberal" interpretation of their powers was legalized.

THE RISE OF THE METROPOLIS

The police commissioners' concern for public services under Brandt's leadership was awakened by the rapid industrialization of Manchester after 1790. Once steam power became available, it was only to be expected that the cotton middlemen would expand their activities from commercial to manufacturing pursuits. They could increase their profits by manufacturing their own yarn on a large scale, and they had the capital available to finance the relatively high cost of the new machinery. Finally, the development of the power loom in the early 1800s led to large industrial concentrations, "mixed firms" combining weaving sheds and spinning mills, consumers as well as producers of yarn. This growth was extraordinarily rapid: in 1794 there were only 3 cotton mills in Manchester; in 1802 there were 26. Moreover, mechanization created a demand for subsidiary activities, particularly the manufacture and servicing of machinery. Numerous firms specializing in engineering and foundry work settled in Manchester during this period, serving not only the town's industries but the cluster's other urbanized areas as well.[22] By 1795 there were at least 6 major foundries of regional importance in Manchester and Salford in addition to numerous smaller establishments still at a handicraft level.

The growth of industry in Manchester, combined with the town's function as a regional market, prompted an increasing interest in transportation. I have already mentioned the importance of the Duke of Bridgewater's canal, which halved the cost of coal through the construction of a first link between the Worsley pits

[20] Minutes of the Manchester Public Commissioners, November 5, 1823. Quoted in S. and B. Webb, *Statutory Authorities*, p. 264.

[21] Manchester Gas Act (5 Geo. 4, cap. 133).

[22] In 1801 there were at least 70 textile mills distributed within the Manchester cluster, in addition to those within Manchester itself.

and Manchester in 1764, and which connected the town to its port of Liverpool in 1776. Industrialization brought an upsurge of canal-building activity. Between 1791 and 1800, 8 acts of Parliament were passed for canal companies in the Manchester region and 6 more between 1800 and 1819. Construction was rapid: in 1801 Salford was connected to Bolton and Bury, and in 1804 the canal between Rochdale and Manchester was completed. The towns of the Manchester cluster were fully connected not only to their overseas markets but also to the rest of England via the Grand Trunk Canal. Improvement of the road network was slower but gained momentum in the first two decades of the century. While only 5 acts were passed between 1793 and 1810, no fewer than 13 were passed between 1801 and 1821.

The lack of continuous statistical series on industrial employment, even in as important a sector of the English economy as the cotton industry, is an obstacle difficult to surmount.[23] Since it is a hopeless task to attempt to estimate the labor force of cottage industries, I have attempted to trace the growth in the number of factory workers in Manchester. These results, summarized in Table 5, show the remarkable increase in factory employment that occurred at the turn of the century. This increase is particularly remarkable in that it is a "deflated" figure, including neither employment in the finishing processes of the cotton trade nor the growing importance of such subsidiary industries as metal and machine fabrication.

A further indication of the development of industry is the more frequent presentment to the Court Leet, starting in 1801, of nuisances directly attributable to factories. In 1801 alone, ten cotton-

---

[23] As early as 1835, Edward Baines expressed his dismay with this state of affairs. "The statistics of the cotton manufacture, as of all the other great manufactures of the country, are very imperfect. Government has never taken measures for ascertaining the number of persons employed and supported by the manufacture, the amount of capital engaged in it, the value of goods produced, the proportions of wages, profits, and cost of raw material which go to make up that value, the relative importance of the several branches of the manufacture, or the localities in which they are carried on. The Population Returns, which might be expected to have shown the number of persons engaged in each department of industry, do not even distinguish between those employed in the manufactures of cotton and silk, in the counties of Lancaster and Chester." *The History of the Cotton Manufacture in Great Britain* (London: Fisher, Fisher, and Jackson, 1835), pp. 363–364.

Table 5. *Growth of Cotton-Factory Employment in Manchester*

	1790	1801	1811	1821
Number of mills	1–2	23	34	66
Number of hands[a]	1240	48,300	28,300	51,800
Percentage of labor force[b]	3.5	90.0	48.0	30.0

[a] Spinners, weavers, and printers. The drop in 1811 reflects wartime conditions.
[b] The labor force is estimated at about 60 percent of the total population, since about 34 percent of the population were children under fifteen (although many of these worked in the mills), and about 16 percent were over fifty years of age. (Thomas Percival, *Observations on the State of Population in Manchester* [Manchester: privately printed, 1789], p. 2.) The 1821 census reported that 87,000 persons (57.5 percent of the population) were employed in "trade, handicrafts, or manufacture."

spinning factories and four other industrial concerns were presented for being

possessed of a certain ffurnace [*sic*] which they used to . . . burn and cause and procure to be burned . . . large quantities of Coal and did thereby then and there [make] great quantities of Smoke and soot which then and there issued from the said ffurnace into and upon the Dwellinghouses of divers of his Majesty's liege Subjects . . . to the great damage and Common Nuisance of the Inhabitants.[24]

A fine of £100 seems to have been standard for this type of offense.

Of more interest are the occasional incursions of the court into the working conditions of the new factories. The first such action occurred in 1806, when David Waddell, owner of a spinning mill, was presented twice to the court for permitting his factory to "remain in a filthy unclean and unwholesome state and Condition to the great Nuisance of all persons dwelling and residing and passing near to the same," in addition to producing an undue amount of smoke. He was fined £20 and threatened an additional fine of £5 if he did not correct these conditions by the subsequent fall sessions.[25]

[24] Earwaker, *Court Leet Records*, 9:174. The number of cases presented varied yearly, probably owing more to indifferent enforcement than to lack of cause. They were: 1801: 14; 1802: 2; 1804: 1; 1805: 2; 1806: 1; 1807: 2; 1808: 3; 1809: 2; 1810: 3; 1814: 4. Ibid., vol. 10.
[25] Ibid., 10:6–8, 15, 16, 18. But the court seems rarely to have taken notice of factory conditions. Between 1800 and 1815, there were only 4 such instances, compared to 34 presentments for smoke, 22 for encroachments, 25 for obstructions of streets, and 1 for "divers fetid stinking and unwholesome smells stenches and vapours . . . from certain boilers and vats." Ibid., p. 118.

I have already mentioned the extraordinarily rapid increase in population that accompanied Manchester's industrialization (see Figure 15), an increase whose full impact was felt only after 1780. The direct result of this population explosion was the extension of the urbanized area beyond the densely settled boundaries of Manchester and Salford. Figure 18 shows the density of settlement in Manchester parish between 1775 and 1831, together with the distribution of textile mills in the area. It should be noted that even after the introduction of steam power, the mills still had to be close to a plentiful source of water, which was used for the boilers and to clean the cotton fiber.[26] The town's piped water supply being hopelessly deficient, proximity to the Irwell, the Medlock, and the Irk was in most cases a necessity for the mills. Since these rivers formed the town's boundaries, the adjacent townships started to urbanize, first Ardwick, Chorlton-upon-Medlock, and Hulme, and later Cheetham, Harpurhey, and Newton, as shown in Table 6. While there were few opportunities for employment in these towns

Table 6. Gross Population Density—Manchester and Suburbs

	1774	1801	1811	1821
		(persons per acre)[b]		
Core				
Manchester	14.3	44.6	50.4	68.5
Salford	3.5	10.1	14.2	19.1
Industrializing suburbs				
Ardwick[a]	0.5	3.6	5.6	7.1
Chorlton-upon-Medlock[a]	0.4	1.1	4.1	11.0
Hulme[a]	0.3	3.3	6.4	8.8
Other suburbs				
Beswick[a]-Bradford	0.6	0.6	0.7	0.6
Cheetham[a]	0.6	0.8	1.3	2.3
Harpurhey	0.5	0.7	1.0	1.8
Newton	0.4	0.9	1.2	1.7

[a] Included in the municipal borough formed in 1838.
[b] Average densities for the townships.

[26] "In some cases engines were used, not to drive the machinery directly, but to raise water to an over-shot wheel." Sydney J. Chapman, *The Lancashire Cotton Industry* (Manchester: Manchester University Press, 1904), p. 56. See also John Aikin, *A Description of the Country from Thirty to Forty Miles round Manchester* (London: John Stockdale, 1795), pp. 174-175.

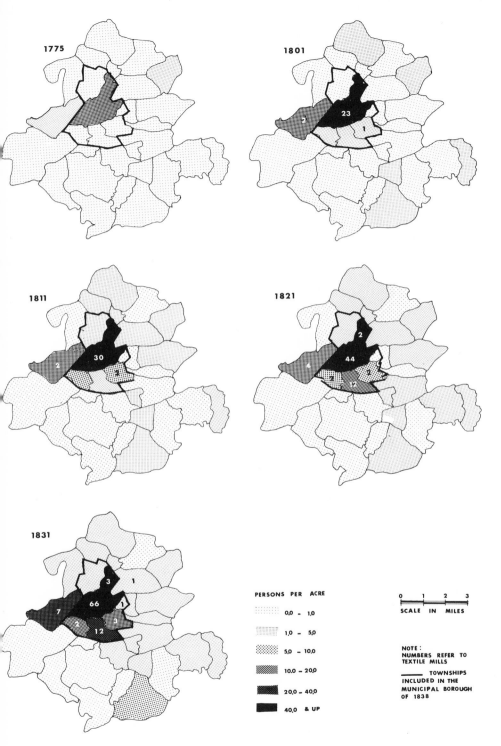

PERSONS PER ACRE

0,0 – 1,0

1,0 – 5,0

5,0 – 10,0

10,0 – 20,0

20,0 – 40,0

40,0 & UP

0   1   2   3
SCALE   IN   MILES

NOTE :
NUMBERS REFER TO
TEXTILE MILLS

——— TOWNSHIPS
INCLUDED IN THE
MUNICIPAL BOROUGH
OF 1838

Figure 18. Manchester Parish, 1775–1831

(with the exception of Chorlton-upon-Medlock, which had twelve mills in 1821) the industry on the Manchester side made them attractively located residential areas for low-income groups as the density of Manchester itself increased.

THE SPREAD OF THE SLUMS

By the turn of the century, crowded conditions were already causing upper-income groups to migrate to suburban locations. Aston's *Manchester Guide* for 1804 mentions that although "Manchester and Salford cannot, as yet, boast elegant squares, they can exhibit two most delightful suburbs." He describes their advantages in rhapsodic terms:

Ardwick-Green, which thirty years ago, was a distant village, is now joined to the town by continued streets. It is perhaps one of the best built, and most pleasant suburbs in the Kingdom, to which its elegant houses—its expanded green—and the lake in its center, all contribute. . . . Salford-Crescent . . . stands upon a spot almost unrivalled for a beautiful, and commanding prospect, which from the nature of the situation can never be interrupted by buildings; and the inhabitants of the charming elevation, will always be sure of rich country scenery, in view of their front windows, however crouded [*sic*] and confined the back part of their buildings may become.[27]

These pleasant surroundings were in sharp contrast to the conditions that prevailed in Manchester itself and in its urbanizing suburbs. The influx of population, attracted by the new factories, had not only caused hitherto unknown levels of overcrowding in the older parts of the town but also an unprecedented building boom of cheap speculative housing next to the industrial districts. Twenty-five hundred new houses were constructed between 1774 and 1788; about 4000 more between 1788 and 1801; and 6000 more between 1801 and 1821. Even then, the workingmen and their families were being crowded into every available cellar and room, partly because of the disparity between the wages they were able to bring home[28] and the rents charged by speculators, and partly because of the

27 *The Manchester Guide* (Manchester: Joseph Aston, 1804), pp. 274–275.
28 In 1833 a Manchester family of seven was paying 3s. 6d. weekly for rent out of a total income of 18s. 1d. This amounted to almost 20 percent for four rooms and was thought to be about average for their class. Great Britain, *Parliamentary Papers*, Series D1, vol. 20 (1833), "Factory Commission Report," pp. 39–40.

necessity to live close to the factories in the absence of any means of public transport. The results were appalling:

> The number of damp, and very ill ventilated cellars inhabited in many parts of the town, is a most extensive and permanent evil.
>
> It may be necessary to explain to gentlemen who have not visited such places, that they each consist of two rooms under ground. The front [room] is used as a kitchen, and though frequently noxious by its damp-ness and closeness, is greatly preferable to the backroom. The latter has only one small window, which, though on a level with the outer ground, is near the roof of the cellar. It is often patched with boards or paper, and in its best state, is so much covered with mud, as to admit very little either of air or light. In this cell, the beds of the whole family, sometimes consisting of seven or eight [persons] are placed. The floor of this room is often unpaved. The beds are fixed on the damp earth. But the floor, even when paved, is always damp. In such places, where a candle is required, even at noon-day, to examine a patient, I have seen the sick without bedsteads, lying on rags. They can seldom afford straw. . . .
>
> The want of proper sewers in several of the streets, and the offal of slaughter-houses, left to putrify before the doors in several places, are nuisances which deserve the serious attention of the [Board of Health].[29]

There were scattered instances of better housing for the workers, four-story row houses with a two-room apartment on each floor, which must have provided reasonably adequate, if crowded, living conditions.[30] But these were exceptional, and the bulk of Man-chester's population was "crowded into one dense mass, in cottages separated by narrow, unpaved streets, in an atmosphere loaded with the smoke and exhalations of a large manufacturing city."[31]

[29] Dr. J. Ferriar, "Report to the Manchester Board of Health, 1796," *Proceedings of the Board of Health in Manchester* (London: T. Cadell and W. Davies, 1805), pp. 12 ff.

[30] See Aston, *Manchester Guide*, pp. 276–277. Considering that there was an average of over four persons per family, even these better low-income houses were exceedingly overcrowded by modern standards. They are cited by Aston as an example of efficient development and judicious siting, as "they all have the advantage of an open prospect to the river, and overlook the garden belonging to the Salford Twist Company, and their elegant factory."

Forty years later these houses are cited again, but this time to illustrate the "crowded and disorderly" method of construction and the close proximity of housing to industry that characterized urban development during the early part of the nineteenth century. Friedrich Engels, *The Condition of the Work-ing Class in England in 1844* (London: Allen & Unwin, 1920), pp. 48–49.

[31] James P. Kay, *Moral and Physical Condition of the Working Classes Employed in the Cotton Manufacture in Manchester* (London: J. Ridgway, 1832), p. 24.

Dr. J. P. Kay (later Sir James Kay-Shuttleworth), in spite of a somewhat conservative attitude toward poor relief, spent the better part of his life doing what we would now call social work.[32] He has given us a graphic description of the continuing deterioration of working-class living conditions, based on his own investigations and on the results of an inspection carried out by the Board of Health in the early 1820s. The abominable conditions he describes had prevailed from the beginning of the century, the result of the uncontrolled and rapid expansion of Manchester.

He speaks of the streets of the poorer sections of the town as "narrow avenues . . . rough, irregular gullies, down which filthy streams percolate; and the inhabitants are crowded in dilapidated abodes, or obscure damp cellars, in which it is impossible for the health to be preserved." There were but the most rudimentary kinds of plumbing, usually shared by many families: even in new housing, it was common practice to build one privy for thirty or more houses. "In Parliament Street, there is only one privy for three hundred and eighty inhabitants, which is placed in a narrow passage, whence its effluvia infest the adjacent houses."[33] The workers' homes were "ill-furnished, uncleanly, often ill-ventilated—perhaps damp: food, from want of forethought and domestic economy is meagre and innutritious."[34] The children who were too young to work in the mills roamed the filthy streets and like their parents were prey to all kinds of diseases from poor food and lack of sanitation; almost none of them attended the Sunday schools. Prostitutes and thieves were to be found in all the poor districts and, together with the profusion of taverns and gin shops,[35] contributed to the

[32] As a medical student at Edinburgh, Kay worked in the slums with Professor Alison. Returning to Manchester, he became senior physician at the Ardwick and Ancoats Dispensary and was also active in the Sunday school movement. In the 1840s, he worked with Chadwick in organizing the National Board of Health and was secretary to the Committee of Education of the Privy Council, which outlined the first steps toward compulsory primary education in England. He was one of the founders of the Manchester Statistical Society.

[33] Kay, *Condition of the Working Classes*, p. 36.

[34] Ibid., p. 25.

[35] In 1775 there were "no less than 193 licensed houses for retailing spiritous and other liquors" (Percival, *Population in Manchester*, p. 40), or one for every 145 inhabitants. Around 1820, there were 430 licensed taverns and inns and at least 322 gin shops, or one establishment for every 144 inhabitants, with the frequency being substantially higher in the working-class districts. Kay, *Condition of the Working Classes*, p. 57.

demoralization of the working class, who spent their Sundays "either in supine sloth, in sensuality, on in listless inactivity.[36]

Yet there were gradations of misery that went beyond these conditions, which can be considered almost normal for the time. The recent migrants, coming to the city in search of employment, with few skills and even fewer resources, were housed in temporary quarters until they could find their own dwellings. There were hundreds of lodging houses around the factories (Districts 2, 3, 11, and 13; see Figure 19), where "without distinction of age or sex, careless of all decency, [the newcomers] are crowded in small and wretched apartments; the same bed receiving a succession of tenants until too offensive even for their unfastidious senses."[37] Others, like the Irish migrants, congregated into ghettos, partly for protection against the still rabid Protestantism of the Lancastrians, partly for the mutual help they could derive from extended family ties or a common birthplace. In "Little Ireland" they led a marginal existence. Many of them were handloom weavers who earned 5s. to 8s. a week[38] and found it daily more difficult to compete in an industrial society. Moreover, the Law of Settlement made many of them ineligible for either indoor or outdoor poor relief, and utter destitution must have been commonplace. Kay describes the Irish settlement in Little Ireland as

. . . a portion of low, swampy ground . . . included between a high bank over which the Oxford Road passes, and a bend of the river Medlock. . . . This unhealthy spot lies so low that the chimneys of its houses, some of them three storeys high, are little above the level of the road. About two hundred of these habitations are crowded together in an extremely narrow space, and are inhabited by the lowest Irish. Most of these houses have also cellars, whose floor is scarcely elevated above the level of the water flowing in the Medlock. The [street drains] are destroyed or out of repair: and these narrow abodes are in consequence always damp, and on the slightest rise in the river, which is a frequent occurrence, are flooded to the depth of several inches. . . . [Little Ireland] is surrounded on every side by some of the largest factories of the town, whose chimneys vomit forth dense clouds of smoke, which

---

[36] Kay, *Condition of the Working Classes,* p. 59.

[37] Ibid., p. 33.

[38] Compare this to the factory wage of 24s. to 29s. for spinners and 15s. to 31s. for other factory workers. Even the average agricultural wage of 11s. was considerably higher than what a handloom weaver could earn. Moreover, the cost of living was increasing rapidly, being at least 30 percent higher than in 1790. See G. D. H. Cole, *Short History of the British Working Class Movement* (London: Allen & Unwin, 1948), p. 133.

hang heavily over this insalubrious region. . . . The habitations . . . are most destitute. They can scarcely be said to be furnished. They contain one or two chairs, a mean table, the most scanty culinary apparatus, and one or two beds, loathsome with filth. A whole family is often accommodated on a single bed, and sometimes a heap of filthy straw and a covering of old sacking hide them in one undistinguished heap, debased alike by penury, want of economy, and dissolute habits. Frequently, the inspectors found two or more families crowded into one small house, containing only two apartments [rooms], one in which they slept, and another in which they eat; and often more than one family lived in a damp cellar, containing only one room, in whose pestilential atmosphere from twelve to sixteen persons crowded. To these fertile sources of disease were sometimes added the keeping of pigs and other animals in the house, with other nuisances of the most revolting character.[39]

Kay, like most of his contemporaries, even those of a liberal cast of mind, tended to attribute at least some of these conditions to what he is fond of calling "improvidence," the lower classes' characteristic lack of economy, "without which wealth is wasted." He attacks the Poor Law for being an impersonal encouragement to idleness, citing the workers' tendency to waste their spare time instead of forming "societies for mutual relief," probably unaware that any such attempt would have been promptly repressed under the Combination Acts. Yet the demands upon the workers' time and energy during the early years of the industrial revolution were such as to all but preclude any other activity. The Manchester factory hand started work at six in the morning (sometimes earlier), had a half hour off for breakfast at eight, and then worked until noon; a one-hour lunch break was followed by a continuation of the working day to seven o'clock at night or later, six days a week. It is no wonder that very little self-improvement took place on Sundays! The absence of any type of recreation other than the street, pestilential and unpaved, or the gin shop, which was at least heated and congenial, helps to account for the numerous brawls and other breaches of the peace that were subjects of wonder to foreign visitors.[40]

These abominable living conditions were due to the overdevel-

---

[39] *Condition of the Working Classes*, pp. 21, 22, 32.

[40] Léon Faucher tells how it was necessary, in the 1820s, to mobilize extra constables on Sundays to protect families who wanted to attend church from rogues (*mauvais sujets*). *Études sur l'Angleterre*, 2 vols. (Brussells: Wouters frères, 1845), 1:198.

opment of housing and overcrowding within individual dwelling units. Figure 19 provides a comparison of these two factors within the fourteen districts defined by the police commissioners. It can readily be observed that in most of the older parts of the town (Districts 3, 5, 6, 9, and 12) overcrowding accompanied a very intensive land-development pattern inherited from the past.[41] In the newer districts, particularly those bordering on the Medlock, the situation was more confused. It has already been mentioned that some of the new housing was of a reasonable quality, but the number of rooms in each unit was certainly inadequate for the large families of the time (the average range was 4.5 to 5.8 members in 1821). Most of the speculative housing built in the newer districts managed to duplicate, if not surpass, the intensity of development in the old town. A developer would subdivide his property into long blocks, about 250 feet by 60 to 90 feet. To provide further access to the interior of these already narrow blocks, he would construct an intricate system of courts and alleys. The row houses were built back to back, so that as many as four houses could be constructed within the width of a block. Of course there was no possibility of adequate ventilation, and in many cases the narrowness of the labyrinthine passages precluded natural lighting.[42]

No attempt whatever was made to control individual developers. Each piece of land within the town was built upon according to the whim of its owner, with no limitation on use except potential marketability. The result was an incredible hodgepodge of land uses that, through a process of natural selection, managed to assume a rough order on a town-wide basis, while remaining chaotic at the neighborhood level. In the eastern portion of the town, the location of industry along existing streams created a centripetal development pattern in which speculative low-income housing tended to nestle close to the mills. By the 1820s the built-up area of Manchester

[41] District 6 is a possible exception, but these are *gross* density figures, so they should be multiplied by about two to take into account the area within the central district used for streets and other purposes. (See Chapter 5, fn. 32.) Similarly, the density shown for the newer districts, particularly 1 and 2, is certainly an underestimate, since a substantial portion of these districts were still undeveloped or in the process of development, while my figures represent the total number of houses, or people, divided by the total area of the district.

[42] Kay reports that the passages in some of the new developments around Portland Street were no more than four feet wide. *Condition of the Working Classes*, p. 36.

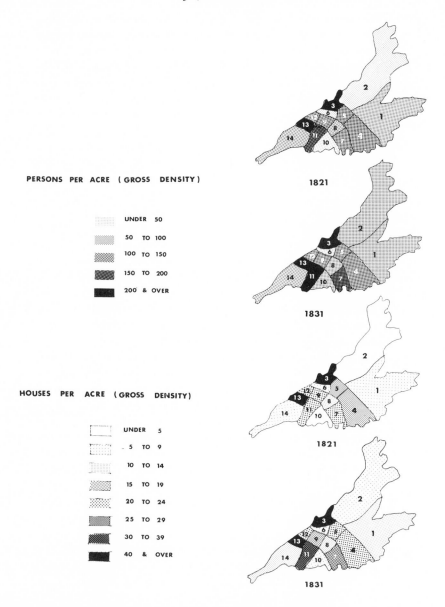

PERSONS PER ACRE (GROSS DENSITY)

UNDER 50

50 TO 100

100 TO 150

150 TO 200

200 & OVER

HOUSES PER ACRE (GROSS DENSITY)

UNDER 5

5 TO 9

10 TO 14

15 TO 19

20 TO 24

25 TO 29

30 TO 39

40 & OVER

1821

1831

1821

1831

Figure 19. Manchester Police Districts

Table 7. *Summary of the Development of the Manchester Area*

	1774	1801	1811	1821	1831
Population	29,159	90,310	110,138	154,712	227,822
Manchester	22,481	70,409	79,459	108,016	142,026
Salford	4765	13,616	19,114	25,772	40,786
Suburbs[a]	1913	6285	11,565	20,924	45,010
Houses	4645	n.a.	n.a.	n.a.	28,555
Manchester	3446	10,109	n.a.	16,653	22,445
Salford	892	2540	n.a.	n.a.	7477
Suburbs[a]	311	n.a.	n.a.	n.a.	8633
Rated valuation (£)	n.a.	n.a.	393,440	n.a.	594,782
Manchester	n.a.	37,082[b]	303,732[c]	313,147	360,121
Salford	n.a.	n.a.	34,058	47,611	80,766
Suburbs	n.a.	n.a.	55,650[d]	n.a.	133,895[e]
Density (persons per acre)	4.0	12.5	15.3	21.5	31.6
Manchester	14.3	44.6	50.4	68.5	90.0
Salford	3.5	10.1	14.2	19.1	80.2
Suburbs[a]	0.5	1.5	2.7	4.9	10.5

[a] Ardwick; Chorlton-upon-Medlock; Hulme; Beswick; Harpurhey; Newton.
[b] Figure for 1794, based upon yield of poor rate. (Probably an underestimate.)
[c] Figure for 1815.
[d] 1815 assessed value. No figure available for Beswick.
[e] 1829 assessed value. No figure available for Beswick.

covered slightly over three-quarters of a circle with a one-mile radius, approximately a threefold areal increase over the preindustrial town of the 1770s (see Figures 16 and 20). Tables 7 and 8 summarize the town's development since 1774 and its condition, by district, in the early 1820s.

It is worth noting that housing conditions in the older and newer districts of the town differed very little.[43] The poor quality of new

[43] Table 8 is a summary of the findings of a survey taken by the Manchester Board of Health in the early 1820s, only a few years after the development of the peripheral working-class districts. The inspectors' report seems to have been extremely conservative, partly because the houses they entered were of generally poor quality. Dr. Kay remarked that "the replies to the questions contained in the inspectors' table refer only to cases of the most positive kind, and the numerical results would, therefore, have been exceedingly increased, had they embraced those in which the evils existed in a scarcely inferior degree." Ibid., p. 31.

Figure 20. Land-Use Structure of Manchester in the 1820s

Table 8. Conditions in Manchester in the 1820s

Districts	1	2	3[a]	4	5[a]	6[a]	7	8
Area (in acres)	404.0	500.0	42.5	131.0	53.0	36.0	59.5	36.0
Population (1821)	21,188	15,479	10,400	13,409	7673	1747	8295	2745
Gross population density (persons per acre)	52.5	31.0	245.0	101.0	144.5	48.5	139.5	76.5
Number of houses	3546	2408	1812	2137	970	306	1390	428
Residential density (houses per gross acre)	8.8	4.8	42.6	16.3	18.3	8.5	23.5	11.9
Percentage of houses in need of major repairs	15.1	11.4	49.8	16.3	19.9	4.1	17.2	22.7
Percentage of houses without adequate plumbing	51.6	41.6	64.2	54.6	33.0	83.2	39.6	44.6
Percentage of houses ill-ventilated	8.2	4.4	24.4	10.6	2.7	—	6.1	16.7
Percentage of streets unpaved	55.4	51.6	4.8	56.0	6.7	b	24.6	12.5
Percentage of streets partially paved	11.4	3.9	4.1	15.2	16.6	b	9.4	6.4
Percentage of streets unscavenged[c]	56.1	51.0	57.1	78.9	40.0	b	32.1	43.7

Table 8 (continued)

Districts	9[a]	10	11	12[a]	13	14	Manchester
Area (in acres)	30.0	74.0	65.5	15.5	27.0	80.0	1,577.0
Population (1821)	3584	855	10,105	2252	5397	4887	108,016
Gross population density (persons per acre)	119.0	11.5	154.5	145.0	210.0	61.0	68.5
Number of houses	613	147	1508	386	887	723	17,287
Residential density (houses per gross acre)	20.5	2.0	23.0	24.9	32.9	9.1	—
Percentage of houses in need of major repairs	25.0	14.3	d	20.4	5.8	2.7	13.8
Percentage of houses without adequate plumbing	38.3	95.3	d	70.0	45.9	45.4	45.4
Percentage of streets ill-ventilated	14.8	.5	d	14.2	7.1	1.5	6.5
Percentage of streets unpaved	—	65.4	d	—	5.5	39.5	36.3
Percentage of streets partially paved	—	—	d	8.3	16.3	—	7.7
Percentage of houses unscavenged[c]	41.6	79.2	d	33.3	41.8	24.2	51.4

a Older districts.
b Only two streets were inspected in this district.
c "Streets containing heaps of refuse, stagnant pools, ordure, etc."
d District 11 was not inspected.
Source: Data calculated from Kay, Condition of the Working Classes, pp. 30–31, and the 1821 census.

construction is apparent in the substantial percentage of recently built houses already in need of repairs or painting, and the neglect of sanitary requirements is amply demonstrated by a comparison of the number of buildings without plumbing. The developers were equally unconcerned with environmental conditions. Excluding the older central districts, between 20 and 70 percent of Manchester streets were either unpaved or partially unpaved in the 1820s, in spite of existing regulations. There is, in fact, little evidence of any but the most sporadic attempts to enforce the town's bylaws, particularly in the newer districts, which by 1821 housed over 76 percent of the population.[44] Similarly, the provision of public services by the police commissioners, especially the scavenging of streets, was certainly selective: the poorer and most densely populated districts received the least attention.

THE APATHY OF LOCAL GOVERNMENT

The failure of local government to guide the development of Manchester is strikingly evident throughout the beginning of the nineteenth century. It showed the same lack of authority when faced with civil disorder. The majority of the population had few outlets for their frustrations. Hopelessly crowded in dismal surroundings and an unwitting prey to technological change and the rapaciousness of landlords, they were buffeted by the frequent economic crises that shook the cotton industy during the Napoleonic Wars and during the wild and ill-fated speculation that followed the return of peace. When faced with rising food prices in 1812 and 1817, they seized potatoes in the markets and stopped incoming carts of meal; when displaced by technological developments or forced to work

[44] The Court Leet's policy for dealing with nuisances was erratic. It seems to have concentrated its efforts, in certain years, either on a particular area of the town or on a specific type of nuisance. For example, in 1813 the court made 17 presentments for street obstructions and inadequate fencing of private property (Earwaker, *Court Leet Records*, 10:108 ff.). In 1815, 13 property owners in Henry and Lever Streets were presented for not keeping the street in front of their property in a good state of repair (ibid., pp. 131 ff.). The 1817–1818 session can well be called the "year of the butchers," since 53 out of 66 presentments dealt with the various failings of that trade (ibid., pp. 175 ff.); and the next year was the "year of the publicans," when 28 liquor dealers were presented, most of them for using false measures (ibid., pp. 212 ff.).

The Marketplace in 1810

Long Millgate

Grammar School Mills

Peter Street in 1830

Market Street in 1828

Market Street—Brook's Bank

for starvation wages, they petitioned Parliament for a minimum wage (in 1804, 1807, 1808, and 1811), and when that proved of no avail, they rioted in the streets. In view of their widespread misery during these difficult transitional years, the cotton workers' reaction was surprisingly restrained. The Manchester weavers struck briefly in 1808, 1811, and 1819, and the spinners in 1810 and 1818. But the mild, pleading tone of their petitions and the more than modest nature of their demands—in 1818 they asked for weekly wages of 9s.—are evident in the following excerpts from the Manchester petition of 1818:

> We the Operative Weavers of Manchester and its Vicinity . . . find ourselves under the necessity of soliciting the aid of those who may be friendly to our cause, in order that such as are out of employ may receive a support from such contributions as are collected by subscriptions.
> It has often been suggested that every Trade ought to afford such Wages as would be a reasonable support without the assistance of Ley Payers; and as it is well known to the Public, the various privations that Cotton Weavers have laboured under, the manner in which we have stood in need of the above support both in times past, and even at the present; and as we feel an inclination to extricate ourselves from this state, we trust we shall meet with universal countenance.[45]

This is hardly the language of the bloodthirsty Jacobins pictured by their employers and the government. In fact, there were many fewer incidents of violence in Manchester than in other northern and Midlands industrial towns. Luddism, or machine breaking, which spread through the Lancashire and Yorkshire industrial districts in 1811 and 1812, never took hold here, perhaps because industrialization arrived later. The difficult transition period between partial and extensive mechanization, with its concomitant displacement of traditional trades, was thus shorter lived in Manchester than in such older manufacturing centers as Bolton, Stockport, Ashton, and Oldham.[46] Economic circumstances were the primary cause of labor unrest in Manchester; fluctuating wages resulting from national cyclical factors,[47] rising costs, and dismal working and living conditions were sufficient incentives for organized protests.

[45] Quoted in John L. and Barbara Hammond, *The Skilled Labourer: 1760–1832* (London: Longmans, Green, 1919), pp. 117–118.
[46] For an excellent résumé of Luddism, see ibid., Chapters 9–11.
[47] The petition of 1807, signed by 130,000 Lancashire weavers, points out that "whenever the demand for goods becomes slack, many Master Manufacturers adopt the expedient of reducing wages." Ibid., p. 74.

The response to these demands was brutal. During the cotton workers' strike of 1808, and again in 1817 and 1818, regular troops were used against the strikers. One weaver was killed by the military in 1808, and 200 people were arrested at an 1817 rally of cotton workers. In 1819, at the Peterloo Field meeting, "six troops of the 15th Hussars, a troop of horse artillery with two guns, the greater part of the 31st Infantry, some companies of the 88th Regiment, the Cheshire Yeomanry, over 300 strong, and about forty of the Manchester Yeomanry" were assembled to deal with a peaceful meeting in support of parliamentary reform. "The Manchester Yeomanry, hot-headed young men who were more or less intoxicated, drew their swords, and dashed into the crowd, cutting and slashing wherever there was an opportunity. . . . Eleven persons were killed and several hundred wounded. Many of these were women."[48] That local police officers did not deal with these civil disturbances was due in part to their divided allegiance. The day police, composed of the deputy constable, the four beadles, and varying numbers of watchmen (fifty-one in 1819) owed their allegiance to the Court Leet; the same individuals, when acting as night watch, were the servants of the police commissioners. In both cases, however, their salaries were fixed by the court and paid out of the commissioners' accounts. This split in responsibility, together with the distressing lack of initiative shown by the Court Leet and the commissioners, could only encourage bureaucratic inaction. The vacuum was filled by the county magistrates, who were empowered not only to call upon regular troops to maintain order but to assume control of the local constabulary in times of emergency. The intolerant response to the well-founded demands of the workers and the use of regular troops against them was thus largely owing to the general inefficiency of local government.

Furthermore, a series of scandals that had shaken their administration made the police commissioners more willing to relinquish their authority to the county magistrates in difficult times. Immediately after the war, members of Manchester's Radical party started a concerted attack upon the commissioners, led since 1810 by Thomas Fleming, a Tory. The discovery of unexplained expenditures for various supplies led to accusations that the commissioners

[48] Axon, *Annals of Manchester*, p. 157. The Regent congratulated the county magistrates on their handling of the Peterloo meeting.

were squandering public funds. Fleming was also charged with adjourning meetings "in the middle of discussion because that discussion may tend to incriminate or expose [members of his administration]" and was accused of repeatedly acting on his own initiative without the approval of his fellow commissioners, and of allowing overpayments for public works undertaken by his friends. Finally, in 1818, a special committee was formed to examine the commissioners' accounts. In spite of the protests of Fleming and his friends, a salaried comptroller was appointed and given the "entire management, direction and responsibility of the General Accounts of the Police and Gas Departments."[49] Fleming resigned at the end of 1819, leaving his accounts in a state of total disarray and with a debit balance of over £2000.

The commissioners' financial difficulties were not entirely due to mismanagement. On the one hand, the economic uncertainties of the war and postwar years were causing wide fluctuations in their revenues;[50] on the other hand, they were investing substantial sums of money in the construction of the gas works. Although it was eventually to yield substantial profits, this first municipal venture in providing a public utility was proving to be expensive in excess of all estimates. The rapid extension of the system necessitated almost yearly inputs of fresh money, in spite of the high charges made for gas.[51] By 1823, the commissioners had invested over £30,000 in the construction of the works, the necessary conduits, and in the purchase of burners, which remained the property of the commissioners; yet £10,000 had to be borrowed in 1824, £5000 more in 1825, and an additional £7000 in 1826. But by that year, the gas directors were able to show a profit of over £2500, "after defraying all current expenses, paying interest on the loans, and making provision for a sinking fund."[52] The following year, the profits had risen to over £4000.

[49] Redford and Russell, *Local Government in Manchester*, 2:270. It is curious, to say the least, that all of the commissioners' records for the period were "lost" about that time.

[50] The police rate was based upon the *rental* value of property rather than upon a fixed assessed valuation. Hence it was quite sensitive to market fluctuations, since it was reassessed yearly.

[51] 14s. per thousand cubic feet. S. D. Simon, *A Century of City Government*, p. 358.

[52] Redford and Russell, *Local Government in Manchester*, 1:293.

In spite of the vociferous protests against the high rates charged by the gas directors—accusations of monopolistic practices, extravagance, and corruption were made by Radical politicians and small users as well[53]—the police commissioners were steadfast in their intention to use the profits from the gas works to help them out of their financial difficulties and to carry out what they saw to be needed improvements in the town. Their first public expenditure was for a new town hall, commissioned in 1820. It became a subject of lively controversy and a glaring example of the commissioners' inefficiency, taking over twenty years to complete. By 1838 it had cost about £50,000, including £6500 for the site, and in spite of its grandiose appearance it "had scarcely a room in it fit for public meetings."[54]

It is symptomatic of their political isolation that the police commissioners embarked on a scheme of such dubious public value while exhibiting little regard for more pressing needs within the town. Although every person assessed a rental of £30 or more was eligible to become a commissioner, few people bothered to take the oath of investiture, and even fewer attended the weekly meetings. The task of operating the town government and making occasional experiments with new techniques or new responsibilities fell upon the shoulders of whichever public-minded men were willing to serve. Naturally enough, the wealthy merchants and manufacturers who composed the permanent active majority of the police commissioners saw the advantages of efficient public services in terms of their own interests. Most of the services provided (paving and sewering the streets, refuse removal, general widening and improvement, and even the provision of gas-lighting) were concentrated in the central parts of the town rather than in the densely settled and rapidly growing peripheral districts that were housing a growing majority of the population.[55]

Paradoxically, it was not the general apathy of local government that aroused popular dissatisfaction with the Tory commissioners, but the high cost of the limited public services they did provide. Starting in 1818, there was an organized effort by the leypayers to

---

[53] See ibid., pp. 294 ff.; S. D. Simon, *A Century of City Government*, pp. 359–360; and S. and B. Webb, *Statutory Authorities*, p. 264. The rate was eventually reduced to 12s. in 1828 and to 10s. 6d. in 1831.

[54] *Manchester Guardian*, February 10, 1838.

[55] 76 percent in 1812; 82 percent in 1831.

control the commissioners when they presented their accounts for approval at the quarterly vestry meetings, where all public officials were theoretically obliged to render detailed accounts, though this requirement, dating back to 1778, had seldom been observed in Manchester. In the early 1820s the vestry became an open arena for public discontent: the accounts were scrutinized closely, and individual items were subjected to fierce discussion and often disallowed, to the great embarrassment of the constables and the commissioners, who had to make up these amounts from their own pockets.[56]

The next step was an attempt sponsored by the Radicals to increase the number of commissioners and thereby gain control of the local government. In 1826, over 1000 new commissioners were sworn in, and by the following year the number had risen to 1800. There was a parallel rise in attendance at the general meetings, prompting one observer to remark, "the numbers . . . have increased from about 50 to 900, thereby infinitely increasing the difficulties."[57] Although the meetings provided an appropriate platform for venting political grievances and attacking the police commissioners, little was accomplished except the introduction of secret balloting. William Whitworth, the Radical leader, was among those who thought such balloting would prevent the ruling oligar-

[56] A local Tory poet expressed his indignation at these proceedings in the following doggerel:

> A meeting convened, in a more legal way
> Was this Spring, in the Church, like a "Row at a Play."
> The Peter's Croft leaven assembled in Church,
> And attempted, e'en there, to light up the torch
> Of rebellion.—Respect for religion pulled down
> 'twould be but mere play, then to pull down the Crown.
> A bull-ring,—Cribb's parlour—a French Chamber sitting,
> Are decorous all, when compared to the meeting
> Held in April to settle the Quarter's Accounts—
> When outrageous disputes about trifling amounts,
> As excuse was sufficient—the sum but a farthing—
> To turn God's Holy Temple into a Beer-garden.

Joseph Aston, *Metrical Records of Manchester* (London: Longman, Hurst, Orme, 1822), p. 65.

[57] Quoted by S. and B. Webb, *Statutory Authorities*, p. 267fn. The minutes of the meeting of January 30, 1828, exemplify the difficult beginnings of the new democracy: "At this meeting nearly four hours were consumed in the appointment of a Chairman, and the meeting finally dissolved [on account of the tumult which took place among the commissioners present] without any business being transacted."

Table 9. Representation under the Police Act of 1829

	Districts							
	1	2	3[a]	4	5[a]	6[a]	7	8
Population	35,850	26,044	15,456	21,501	7275	1274	2744	9784
Number of voters	183	112	194	259	598	749	145	307
Percent voters to population	0.5	0.4	1.3	1.2	8.2	58.7	5.3	3.1
Number of commissioners	15	9	15	15	27	36	12	15
Population per commissioner	2390	2900	1030	1430	270	35	228	655
Assessed value (£)	38,668	16,410	17,001	27,212	39,017	45,425	17,031	24,080
Police rate (£)	2280	9700	1062	1600	2300	2680	1003	1415
Percent of total rate	10.6	4.3	4.7	7.4	10.7	12.5	4.7	6.6
Percent of population to total	21.8	15.8	9.4	13.1	4.4	0.8	1.7	5.9
Cost of improvements (£)	—	—	11,647	71	—	600	5469	—

[a] Older districts.

chy from exerting undue pressures on individual commissioners. These confused and occasionally violent proceedings were extended to the vestry, which also transformed itself from a financial controlling body into a political forum. When the boroughreeve and constables came to present their accounts, they were now faced with a "howling mob of several thousand persons, who filled the whole building, perched themselves on every coign of vantage, and vigorously applauded the speeches of their champions. . . ."[58]

Realizing that they were losing control of the town government, Tories and Whigs petitioned Parliament for a new Police Act, which paid lip service to the Radicals' demands by lowering the property qualifications for voters to £25, but raised the minimum for holding office to £35. Even under these more liberal voting qualifications, only 3800 persons, or just over 2 percent of the population, would have qualified as voters; and of the present commissioners, at least one-fourth, many if not most of them Radicals, would have been disqualified. After much discussion in the Commons, the House of Lords, and locally, a compromise act (9 Geo. 4,

[58] S. and B. Webb, *The Parish and the County*, p. 100.

Table 9 (continued)

| | Districts | | | | | | |
	9[a]	10	11	12[a]	13	14	Manchester
Population	3318	3886	13,635	11,859	7269	14,648	164,543
Number of voters	857	153	204	163	169	149	4242
Percent voters to population	25.8	3.9	1.5	8.8	2.3	1.0	2.6[b]
Number of commissioners	36	9	15	12	12	12	240
Population per commissioner	95	430	915	155	605	1220	688
Assessed value (£)	54,061	15,813	22,759	11,503	14,665	27,342	365,990
Police rate (£)	3180	932	1340	676	865	1310	21,540
Percent of total rate	14.8	4.3	6.2	3.1	4.0	6.2	100.0
Percent of population to total	2.0	2.4	8.3	1.1	4.4	8.9	100.0
Cost of improvements (£)	2000	—	229	—	—	40	20,057

[a] Older districts.
[b] Equivalent to 8.5 percent of male adults.
Source: Calculated from Wheeler, Manchester, pp. 264–310. All figures are for 1834–1835.

cap. 117) was passed in 1829, which set the minimum requirement for voters at £16 and for holding office as a commissioner at £28.[59]

Although the new act represented a partial victory for those who urged a more democratic approach to local government, it hardly achieved popular representation. By 1835 the total number of voters in the fourteen districts of Manchester, which had been extended to include parts of adjoining townships, was only 4242, or 8.5 percent of the adult males in the population. Moreover, there were gross discrepancies among the districts in the ratio between population and number of voters (the poorer districts being all but disqualified by the minimum property requirement), the number of commissioners elected, and the share of the police rate paid (see Table 9). Even accepting the restrictions of the property requirements for voters—and the more liberal Whigs and all but the most rabid Radicals did, the main topic of dispute being the amount required—the Act of 1829 was grossly unfair. Working-class in-

[59] See James Wheeler, Manchester: Its Political, Social, and Commercial History, Ancient and Modern (London: Whittaker, 1836), pp. 312 ff., for a summary of the provisions of the act.

habitants of the peripheral districts (1, 2, 4, 7, 10, 11, 14) made up only 28.3 percent of the town's voters although they paid 43.7 percent of the police rate. Conversely, the older and more affluent districts (3, 5, 6, 9, 12) contained 60.5 percent of the voters, who represented 17.8 percent of the population and controlled a majority of 126 out of 240 commissioners. Indeed, it comes as no surprise to find that the newly appointed Improvement Committee of the commissioners continued to concentrate their efforts on the central districts, to the obvious detriment of the needy portions of the town. In 1835, 71.5 percent of the total capital-improvement budget was allocated to the central districts, in spite of their paying only 45.8 percent of the police rate.

Throughout the history of their administration, the commissioners' main concern was with projects that would directly benefit members of their own class: the gas works, the improvement of the central streets, and the construction of an expensive new town hall. Although it has been claimed that Manchester was governed by a "really energetic and successful body of Improvement Commissioners,"[60] their energy was not only intermittent but highly selective. Supposedly endowed both with popular support (under Brandt's leadership in 1800, and after the passage of the new Police Act in 1829) and with a substantial source of revenue after 1825, when the gas works started yielding an increasing yearly profit, the Manchester police commissioners could have achieved a notable degree of control over the forces that were shaping their town. For example, had they only heeded Dr. Kay's recommendations to pave and sewer the streets, to remove the "years' accumulation of filth," and to oblige landlords to install plumbing facilities, they might well have avoided the cholera epidemic of 1832, which caused 674 deaths, "chiefly confined to the district of Angel Meadow, Deans-

----

[60] S. and B. Webb, *Statutory Authorities*, p. 256. There is little reason to share the Webbs' admiration for the Manchester police commissioners. It is difficult to believe that the "municipal gas-works [was] the most remarkable of all municipal experiments prior to 1835," and that it "gave to the new Town Council an impetus which was not spent for a whole generation" (p. 258). Although interesting conceptually, municipal ownership of the gas works can hardly be said to have benefited the public at large: the rates were exorbitant and the profits from the works squandered on what was probably the kingdom's most expensive town hall. As for the commissioners' energy, so much admired by the Webbs, we have seen that it was expended more on maintaining the *status quo* than in undertaking needed reforms.

gate, Portland Street, Little Ireland, and Bank Top,"[61] all working-
class quarters. Even in the face of this serious epidemic, the
commissioners were timid: when the Board of Health asked them
to scavenge the streets in the affected districts to prevent the spread
of the disease, they suggested "that the owners of them should be
compelled by indictment to cleanse them; and perhaps . . . it may
be properly recommended to authorize the Churchwardens to assist
in cleansing the unpaved streets."[62] This apathetic response to crisis
does not even exhibit the administrative cooperation cited by
Marshall as part of the evolutionary process heralding the appearance of a liberal mode of thought.[63] There is thus no evidence that
the more representative legislative formula achieved by the Police
Act of 1829 made the commissioners more responsive to public issues.

It is true that whatever social struggles that occurred during the
first half of the nineteenth century were aimed principally at obtaining economic gains for the working class rather than greater
participation for it in local affairs and that there was little articulate
public demand for better local government. Yet even in the absence
of local pressures, the forty years of the Manchester police commissioners' administration that I have traced are hardly commendable
either for a vigorous approach to social problems or for efficiency
in carrying out daily administrative responsibilities. This is all the
more disappointing in view of the fact that the governmental institutions of Manchester were forged to deal with the very problems
of rapid urbanization that its antiquated Court Leet was unable to
resolve. It might be expected that such *ad hoc* institutions would be
endowed with the popular support, the resources, and, most important, the leadership required to carry out their responsibilities.
But the Manchester police commissioners, in spite of the obvious
organizational advantages of a special-purpose authority, were no

[61] Axon, *Annals of Manchester*, p. 185.

[62] Quoted by Redford and Russell, *Local Government in Manchester*,
1:336.

[63] "The revolution in local government was not a product of a clearly
articulated public opinion. Nor was it the result of a social struggle between
divergent interests in the community. On the contrary, representatives of
conservative interests generally cooperated with those who sought to extend
and improve the services rendered by local government. This tendency to
cooperative experimentation together with the decline of the ancient institutions made Manchester's government in 1820 the product of evolutionary
processes." L. S. Marshall, *Public Opinion in Manchester*, p. 104.

more successful in creating a tolerable urban environment for the new industrial workers than were their more tradition-oriented colleagues on the Liverpool municipal council.

As an elected body, theoretically representative of the aspirations of the new industrial middle class, the Manchester commissioners should have been able to marshal public support behind enlightened policies to offset the negative consequences of industrial urbanization. In fact, the failure of the commissioners to present issues suitable for community discussion and choice alienated the voters, as demonstrated by the low attendance both at their own and at the vestry meetings until the Radical campaign of the 1820s. Reform-minded "outsiders," such as Dr. Ferriar and Dr. Kay, presented well-documented evidence on the rapidly deteriorating conditions within the town and even suggested remedies that paralleled the most enlightened current approaches to low-income housing.

What I now propose to the committee can be regarded as a measure palliative of the most urgent evils, for *the only method of furnishing the poor with healthy habitations*, which shall effectively stifle the germs of infection, *would be that of erecting small houses, at the public expense*, on the plan of barracks, or caserns, *to be let at small rents, or gratuitously, according to the circumstances of the person applying.*[64]

But the commissioners, whether by choice or through inertia, never transformed the information at their disposal into programs that might have gained public support. Rather, they sat in splendid isolation, formulating policies ex cathedra—on the gas works, on the construction of an unnecessarily ornate town hall, and on public works and services in parts of the town selected for personal convenience rather than general need—policies that aroused the ley-payers' ire on those rare occasions when they were not met with indifference.

Although the police commission had grown out of a genuine middle-class desire to create a government able to deal with the problems of rapid urbanization, within a few years of its inception the commission was operating in the same self-interested manner as the Liverpool council. But while the Liverpool aldermen could claim that they were defending the traditional interests of their corporation, the evolution of the Manchester commissioners was in

[64] Dr. Ferriar, "Report to the Manchester Board of Health, 1796," p. 7 (my italics).

direct opposition to the spirit of reform that had led to their creation. The failure of local government in Liverpool was due to the
inability of an oligarchy to adjust to the changes brought by the
industrial revolution. That failure can therefore be largely ascribed
to the rigidity that had overcome local government rather than to
an unwillingness to institute change on the part of the men who
composed it. Manchester's failure, however, was a failure of men
rather than of institutions, since neither its police commissioners
nor its middle-class voters thought it fit and proper to utilize the
institution they had created to govern their town effectively.

CHAPTER SEVEN

The Pressure for Reform

The full impact of the industrial revolution was felt throughout England by the middle of the nineteenth century. Although many changes were still in the future, most of the qualitative characteristics of a highly urbanized, highly industrialized country were present. Forty-two percent of England's population lived in the urban areas that formed an almost uninterrupted spine from London to Lancashire (see Figure 21), and the median size of the new industrial cities, most of which were already joined by the rapidly increasing network of railroads, was on the order of ten to twenty thousand people. The economic expansion that followed the end of the Continental Wars, the widespread acceptance of the new machines, and the development of rail transportation had opened new vistas that received the encouragement and support of government. Although the bounties of the industrial age were certainly unevenly shared, the repeal of Pitt's Combination Acts in 1824 had begun to pave the way for a somewhat more productive relationship between capital and labor.[1] The phenomenal increase in labor productivity that followed was due not only to the greater effi-

---

[1] "The five years from 1815 to 1820 were a season of blind and desperate reactions to intolerable distress. The decade from 1820 to 1830 was the seeding-time of working class ideas and organization . . . . By 1830, Socialism had already gone far towards taking shape as a movement aiming at the communal control of the new forces unleashed by the Industrial Revolution." G. D. H. Cole, *A Short History of the British Working Class Movement, 1789–1947* (London: Allen & Unwin, 1948), p. 52.

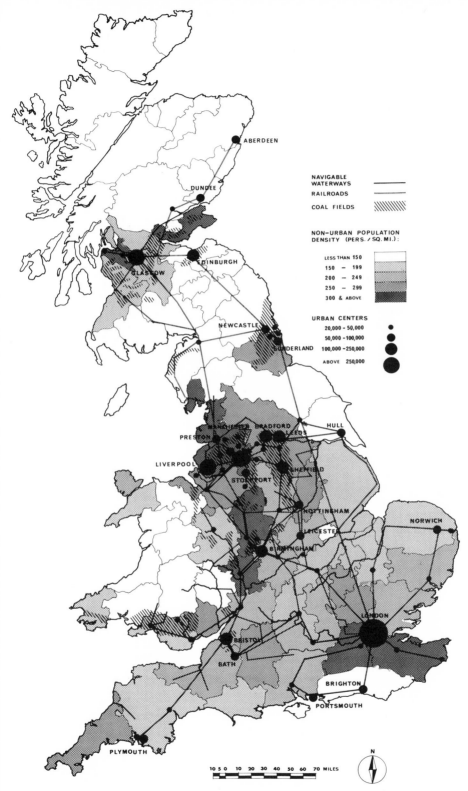

Figure 21. Population Distribution in Great Britain—1851

ciency of the machines themselves but to the willingness to utilize them to their full capacity, a willingness that had not been present in all industrial sectors during the painful transitional years at the turn of the century.

Contemporary English and foreign observers alike were aware of the impact of technological change. Von Raumer, a professor of history at the University of Berlin, estimated that the industrial worker of 1835 had achieved a productivity 266 times greater than that of former times: "And some people want this wondrous augmentation of human power and human dominion over matter . . . destroyed, or denounced as a calamity!"[2] Léon Faucher, a French visitor, deplored some of the social evils brought by industrialization, but was quick to remark that England had become the prime example of a "modern society" and that its industrialization could teach important lessons to European nations on the verge of a similar experience.[3]

If the last quarter of the eighteenth century was the age of the canals, the middle of the nineteenth century was the age of the railroads. Stephenson's steam locomotive appeared in 1813, though it was not until rolled wrought-iron rail sections were manufactured by the Bedlington Ironworks in 1820 that a roadbed smooth enough to accommodate the relatively high speed and the heavy loads of the trains could be economically constructed. The beginning of the railroad era, like that of the canals, was the opening of the Liverpool to Manchester line in 1830. Constructed at a cost of over £992,000, the line reduced to a couple of hours the travel time between the two towns, a dramatic improvement over the thirty-six hours or more that the Bridgewater Canal required. In fact, the canals had become unable to handle the ever-increasing traffic, and the long delays in moving goods on crowded canals, the slow speed of the horse-drawn barges, and the overcharges of the canal com-

[2] Friedrich von Raumer, *England in 1835* (Philadelphia: Carey, Lea, and Blanchard, 1836), pp. 293–294.

[3] "Ce n'est guère que là que l'on trouve un champ d'expérience assez vaste pour étudier les problèmes qui pèsent sur les sociétés modernes, tels que la condition des classes pauvres et laborieuses, le mouvement de la population, l'état des grandes villes, la prostitution, le crime, le travail des enfants, l'avenir de l'industrie, l'assiette de l'impôt, les rapports du pouvoir avec la liberté." *Etudes sur l'Angleterre*, 2 vols. (Brussells: Wouters frères, 1845), 1:20.

panies provided much of the incentive for private investment in rail-road construction.[4]

Both the capital investment to be provided and the engineering problems to be solved were staggering. Over the 30 miles of line between Manchester and Liverpool, 2 tunnels were pierced, 63 bridges constructed, and 928 million cubic yards of earth and rock excavated.[5] Although they were developed in much the same way as the canals—by companies chartered under a private parliamentary act, with the power of eminent domain along the projected route—the early railroads encountered vigorous local opposition, which increased their development costs. Foremost was the lobbying in Parliament undertaken by the canal companies, who were quick to see the threat to their monopoly on long-distance transportation. The Manchester and Liverpool railway bill, for example, languished in Parliament for almost two years and was rejected once before being approved. Additional opposition came from landowners who objected forcefully to having the lines pass through their property, fearing "that all sorts of vagabonds would be brought . . . into contiguity with their estates, and that the beauty of their drawing-rooms would be defaced by so unseemly an object as a steam-engine."[6] Much of the high cost of the early railroads can thus be attributed to the influence of the country gentry in a Parliament that overwhelmingly represented their interests. The early railroad acts not only required excessive land-acquisition payments but in many instances obliged the railroad companies to lengthen their routes and undertake the construction of costly viaducts and bridges

[4] "In the 1820's, cotton lay at Liverpool for weeks waiting for transport and took longer to move from Liverpool to Manchester than to cross the Atlantic." Christopher I. Savage, *An Economic History of Transport* (London: Hutchinson, 1959), p. 34.

[5] For a detailed and amusing contemporary description of the Manchester to Liverpool railroad, see James Wheeler, *Manchester: Its Political, Social, and Commercial History, Ancient and Modern* (London: Whittaker, 1836), pp. 279 ff. Referring to the viaducts, 50 to 70 feet high, that were constructed to span a number of small valleys, he mentions that they "have a fearful aspect to the stranger who travels for the first time on the railroad, and perhaps many are unable to divest themselves of the idea that the carriages may diverge from the line of propriety, and try the descent" (p. 284).

[6] Ibid., p. 280.

to protect individual landowners.[7] It was not until 1845 that Parliament attempted to establish a standard procedure for land acquisition, in which independent appraisers, appointed by the companies and the landowners, were given the responsibility of establishing the fair value of land.

In spite of the handicaps of high development costs and opposition from vested interests, the railroads were an immediate success and experienced two periods of intense activity, similar to the earlier canal booms. The first of these (1836–1837) followed the opening of the Liverpool and Manchester line, when it was realized that, contrary to earlier predictions, the railroads could be used to transport not only goods but passengers as well. During the first three months of the operation of the line, 130,000 passengers were conveyed between the two towns, and by 1833 close to 400,000 passengers were transported annually.[8] Spurred by this unexpected success, 29 bills were passed in 1836 for new railroad companies, representing a capitalization of £17.5 million; and 16 additional bills were passed in 1837. By 1841, 71 railroad lines were completed and 9 more partially opened, representing a total length of 1581 miles, with an additional 606 miles authorized by Parliament.[9] The pace continued unabated. By 1845 the government had authorized 5781 miles of railroad, with a capital value of £163.8 million, and 42 percent of the authorized mileage had actually been constructed.[10] The major cities of the industrial counties were interconnected, as were the southern towns with London.

During the second railway boom (1845–1847), the smaller lines consolidated into regional companies, the one important exception being the Great Northern Railway, authorized in 1846, which was to link London to York and the northern network. By 1851, almost 7000 miles of lines were open, and all the major English cities were interconnected. Within twenty years, all the major components of the British railroad system had been constructed, and on the main

---

[7] "Some Acts even required that screens should be erected so that railway locomotives should not frighten the horses on adjoining roads!" Savage, *Economic History of Transport*, p. 41.

[8] Wheeler, *Manchester*, p. 294. Passenger fares amounted to 54 percent of the total revenue of the line.

[9] *Journal of the Manchester Statistical Society* 4, no. 2 (July 1841):176–177.

[10] Savage, *Economic History of Transport*, p. 46.

lines it was now possible to travel at an average speed of over forty miles an hour.

The major effect of the canals had been to generate the development of industrial clusters, because lower transportation costs allowed a pattern of interdependence among industrial areas. The railroads strengthened this pattern and, in addition, had profound social effects. In order to capture as much traffic as possible, the railroads set their rates substantially below those of the canals. The result was a general reduction of all transportation costs by as much as 50 percent, since the canals were forced to cut their rates drastically once their monopoly was broken.[11] The second effect of the railroads was to ensure rapid and cheap mail communications. As early as 1838, Parliament became aware of the advantages of having the railroads carry the Royal Mail and passed an act requiring them to provide adequate mail-carrying facilities. In 1840 the "penny postage" was introduced and the first postage stamps were printed. This was indeed a major improvement for personal as well as business communications: for example, a letter could now be sent overnight from London to Edinburgh for 1d. instead of the former charge of 1s. 4½d. Last and perhaps most important, for the first time in history cheap transportation was made available to the masses. The Railway Regulation Act of 1844 established a maximum rate of 1d. per passenger-mile, thereby allowing long-distance travel, as well as the spread of low-income residential suburbs from which workers could travel inexpensively to their factories.

In Lancashire, the coming of the railroads accelerated the centralization of the cotton industry. The canals, following by a few years the original industrialization of the county, were laid out to serve their scattered customers, generating new growth around these original rural locations while permitting industrial development beyond their immediate service area. The early railroads, be-

---

[11] "The Grand Junction canal, for example, cut its coal rate to London from 9s. 1d. to 2s. 0 1/4d. a ton." Savage, *Economic History of Transport*, p. 50.

The canals had never reduced their rates from the generous upper limits prescribed in the parliamentary acts. The Duke of Bridgewater's canal, for example, which had cost £220,000 to construct, was bringing in an annual profit of about £100,000. Ernest L. Woodward, *The Age of Reform, 1815–1870* (Oxford: Clarendon Press, 1938), p. 45.

cause of their higher development costs,[12] had fewer routes and limited themselves to serving the existing industrial concentrations. As a result of their improved accessibility, all new factories built after 1830 were located in existing urbanized areas. The new textile factories became considerably larger, to take advantage of faster and cheaper movement of goods. By 1845 the average cotton mill in Manchester, which now usually combined spinning and weaving, employed between 300 and 1000 workers.[13] Moreover, the more flexible choice of routes offered by the railroads encouraged the reorganization of certain traditionally located marketing functions whose efficiency had become questionable. For example, Manchester lost its predominance as a cotton market in the 1830s, largely as a result of the railroads; it was now possible to ship cotton directly from the Liverpool docks to all of the Lancashire textile centers.[14]

The highly competitive cotton industry, sensitive to small price changes in its raw material and finished product, reacted quickly to improved communications. Manufacturing processes themselves were greatly accelerated, and full advantage was taken of the speed of the railroad:

Bleaching, formerly a process occupying weeks, might now be almost completed in the course of twenty-four hours, so that calicos which a Manchester manufacturer dispatches to his bleacher on the outskirt of the town early on one day, he *might* receive on the next—they might pass through the hands of the manufacturer in the evening—be conveyed on the same night (as is by no means uncommon) along the railway to the docks at Liverpool, and by a rapid shipment be on their voyage to a distant country within little more than forty-eight hours![15]

[12] The Bridgewater Canal between Manchester and Liverpool cost £220,-000 to construct; the railroad between these same two towns cost £992,000.

"It should be emphasized that the cost-reducing effects of the extension of the British railway system were evident in the fairly short run. The lines were laid to connect areas already highly industrialized, and prepared, almost immediately, to take full advantage of cheapened transport and communication facilities." Arthur D. Gayer, Walt W. Rostow, and Anna J. Schwartz, *The Growth and Fluctuation of the British Economy, 1790–1850*, 2 vols. (Oxford: Clarendon Press, 1953), 2:650.

[13] B. Hoselitz, "The City, the Factory, and Economic Growth," *American Economic Review* 14, no. 2 (May 1955):166–184.

[14] See Sydney J. Chapman, *The Lancashire Cotton Industry* (Manchester: Manchester University Press, 1904), pp. 114 ff.

[15] Wheeler, *Manchester*, p. 168.

Cheaper transportation also allowed greater flexibility in the supply of labor. Not only were the industries able to draw upon a larger labor market but the urban worker was free to move from one job to another. For the first time, he was able to respond to a temporary layoff, perhaps owing to local economic fluctuations, by seeking employment elsewhere, instead of waiting for an improvement in the situation, depleting his meager savings and becoming dependent upon poor relief. Mobility of labor, hitherto restricted to the skilled crafts, became a characteristic of mid-nineteenth century England. It softened the workers' economic plight and provided a safety valve for social unrest during the transformation and mechanization of industrial processes, since the transition from handicrafts to machines, although rapid, was far from universal, and the old and new systems of manufacturing existed side by side during most of the century. In the cotton industry, for example, there were about 100,000 power looms in 1833; but the number of handlooms was approximately 250,000 and was "believed not to have diminished between 1820 and 1834, but rather to have increased."[16]

The coexistence of large urban factories with small, old-fashioned workshops was due to the peculiar economic conditions of the time. The wide fluctuations in prices and the uncertainty of foreign markets after the return of peace, the heavy investments entailed by the new machines, and the scarcity of capital all contributed to the survival of the old system and of an exploitative attitude toward labor.[17] Part of the attraction for factories of an

[16] Edward Baines, *History of the Cotton Manufacture in Great Britain* (London: Fisher, Fisher, and Jackson, 1835), p. 237.

[17] "Up to nearly the middle of the century, though wealth was accumulating fast and average rates of profit were high, industry suffered from a severe shortage of capital. Banking was hardly put on secure foundations adapted to the new needs of industry for credit until after the Bank Charter Act of 1844. And, although the joint stock company as a form of organization was extending its scope throughout the century, it was not securely established, or made into a flexible instrument for the raising of capital for ordinary business, until the principle of limited liability was generally conceded to shareholders by the Acts of 1855 and 1862.

"The ordinary employer was thus under the necessity of financing his business either by finding rich partners . . . or by borrowing on his own personal resources and security, or by accumulating out of profits the means wherewith to finance the expansion of his trade. Under these conditions . . . the smaller employer often pinched and saved in order to put every possible

urban location was the availability of an ample supply of "free" children, that is, children whose labor was not regulated by the Health and Morals of Apprentices Act, which limited the workday of parish apprentices (the main source of child labor in the rural mills) to twelve hours. The dependence of the new industrial system on this somewhat tenuous base was in part artificially fostered by the willingness of working-class parents to put their children to work at an early age, but it also reflected the financial difficulties of individual entrepreneurs, which explains the antipathy of the factory owners to reform and the willingness of Parliament to lend a sympathetic ear to their arguments. At the parliamentary hearings, the manufacturers' response to the heartrending descriptions of the abysmal working conditions and the long hours demanded of children was always to claim that the industry would go bankrupt and a financial crisis be precipitated by any shortening of the workday. Since the postwar government policy, supported by opposition Whigs as well as by the ruling Tories, was a stable currency, a reduction of public expenditures, and the quick retirement of the war debt,[18] the manufacturers' line of argument was obviously persuasive, particularly in the House of Lords, many of whose members owned factories or had financial interests in them.

The urban working class itself was not able to bring much pressure to bear upon the government. The workers were not represented in Parliament; their attempts to unionize were largely ineffective, and their vulnerability to economic fluctuations (wages varying erratically from mill to mill and from time to time, according to the demand for the finished product) made the employment of their children seem an indispensable part of their struggle for survival. Finally, the workers lacked dynamic leadership and tended toward individual conservatism, partly through tradition and partly through ignorance and an inability to understand the larger forces

---

penny back into his business. And if he pinched himself, he was not likely to have too much compunction about pinching his work-people a good deal harder, though the reward of their abstinence, as well as his own, went in the end to swell his wealth." Cole, *British Working Class Movement*, p. 123.

[18] In the 1820s the interest paid on the outstanding debt was on the order of £30 million a year, or about half the government's total revenues. Woodward, *Age of Reform*, p. 68.

that were affecting their daily lives.[19] Even after the repeal of the Combination Acts in 1824, the working class made few attempts to organize on a large scale, and discontent manifested itself locally.[20] The first industry-wide union, the Grand Union of All Operative Spinners of the United Kingdom, founded in Manchester in 1829, lasted little more than a year; and the first country-wide union, John Doherty's National Association for the Protection of Labour, also founded in Manchester in 1830, never marshaled any extensive support and withered away within two years. The National Association's successor, the Grand National Consolidated Trade Union, founded in 1834 under the influence of Robert Owen, combined political, economic, and social aims. One of its intentions was to establish communal working-class communities along the lines of Owen's New Harmony, where the workers would own the means of production and achieve local self-government. Owen saw the Grand National as a way of extending his concept of an ideal industrial society to the country as a whole, in which each craft and industry would have its own communal settlements, exchanging their specialized production for other goods on the basis of the value of labor added in production. This scheme succeeded in winning wider support than did its predecessors, principally through offering the promise of an immediate improvement in the workers' way of life. Yet it too collapsed; the Grand National sponsored a large number of local and industry-wide strikes soon after it was organized, before it had accumulated sufficient funds to meet the vigorous response of factory owners and government.

Early nineteenth-century reforms, therefore, can be ascribed neither to pressures exerted by the new urban working class to improve its conditions nor to dynamic and farsighted leadership by government. Such reforms resulted from the efforts of individuals, usually members of the ruling class influential in Parliament, who were concerned with specific problems that suggested equally

[19] "Poor men, without education, reason in and around their own humble interests and needs . . . . The better-paid artisans [who could have provided leadership] distrusted the violence of the chartist leaders, though they agreed with their aims." Ibid., p. 121.
[20] "In Lancashire, from 1810 to 1829, numerous local strikes were set on foot, but no traces of a combination of any importance can be found." Chapman, *Lancashire Cotton Industry*, p. 201.

specific remedies. In 1819 the personal intervention of Sir Robert Peel, himself a factory owner, led to the application of the twelve-hour workday to all children under sixteen and the prohibition of factory employment for children under nine years of age (59 Geo. 3, cap. 66). The long parliamentary fight for a ten-hour day for women and children was conducted by Lord Ashley. Although it was not enacted until 1847 (10 Vict., cap. 29), it generated a series of intermediate acts, including the prohibition of night work and the provision of two hours of compulsory education for factory children.[21] However, the reformers' fight in Parliament was rarely paralleled by any concerted social action in the industrial districts. The testimony of the workers was even used by opponents of reform as an indication of pernicious Jacobinism. Indeed, it is probable that supporting strikes, for example, would have caused the workers' advocates in Parliament to have second thoughts, since they wanted to remedy social evils, not to support government interference in the private sector.[22] Moreover, labor's support for the shorter work-week often seems to have been prompted more by the fear of un-employment than by the desire to obtain more humane working conditions. While Malthus urged the working classes to "cease to beget children," labor organizations such as the Society for National Regeneration responded to the population explosion by advocating a reduction in the workweek, so that "those who have too much

[21] For an excellent account of Ashley's struggles to shepherd his reform bills through Parliament, including pertinent extracts from his diaries, see Robert A. Rosenbaum, *Earnest Victorians* (New York: Hawthorn Books, 1961), Chapter 1.

[22] "A distinction was drawn early in the nineteenth century between interference with industry as a matter of general policy and special action to prevent particular evils . . . . In many cases, [it was believed] that a problem was insoluble, or that it must be endured because no one could think of any method of solving it. From this point of view, the policy of *laissez faire* was not the result of a new and optimistic belief in the progress of society through private enterprise. It was rather an acknowledgement that the fund of skill and experience at the service of society was limited, and that in the management of their common affairs men would not be able to find the elasticity and adaptiveness which individuals showed in devising schemes for their own self-interest . . . . If a practical solution suggested itself, if a tentative experiment could be made, the doctrine of *laissez faire* would be thrust aside, only to be used again after another failure to discover the way out of a difficulty." Woodward, *Age of Reform*, pp. 14–15.

work can spare a little to those who have none, and still there will be enough for all."[23]

Within Parliament, attitudes toward reform were not divided entirely along party lines. Although they represented vested landowning interests, the Tories were not averse to all reform: Lord Ashley, for example, was a Tory aristocrat and disliked trade unions, but he took a leading role in alleviating what he considered shocking inequities in working conditions. The Whigs did not differ substantially from the Tories in their attitude toward strikes and other forms of social unrest. The Radicals claimed to represent the interests of the working classes but had no clear mandate because of the restrictions on suffrage. They were forced to adopt an intellectually aloof position, championing their own interpretation of the desires of the masses. Indeed, the formulation of a satisfactory reform policy could hardly take place until Parliament itself had been reformed and a more representative voice given to the urban areas, which now played the leading role in the country's economic life but had no political voice.

The first tremors in the movement for parliamentary reform occurred soon after the return of peace. In 1819 a Select Committee of the House was appointed to investigate the petition of Scottish royal boroughs for the right to elect members to Parliament. In 1821 and again a year later, Lord John Russell, a Whig, attempted to convince the House that "the present state of the representation of the people requires most serious consideration." He advocated the disfranchisement of rotten boroughs and the transfer of their seats to the new industrial urban areas. But the question of reform met with general apathy within the House. The benches were empty during the 1821 debate; in 1822 barely half the House was present and divided on the issue; and again in 1823 and 1826 there was no support for the introduction of a reform bill.

The defeat of Wellington's Tory government in 1830 paved the way for reform. Lord Grey, the Whig prime minister, stated publicly that his administration intended to effect reform; and in 1831 Lord Russell introduced a bill calling for the disfranchisement of all boroughs with populations under 2000 and the semidisfranchisement of boroughs with populations between 2000 and 4000.

[23] Quoted by Chapman, *Lancashire Cotton Industry*, pp. 97 ff.

Of the disfranchised seats, 109 out of 167 were to be redistributed (only 44 being allocated to previously unrepresented towns), and the remainder abolished; on the other hand, the right to cast a vote was to be given to each householder in the rural counties. Although the bill proposed to add some 217,000 voters to an electorate of 435,000, it fell short of the principle of universal suffrage, since the country's population had passed the 14-million mark. Yet it generated violent arguments in spite of its mildness.

The Radicals had not dared to expect, the Tories, in their wildest fears, had not apprehended, so complete a measure. Enthusiasm was visible on one side of the House; consternation and dismay on the other. At last, when Lord John [Russell] read the list of boroughs which were doomed to extinction, the Tories hoped that the completeness of the measure would ensure its defeat. Forgetting their fears, they began to be amused, and burst into peals of derisive laughter.[24]

The bill was carried in the House by one vote on its second reading but was finally defeated on its third reading. Parliament was dissolved and general elections called. Demonstrations in favor of the reform bill and the liberal members who had supported it were held throughout the country, particularly in the industrial towns. Opponents of the bill fared badly: for example, Gascoyne, the Tory member for Liverpool, was subjected to violent abuse for his opposition to the reform bill and defeated, as were many others, including "ardent Reformers" who had not fought as hard as popular enthusiasm required. The reformers were given a large majority, and in June 1831, three days after the new Parliament was opened, a new reform bill, essentially similar to the first, was introduced. In spite of the opposition's delaying tactics, it was passed on September 21, 345 to 236, and forwarded to the Lords. But the Tories' majority in the upper house allowed them to block the bill successfully, and at the beginning of October it was rejected by 199 to 158 votes. The country's growing impatience for reform manifested itself at once: "The news of the division reached Birmingham at 5 o'clock in the afternoon. The bells were immediately muffled and tolled. The mob at Derby, irritated at the announcement, broke out into open riot. The gaol at Nottingham was burned down."[25] Civil troubles spread

24 Spencer Walpole, *A History of England*, 6 vols. (London: Longmans, Green, 1878), 2:640.
25 Ibid., p. 655.

throughout the country and in cities like Bristol reached the level of an armed insurrection. The riots were further aggravated by an epidemic of cholera that ravaged the densely packed industrial cities. Troops had to be used repeatedly, not only to control the mobs but to cordon off areas affected by the epidemic.

Partly as a means of reducing popular pressures, the government introduced a new measure at the end of December, which was passed without a division on March 23, 1832. Threatened with the creation of new Whig peers to ensure a majority, the Lords approved the Reform Bill on June 7, 1832 (2 Will. 4, cap. 45). Fifty-six boroughs were disfranchised and an additional 30 lost one of their two members; 42 new boroughs were created, 22 sending two members to Parliament and 20 sending one member. The new boroughs accounted for nearly one-quarter of the country's total urban population, hitherto unrepresented. In addition, some counties that elected members at large increased their representation. For the first time, precise procedures were established to prevent electoral irregularities. The overseers of the poor were made responsible for keeping a register of voters in parishes and townships, and the county assizes for keeping county lists; the town clerks were given similar responsibilities in cities and boroughs. Voters were permitted to be questioned only about their identity and right to cast a vote, and voting booths were provided at specified places.

The Parliamentary Reform Act satisfied the urban masses insofar as it was a first step toward the liberalization of electoral procedures, but it did little to ensure adequate communication between the urban population and the government. The power of the conservative Tory party, representing the large landowners, was certainly damaged, but the number of seats representing urban areas actually dropped: under the new act, 264 seats out of 658 represented urban areas, as opposed to 400 prior to the act.[26] For a long time, members of the upper class continued to be nominal spokesmen for the urban population, although in terms of education, tradition, and personal interest they were probably more representative

[26] "The Whigs in 1830 were reckoned to hold 60 out of the 200 rotten borough seats which they destroyed by the Bill. About 140 of these 200 were abolished altogether, and about 60 more had their electoral character restored by the new ten pound franchise." George M. Trevelyan, *History of England*, 3rd ed. (London: Longmans, Green, 1947), p. 635fn.

of the landed gentry.[27] Moreover, the £10 minimum property requirement excluded all but a fraction of the urban population from participating in the electoral process.[28] Whatever interest in urban problems was generated, appropriate solutions still depended upon an upper class largely removed from these problems. There were still no channels for transmitting local pressures to the central government. But whatever its failings may have been, the Reform Act represented the first official recognition that times were changing, that the "population, moving towards the coal-fields, were creating a new England in the Northern Counties, while the little agricultural towns and fishing villages of the South were stagnating in a stationary and inelastic torpor."[29]

MUNICIPAL REFORM

The decision to extend reform to the country's local administrative structure was also due to the efforts of a small group of Whig reformers led by Lord Russell. Although the parliamentary inquiry into conditions in the rotten boroughs had cast most urban administrative practices under a cloud, at least by implication, further parliamentary intervention in local affairs remained contrary to what was considered the normal scope of governmental activity.[30] The traditional division of England into an administrative hierarchy charged with specific responsibilities—the county, the hundred, and the parish—established a series of vested interests opposed to any reform that would strip them of their influence, even though the

[27] "The act of 1832 did not have much immediate effect upon the composition of parliament. The new parliament which met in 1833 contained 217 sons of peers or baronets; in 1865 the number was 180; the landed interests which were nearly 500 strong in 1833 had about 400 representatives in 1865." Woodward, *Age of Reform*, p. 87.

[28] In Manchester, only 15.6 percent of adult males satisfied the minimum property requirement, 13.5 percent in Birmingham, and 12.1 percent in Sheffield.

[29] Walpole, *History of England*, 2:647.

[30] "Parliament itself had no tradition to help the creative spirit. The ruling mind of the eighteenth century looked on local life as the province of the country gentleman, aided by overseers and parish constables. Parliament itself was regarded rather as a checking and limiting body than a legislative body. It existed to abate grievances. It was a bridle on the executive power. . . ." John L. Hammond, "The Social Background," in Harold Laski, W. Ivor Jennings, and William A. Rabson, eds., *A Century of Municipal Progress* (London: Allen & Unwin, 1935), pp. 38–39.

powers contained in each level were not particularly extensive. The county's principal function was to levy the rate necessary to administer justice, to construct and repair bridges, and to build and maintain jails and houses of correction; the hundred was a judicial body that acted through the quarter sessions as well as being an intermediary between the county and the parish; the parish, having evolved from a purely ecclesiastical role, was the most powerful local administrative unit. It was responsible for enforcing and interpreting the Poor Laws, levying the poor rate, maintaining highways, and providing other communal services that were needed. The resistance of the parishes to change is exemplified by the failure of the Gilbert's Act (22 Geo. 3, cap. 83). Passed in 1782 as England's first general enabling legislation, it empowered parishes to unite for the purpose of maintaining a common workhouse. The act could be applied locally, without further parliamentary approval, if a majority of the parishes' ratepayers assessed at £5 or more voted in favor of a common venture. The only limitation was that no parish could be more than ten miles from the site of the workhouse. The financial advantages of such a plan were obvious.[31] However, the act was not used until well into the nineteenth century, and finally fewer than one thousand parishes, or 6 percent, took advantage of it.

The commissioners inquiring into the practices of municipal corporations turned up damaging evidence of inefficiency, neglect of duty, and corruption. These findings are summarized eloquently in the last paragraph of their report, which I shall quote in full:

In conclusion, we report to Your Majesty that there prevails amongst the inhabitants of a great majority of the incorporated towns a general and, in our opinion, a just dissatisfaction with their Municipal Institutions; a distrust of the self-elected Municipal Councils, whose powers are subject to no popular control, and whose acts and proceedings being secret, are unchecked by the influence of public opinion; a distrust of the Municipal Magistracy, tainting with suspicion the local administration of justice, and often accompanied with contempt of the

---

[31] "Of the 15,635 parishes at the 1831 Census, 6681 had less than 300 population, 1907 under 100, and 737 under 50. Such parishes could not maintain a proper poor-house if they tried to; it was 'a miserable abode, occupied rent-free by three or four dissolute families, mutually corrupting each other.' Even the 5353 parishes whose population ranged from 300 to 500, could not have an efficient poor-house except at disproportionately heavy expense." Vivian D. Lipman, *Local Government Areas, 1834-1945* (Oxford: Blackwell, 1949), p. 41.

persons by whom the law is administered; a discontent under the burthens of Local Taxation, while revenues that ought to be applied for the public advantage are diverted from their legitimate use, and are sometimes wastefully bestowed for the benefit of individuals, sometimes squandered for purposes injurious to the character and morals of the people. We therefore feel it to be our duty to represent to Your Majesty that the existing Municipal Corporations of England and Wales neither possess nor deserve the confidence or respect of Your Majesty's subjects, and that a thorough reform must be effected, before they can become, what we humbly submit to Your Majesty they ought to be, useful and efficient instruments of local government.[32]

The most important recommendation of the commissioners was that there be popular representation in local government, not only to ensure efficient administration but as the only way to remedy the alienation between the voters and the municipal oligarchies. This important point, examples of which have been seen both in Liverpool and Manchester, was emphasized forcefully and repeatedly.

The most common and most striking defect in the constitution of the Municipal Corporations of England and Wales is, that the corporate bodies exist independently of the communities among which they are found. The Corporations look upon themselves, and are considered by the inhabitants, as separate and exclusive bodies; they have powers and privileges within the towns and cities from which they are named, but in most places all identity of interest between the Corporation and the inhabitants has disappeared. This is the case even where the Corporation includes a large body of inhabitant freemen; it appears in a more striking degree, as the powers of the Corporation have been restricted to smaller numbers of the resident population, and still more glaringly, when the local privileges have been conferred on non-resident freemen, to the exclusion of the inhabitants to whom they rightfully ought to belong.[33]

Yet the Municipal Reform Bill, as originally presented, went only part of the way to enact this recommendation. All persons who had paid the poor rate for three consecutive years were, for the purposes of the act, to be considered burgesses of the town and entitled to vote. More important, the new councils were elected for three-year terms, renewable in thirds, abolishing the self-perpetuating municipal councils. As in the case of parliamentary elections, however,

---

[32] Great Britain, *Parliamentary Papers*, vol. 23 (1835) (*Reports from Commissioners*, vol. 3), "Report of the Royal Commission on Municipal Corporations," p. 49.

[33] Ibid., pp. 32–33.

only male residents living in properties assessed at £10 or more were in fact eligible to vote, a small minority of the total population, although the act did contain a clause (5 and 6 Will. 4, cap. 76, para. 11) permitting residents of nonassessable properties to become voters through voluntary payment of the poor rate.

In spite of the telling case presented by the commissioners, the Reform Bill encountered strong opposition in both houses. The Tories' objection to what they considered a nefarious increase in the influence of the "ten-pound voter" led to the incorporation of an amendment requiring more stringent property requirements for holding office. Strangely enough, the minimum was set at a higher level in the larger towns (£1000 or an assessed value of £30) than in the smaller ones (£500 or an assessed value of £15), probably as a way of preventing radical-minded champions of the working class from holding office. Additional clauses in the act defined the traditional powers of municipal corporations: keeping the peace, administering justice, making by-laws, and undertaking such public improvements as might be authorized by prior or subsequent acts. Similarly, certain restrictions were put upon the disposal of the corporate estate, and auditing procedures suggested.

Although revolutionary in concept, since it represented an effort at uniform legislation on a national basis, the Municipal Reform Act did little except codify a limited form of local autonomy and restore to the burgesses the prerogatives they had lost.[34] The powers of the reformed municipal corporations were still severely constrained, in that existing statutory authorities were allowed to retain their powers until such time as they might voluntarily surrender them. This led to a prolonged period of ambiguous relations between the new borough councils and the various other bodies responsible, at least in part, for municipal services. Moreover, the act applied only to 178 out of the 246 existing boroughs; the large, new, unincorporated industrial towns, such as Birmingham and Manchester, were totally ignored and had to petition the Crown for a charter that would extend the provisions of the act to them.

These restrictions did not merely reflect the pressure of local

[34] It is symbolic of parliamentary concern that the enactment of the Municipal Reform Act on September 9, 1835 was sandwiched between an amendment to the law "as to the tithing of Turnips" and the repeal of a duty on the import of flint glass.

vested interests or legislative obtuseness; they arose from a deep distrust of the new authorities. Not only might they repeat their predecessors' mismanagement, but their "democratic" constitution might mean the eventual control of local politics by the new urban voters.[35]

[35] "Morpeth said that the Government had been afraid that the new town councils would be political. Apart from this there was great anxiety on the part of all the vested interests, water companies, railway companies, even burial companies, in addition to the general alarm of property. . . . On the other side, local authorities were very jealous of their independence, and many of them resisted obstinately all proposals for setting up a central department." J. L. Hammond, "The Social Background," p. 41.

Liverpool in 1847
Courtesy of Henry Young and Sons, Liverpool

CHAPTER EIGHT

The Reformed Corporation of Liverpool

The twenty years that elapsed between the end of the Continental Wars and the Municipal Reform Act were years of prosperity and expansion for Liverpool. The growth of the Lancashire cotton industry, dependent upon the port of Liverpool for the import of its raw materials and the export of its finished goods, caused a two-fold increase in the town's docking facilities,[1] and the population grew from 121,000 to about 202,000. Much of this expansion took place in such suburban townships as Everton, Kirkdale, West Derby, and Toxteth Park, which in a few years had been transformed from sleepy villages into urban middle-class districts or even, in the case of parts of Toxteth Park, dense urban slums. These four Lancashire townships and Birkenhead, the rapidly developing shipbuilding center on the Cheshire bank of the Mersey, had a combined population of about 41,000 people, representing over 50 percent of the total growth during this period. The development of the periphery had been encouraged by the very high densities that prevailed in the Old Borough[2] and by the new omnibus lines, which, by 1831,

[1] In 1816 the area of the 7 major basins comprising the dock estate was equal to 33.5 acres, and about 8000 ships were cleared yearly. In 1832 the area of the 10 major basins was 66.4 acres (in 1826 the Old Dock was filled in), and over 12,000 ships were cleared yearly, the average tonnage of ships having increased from about 100 tons to about 125. See James A. Picton, *Memorials of Liverpool*, 2 vols. (London: Longmans, Green, 1875), 1:551 ff.

[2] The gross density within the borough was 89 persons per acre, or between 160 and 200 persons per net residential acre.

provided ready access to the center of town from the ring of suburbs stretching from Bootle to Aigburth.

As might be expected, such rapid expansion resulted in a further deterioration of the living conditions of the lower classes, whose ranks were being swelled by a continuous flow of Irish migrants. Dr. Duncan's testimony before the commissioners on municipal corporations gives a disheartening description of living conditions within the borough: he reported that at least 20,000 persons lived in cellars and 40,000 more were crowded, 5 or 6 to a room, in the medieval courts and alleys behind the town's main streets. In other words, no fewer than 40 percent of the borough's inhabitants were living in appalling slums, and many more shared their fate in the new speculative subdivisions in Toxteth Park and Birkenhead, which were so carelessly designed that they deserved to be called planned slums.

. . . The soil is subdivided into a multitude of holdings, and a man runs a new street, generally as narrow as he possibly can, through a field, not only to save the greater expense of soughing and paving, which, in the first instance, falls upon himself, but also that he may have a greater quantity of land to dispose of. The next owner continues that street, if it suits him, but he is not obliged to do so, and . . . the growth of narrow thoroughfares, the utter neglect of proper sewerage, the inattention to ventilation, and that train of evils which is so much to be deplored, is the inevitable consequence.[3]

Although these conditions were typical of the new industrial towns, as has been shown in the case of Manchester, the Liverpool poor were surviving under conditions that were probably even more marginal. The specialized economy of Liverpool offered limited opportunities for workers other than skilled shipbuilders: less than 5 percent of the labor force worked in the town's few industries,[4] casual employment on the docks being the only avenue open to the immense majority of the population. Their wages were on the order of only 1s. a day,[5] and they were highly vulnerable

[3] Testimony of Samuel Holme, a builder, in Great Britain, *Parliamentary Papers*, vol. 17 (1844) (*Reports from Commissioners*, vol. 3), "Report of the Commissioners of Inquiry into the State of Large Towns and Populous Districts," p. 186.

[4] Brian D. White, *A History of the Corporation of Liverpool, 1835–1914* (Liverpool: Liverpool University Press, 1951), p. 2.

[5] A Manchester spinner's wages in 1831 ranged from 19s. 8d. to £1 14s. 9d. per week; dressers were paid £1 10s. 6d. and weavers 12s. *Return of Wages* (London: H.M.S.O., 1887), p. 8.

to seasonal and secular economic fluctuations. During the depression of 1842, for example, 28 percent of the families in Liverpool's Vauxhall Ward were unemployed, and over one thousand families "were supporting themselves by pawning, prostitution or charity."[6] And unlike their industrial counterparts, the casually employed Liverpool workers had little opportunity to organize themselves into protective labor associations, which, in spite of their doubtful effectiveness in improving wages and working conditions, did help their members in difficult times and provided a forum for political action.[7]

The storm that was about to break on national politics with the introduction of the Parliamentary Reform Bill was heralded by the election of 1830. Much of the impetus for reform was a reaction to the widespread bribery that had become characteristic of Parliamentary elections, not only in the rotten boroughs but in all the larger towns as well. In Liverpool, for example, both the reform candidate, William Ewart, and the antireformer, John Denison, spent large sums to purchase the vote of the town's freemen, the price rising during the seven days of polling from £5 to £40 per vote. Ewart was finally elected with a majority of only twenty-nine votes, after spending £15,000 more than his opponent. The following account of the election can be taken as representative of the mores of the time.

Out of 4401 freemen, not 1000 voted without being bribed. The resident voters received sums varying from £5 to £40 each. Some of the non-resident freemen having to come from a distance received larger sums. The highest on the list is a person from Belfast, styled a "merchant," who voted for Mr. Denison, and received £80. A resident freeman in Liverpool, who voted for Mr. Ewart received £50. The cost of the election, it may well be supposed, amounted to a very large sum. Mr. Ewart's expenses were defrayed by himself and family. Mr. Denison's outlay was not reckoned at more than £50,000, towards which it was said Colonel Bolton contributed £10,000.[8]

Even the unreformed Parliament was shocked by these loose electoral practices. Several parliamentary inquiries were held, and the lord chancellor was moved to remark that "the corruption and bribery

[6] White, *Corporation of Liverpool*, p. 5. See also J. Finch, *Social Statistics of Vauxhall Ward* (Liverpool: Anti-Monopoly Association, 1842).

[7] The highly organized Liverpool building trades were an exception. They provided prototypes for many of the trades councils that were formed at the end of the century.

[8] Picton, *Memorials of Liverpool*, 1:424.

practised [in Liverpool] surpassed in openness and audacity all that had ever been recorded in the annals of electioneering."[9]

Although the Reform Bill received support in Liverpool, agitation in its favor during the seesaw contest between the two Houses was considerably milder than in many other towns. There were no popular riots akin to those in Nottingham and Bristol, support coming mostly from members of the mercantile middle class, who were content to hold orderly rallies at which petitions to the King and the House of Lords were circulated. Parliamentary reform seems to have been identified not so much with a broadening of the national electoral base as with the continuing struggle for representation between the new urban middle class of Liverpool and the closed corporation. Yet the enfranchisement of £10 voters had a substantial effect, shifting the balance of power to the moneyed classes. The number of potential voters leaped from 4400 to over 16,000,[10] and many of the traditional electors, small artisans whose prerogatives as hereditary freemen had allowed them to vote even though they were of modest means, were disfranchised. In the elections of 1832, 24.5 percent of the voters belonged to the upper class of professionals and businessmen, 39.4 percent to the mercantile middle class, and 36.1 percent were "mechanics and labourers."[11] The voters participating in the parliamentary election of 1832 numbered 9091, or 55 percent of the householders occupying dwellings assessed at £10 or more. This low ratio can be attributed to the minimum requirement of one year of residence, the compounding of rental properties, and a lack of information about registering under the new procedures. Although far from dramatic, the shift in the electoral structure was sufficient to arouse the anxiety of the corporate oligarchy. While their opposition to parliamentary re-

[9] Lord Brougham's speech of March 23, 1831 in the House of Lords. Ibid., p. 427.

[10] In 1832, out of a total of 27,749 dwellings, 16,485 were assessed at £10 or more. Commissioners on Municipal Corporations in England and Wales, *Report on the Corporation of Liverpool* (London: H.M.S.O., 1833), p. 2737.

[11] Thomas Baines, *History of the Commerce and Town of Liverpool* (London: Longman, Brown, Green and Longmans, 1852), p. 633.
Many of the "mechanics and labourers" and some of the mercantile middle class were freemen, but only a small portion of the upper class belonged to the politically privileged group: "A large majority of the wealthiest merchants who had made the prosperity of the boroughs were not Freemen; nor were most of the professional classes." J. Ramsay Muir and Edith M. Platt, *A History of Municipal Government in Liverpool* (Liverpool: Liverpool University Press, 1906), p. 135.

form had remained within the bounds of party politics, their opposition to municipal reform was on a grander scale.

Prior to the introduction of the Municipal Reform Bill, a Committee of Inquiry had been appointed in the House to investigate the corrupt practices that prevailed in parliamentary and municipal elections in Liverpool. The conclusions of the committee were strongly critical. After reporting that "bribery and corruption have existed in the elections of Members of Parliament and Chief Magistrates for the borough of Liverpool," the committee had recommended the introduction of a special bill "to restrict the franchise, and to alter the whole system of elections in that borough."[12] The matter was dropped, although it had been approved by the Commons, because of the impending Municipal Reform Bill, which would have automatically caused the final disfranchisement of the Liverpool freemen; but this threat to local prerogatives was sufficient to marshal corporate establishment's opposition to the bill. While it was under consideration by the House, petitions against the bill were received from the Mayor of Liverpool, the Liverpool Sons of Freemen, the Burgesses (freemen) of Liverpool, and the Clergy of Liverpool. Support for the bill came from the Churchwardens of Liverpool, the Inhabitants of Liverpool (who forwarded a petition with eighteen thousand signatures), and such liberal groups as the Reform Association and the Free Burgesses of Liverpool.

The stream of accumulated feelings against the exclusive and self-perpetuating borough council manifested itself in the election of December 1835. The first reform council was overwhelmingly dominated by Whigs (15 out of 16 aldermen and 43 out of 48 councilors), and only two members of the old council succeeded in their bid for reelection. This was glaring proof that the commissioners had been correct in their estimation of the chasm between the old council and the borough's inhabitants:

While we find the highest tributes paid (and justly) to the personal characters and individual motives of action of the members of the common council, they are shown, as a body, to be perpetually subject to the bias of some unbecoming influence or partizanship, standing aloof from the commonalty, and looking mainly to the aggrandizement of the select few.[13]

Despite its clear mandate, the first Whig reform council did

[12] Quoted by Picton, *Memorials of Liverpool*, 1:449–450.
[13] *Report on the Corporation of Liverpool*, p. 2741.

little to remedy the paucity of public services in the borough. Their most forceful step was to provide better police protection. The night watch of 170 "Old Charlies"[14] was replaced by a new police force modeled after Sir Robert Peel's Metropolitan Police. The 318 policemen and 40 firemen were increased to 574 within three years, and the police budget rose from the £2600 spent prior to reform to more than £24,000. In 1836 the Liverpool freemen's last privilege, exemption from the town tolls, was taken away from them. In 1839 the council enacted, as a local bylaw, the major provisions of an earlier act (6 Geo. 4, cap. 57; 1825) setting forth a series of minimum standards for new buildings, but which had never been enforced by the old council.[15]

The general inaction of the reform council was due to two

[14] They were, for the most part, "so aged and feeble that the inhabitants could only account for their filling the post by supposing that when men were considered too decrepit for any other employment they were elected guardians of the public safety." H. M. Walmsley, *Life of Sir Joshua Walmsley,* quoted in White, *Corporation of Liverpool,* pp. 11–12.

[15] This was indeed a modest attack upon the conditions that, ten years later, and after a serious attempt to change them, still caused a French visitor to castigate the "carelessness" of the municipal authorities:

"L'état de la voie publique atteste . . . l'incurie de l'autorité municipale: les immondices de toute nature restent, la semaine entière, étalées en plein air, et les rues n'ont pas d'égouts. . . .

"Les logements des ouvriers, à Liverpool, sont encore plus insalubres qu'ils ne sont misérables. Leurs familles vivent en majeure partie, dans des caves (*cellars*) ou dans des cours fermées, et manquent d'air avant de manquer de pain . . . . Représentez-vous des espèces de trous de dix à douze pieds carrés de surface, ayant souvent moins de six pieds anglais de hauteur, en sorte qu'il est difficile à un homme de s'y tenir debout. Ces tanières n'ont pas de fenêtres; l'air et la lumière n'y pénètrent que par la porte dont la partie supérieure est généralement au niveau de la rue. On y descend, comme dans un puits, par une échelle ou par un escalier presque droit. L'eau, la poussière et la boue s'accumulent au fond; comme le sol est rarement parqueté, et qu'aucune espèce de ventilation n'y est possible, il y règne une épaisse humidité. Dans quelques endroits, la cave a deux compartiments, dont le second, qui sert de chambre à coucher, ne reçoit de jour que par la première. Chaque cave est habitée par trois, quatre et jusqu' à cinq personnes. Le loyer coute deux schellings par semaine. . . .

"Un autre trait distinctif de Liverpool est la construction de ces cours fermées qui doublent en quelque sorte les rues. Elles se composent de deux rangs de maisons à trois étages d'élévation, qui se font face et qui sont adossées à d'autres édifices. Un espace, qui varie de six à quinze pieds, sépare les deux côtés, et la cour ne communique avec la rue que par un étroit corridor sous lequel on entre en se baissant comme par la porte d'une prison." Léon Faucher, *Etudes sur l'Angleterre,* 2 vols. (Brussells: Wouters frères, 1845), 1:153–155.

interrelated causes: the division of administrative responsibility that had occurred at the end of the eighteenth century and the consequent stringent limitations on borough finances. The abortive attempts to control the activities of the Liverpool corporation, first by the freemen in 1791 and later by the merchants, had resulted in the establishment of a series of relatively autonomous authorities to carry out the business of the borough (Figure 22). At the time of the passage of the Municipal Reform Bill, the corporation was responsible only for the "ancient streets of the borough," the administration of justice, and the supervision of the markets. Poor relief, the watch (including scavenging and lighting), and the paving and sewering of the streets was under the control of separate boards of commissioners, the majority of whom were appointed by the churchwardens. The corporation had agreed to the establishment of these boards and was represented on them (in the case of the Highway Board, the corporation even made an annual payment of £5000 toward the cost of street maintenance and improvement), but the boards were independent of the corporation. Instead, the commissioners owed their allegiance to the parish vestry, which controlled and financed their expenditures from the general rate. In fact, the vestry had emerged as the natural forum for the discussion of municipal affairs, the approval of the churchwardens' accounts having become, as in the case of Manchester, an excuse for airing conflicting views, which were settled by recourse to parish polls. The frequency of these polls in Liverpool and many other towns is indicative of the growing frustration felt by the middle class at their inability to participate in local government prior to the Municipal Reform Act. In 1832, for example,

. . . no less than eight of these polls were taken [in Liverpool], on such questions as the amounts of salary to be paid to an official, the election of Churchwardens and Sidesmen, the assessment of the owners of cottage property, and whether the Churchwardens' accounts should or should not be passed. The active spirits who, in the heated years of the Reform controversy, carried the Open Vestry meetings, were habitually defeated at the poll. They revenged themselves on the Tory party by turning the half-yearly meeting at the old Parish Church into a pandemonium.[16]

16 Sidney and Beatrice Webb, *Statutory Authorities for Special Purposes* (Hamden, Conn.: Archon Books, 1963), p. 448.
The defeat of the reform-minded wing of the parish vestry at the polls

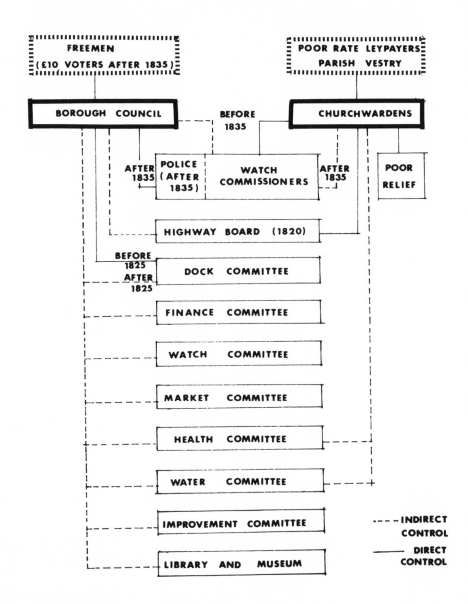

Figure 22. Administrative Organization of Liverpool

Moreover, since control of the police force was the only specific responsibility assigned to a corporate body by the act (clauses 76 to 81), and since transfer of the powers vested in statutory authorities was left to the discretion of the trustees of these authorities (clause 75), the reform council was limited in its ability to assume the reins of power quickly.

Despite its substantial revenues and limited responsibilities, the Liverpool corporation had managed to accumulate an outstanding debt of £792,000 by 1833, which was costing £34,000 per year to service, or almost half the corporation's revenue. The yearly operating deficit was approximately £27,000, in spite of the fact that the town dues (the tolls collected on the mercantile activities of the nonfreemen) had been increasing steadily, from £19,668 in 1800 to £35,903 in 1833. As Table 10 shows, the salaries paid to corporate officers and the general administrative costs of the council, including several thousand pounds spent on the maintenance of the Town Hall,

Table 10. Accounts of the Liverpool Corporation, 1832–1833

	£	%		£	%
Receipts	78,802	100.0	Expenditures	104,299	100.0
Town dues	35,903	45.7	Salaries, etc.	15,117	14.4
Leases and rents	17,358	22.0	Police	2616	2.5
Land sales	3503	4.4	Corporate estate	13,555	13.1
Markets	3144	4.0	Streets and		
Ports, docks, and			sewers	8479	8.1
warehouses	14,034	17.8	Public works	10,352	9.9
Miscellaneous	4860	6.2	Schools	604	0.6
			County leys	6847	6.5
			Debt service	34,845	33.2
			Miscellaneous	11,884	11.4

Source: Commissioners on Municipal Corporations in England and Wales, *Report on the Corporation of Liverpool*, p. 2717.

was due to the multiple-vote system, depending on the ratable value of property, introduced by the Sturges-Bourne Act. Although the purpose of the act had been to uphold the political influence of the larger property owners, its mandatory referendum clause caused considerable confusion and increased the need for full discussion of every aspect of the parish's activity: "Any section outvoted at the meeting immediately claimed a poll of the Parish; and this had to be granted as a matter of legal right." Ibid.

the mayor's carriage, and the corporate wine cellars, formed the major part of the corporate expenditures after servicing of the debt.

The corporation had found itself in financial difficulties after its extensive land purchases around Birkenhead on the opposite side of the Mersey. At the same time, it had lost absolute control over the dock estate. The "Wallasay Pool" purchase, made in order to forestall the construction of a rival port on the Cheshire coast, was very much in keeping with the active role played by the corporation in developing the Liverpool docks. However, the land was allowed to lie idle for many years, and over £5500 interest was paid annually on the £157,925 bond issue used to finance its purchase.[17] In the meantime, the pressure put upon the corporation by shipowners and merchants had resulted in the legal separation of the dock estate in 1826 (7 Geo. 4, cap. 187), abolishing the automatic transfer of funds from one account to another. Although the council appointed thirteen of the Dock Committee's twenty-one members and retained a veto over the committee's decisions, the presence of representatives from the shipowners and merchants, as well as separate auditing procedures, ensured a more rigorous management.[18] Nevertheless, the corporation had lost exclusive control of an estate with a capital value in excess of £1.5 million. By 1840, when the reform council was attempting to cope with the extensive public investments required to improve the borough, the yearly revenue of the dock estate had gone up to £178,197. Although the better part of the income went to debt service and retirement, and to extension of the port facilities, the Dock Committee was twice able to reduce its charges. However, the only money that accrued to the corporation from the port facilities that they had created with public funds was now limited—at the time when it was most needed—to a few thousand pounds from the warehouses and graving docks remaining in the corporate estate.

[17] The commissioners on municipal corporations spoke at length of this venture and the strong opposition it had encountered from merchants and freemen alike. In their report, the commissioners qualified the purchase as "an expenditure of the corporate income [requiring] more particular animadversion"—a striking departure from their usual tolerance, at least in matters of corporate finances. *Report on the Corporation of Liverpool*, pp. 2727 ff.

[18] The former Dock Committee had been "formed out of the common council, the members of which were self-elected for life, and were practically irresponsible. Abuses had crept in. Frauds and speculations of rather a serious nature had been discovered, and more were suspected." Picton, *Memorials of Liverpool*, 1:563.

Limited financial resources, together with the prevailing popular expectation of more efficient and economical municipal government, hampered the reform council; but divided responsibility rather than lack of means was the most serious obstacle to public action. Many of the extravagant expenses of the old council had been abolished, and several of its highly paid servants dismissed; in addition, the most costly of the borough's activities continued to be defrayed out of the poor rate.[19] In fact, only the police and the scavenging of streets, together with the traditional watching of markets, were paid out of corporate revenues. Although it was found politically expedient not to levy a regular borough rate until the 1860s, there was no difficulty in raising special rates to carry out various improvements in the 1840s, and the corporation's credit was undiminished. For example, barely two years after their election, members of the reform council obtained an act of Parliament (1 Vict., cap. 115; 1837) permitting them to borrow more than £100,000 for the construction of a new public building, St. George's Hall, which was to contain a vast auditorium "sumptuously constructed in the Corinthian style of architecture."[20] Since approximately 30 percent of the borough's population lived in cellars or ill-ventilated and unpaved courts, this allotment of public funds was another example of the profligacy that had characterized Liverpool's local government for so many years.

The construction of St. George's Hall aroused the justified ire of Edwin Chadwick, the public health reformer, who remarked that the same sum "would, if so applied, serve to sweep and cleanse in perpetuity, and make decent, the filthy by-streets of upwards of 23,000 houses, out of the 45,000 houses, which are under the corporation's jurisdiction."[21] One might add that a more productive use of corporate funds was well within the council's prerogatives, the Municipal Reform Act specifically empowered "the Council or any Borough to make such Bye Laws as to them shall seem meet for . . . Prevention and Suppression of all such Nuisances as are not already punishable" (clause 90). But Chadwick's was a lonely point of view, which was not shared by many of his contemporaries.

[19] The imposition of a borough rate was not contemplated until the town dues were ruled illegal in 1856.

[20] Hugh Gawthrop, *Fraser's Guide to Liverpool* (London: W. Kent, 1855), p. 187.

[21] Quoted in T. Baines, *History of Liverpool*, p. 676.

A few years after his remarks, the new hall was eulogized by the author of *Fraser's Guide to Liverpool:*

There is no drawback to damp the ardour of enthusiastic admiration: these stones, at least, are not cemented with the blood of negroes; these ornaments and decorations are not insulting trophies of grinding oppression; this massive pile has not been raised by successful appeals to demented superstition—extracting the hard-earned coin through fears of supernatural terrors. The fountain of wealth expended in erecting this pile was unpolluted; it is a temple erected to the genius of Commerce—bartering fairly, justly, freely—guided by the sanctifying influences of an enlightened Christianity.[22]

Instead of the "blood of negroes" or the "fears of supernatural terrors," it was the high mortality, the diseases, and the hopelessness of the majority of Liverpool's inhabitants that had paid for this monument to the genius of Commerce and the frivolity of the borough council.

The first attempts to deal with overcrowded and unsanitary housing did not occur until 1842. The so-called "Health-of-the-Town Act" (5 and 6 Vict., cap. 42), obtained that year, was principally intended to control the activity of developers and speculators by imposing environmental and space standards on new construction. A minimum width of 25 feet was prescribed for new streets and of 15 feet for courts, whose openings had to be at least 6 feet; new houses were to have at least one room with an area of 100 square feet, no ceiling could be lower than 8 feet, and each room was to be ventilated by a window 3 by 5 feet; no inhabited cellar could be located in a court or have a ceiling height of less than 7 feet. Despite the strong opposition of landlords, two clauses of the act applied to existing housing: no cellar was to be let after 1844 unless it met the criteria of new construction, and the owners of the courts *could* be compelled to pave them and provide privies, at the council's discretion. They need not have feared: the mild enforcement of the act permitted the worst type of slum houses to be constructed until 1868.[23]

---

[22] Gawthrop, *Fraser's Guide to Liverpool*, pp. 187–188.

[23] Sir Ernest Simon, "Housing and Civic Planning," in Harold Laski, W. Ivor Jennings, and William A. Rabson, eds., *A Century of Municipal Progress* (London: Allen & Unwin, 1935), p. 203. See also the excellent chapter on housing in C. D. Jones, ed., *The Social Survey of Merseyside* (Liverpool: Liverpool University Press, 1934), pp. 251–268.

Simultaneously, the council, through its Health and Improvement Committees, continued the sewering of the borough, an undertaking that had been started somewhat lackadaisically by the old council. The magnitude of this task, and the laxity of previous administrations, are shown clearly in the progress report given in 1835 by Dr. Duncan, a physician at the Liverpool Infirmary. Although more than £100,000 had recently been expended, only 235 out of 566 residential streets had been sewered, most of them in midlde- and upper-class districts. While 4 out of 20 miles of working-class streets in the borough were sewered (but none of the courts), the sewerage of 21 out of 37 miles of upper-income streets had been completed.

An even more serious problem was the provision of water. The high rates charged by the two private companies that supplied the town, together with their inadequate distribution system, had created appalling conditions in the slums:

There is one circumstance which very much affects the atmosphere in those districts in which the cellars are particularly; there is a great deal of broken ground, in which there are pits; the water accumulates in those pits, and of course at the fall of year there is a good deal of water in them, in which there have been thrown dead dogs and cats, and a great many offensive articles. This water is nevertheless used for culinary purposes. I could not believe this at first. I thought it was used only for washing, but I found that it was used by the poorer inhabitants for culinary purposes.[24]

Yet, it was not until 1847 that the borough council became sufficiently preoccupied with the chronic water shortage in the town to appropriate £200,000 to purchase the two companies and plan the extension of the water supply. But

. . . a storm of opposition broke out which found considerable support within the Council, caused several prominent Council members of both parties . . . to lose their seats, and delayed the beginning of the work on the Rivington [extension] scheme for five years.[25]

The reformed corporation of Liverpool proceeded carefully indeed in its efforts to clean the Augean stables it had inherited

[24] Testimony of J. Riddal Wood, in Great Britain, *Parliamentary Papers*, vol. 11 (1840) (*Reports from Committees*, vol. 8), "Minutes of Evidence Taken before the Select Committee on Health and Towns," p. 132.

[25] White, *Corporation of Liverpool*, p. 56.

from its predecessor. Once they had gained control of local government, the newly influential merchants were willing to continue
spending vast sums on the further development of their port—well
over £1 million was invested in the dock estate between 1835 and
1845—or on such sumptuous edifices as St. George's Hall; but the
strictest economy governed other municipal affairs. Not only were
new policies formulated slowly and sporadically, but the broad
powers granted under the Municipal Reform Act and the several
improvement acts remained unused.

Manchester in 1843

CHAPTER NINE

The Municipal Borough of Manchester

The Municipal Reform Bill of 1835 had been actively supported in Manchester even though the town, as an unincorporated borough, did not come under its aegis. More than twenty-two thousand signatures in support of the Reform Bill were sent to London.[1] Nonetheless, it was three years before the first attempts were made to obtain a municipal charter under the provisions of paragraph 141 of the act.[2] The proponents of more efficient municipal government, who were agitating for incorporation under the leadership of Richard Cobden, had to reckon with the opposition of various

[1] Pointed questions were asked in the House of Lords regarding the validity of the petitions. The supporters of the bill could not deny the accusation that "such petitions very frequently [contained] the signatures of persons who were perfectly incompetent to affix their signatures to it. . . . [Petitions were obtained] by placing tables at the corners of the public streets and getting at such persons as could just scribble their names . . . not one of them knowing what they were signing." Quoted in Shena D. Simon, *A Century of City Government* (London: Allen & Unwin, 1938), p. 73. However, since there were only 4242 registered voters at the time (Table 9), there is no doubt that there was enthusiastic support for the Reform Bill.

[2] "And whereas sundry Towns and Boroughs of England and Wales are not Towns Corporate, and it is expedient that several of them should be incorporate; be it enacted, That if the Inhabitant Householders of any Town or Borough *in England and Wales* shall petition His Majesty to grant to them a Charter of Incorporation, it shall be lawful for His Majesty, by any such Charter, if He shall think fit, by Advice of His Privy Council, to grant the same, to extend to the Inhabitants of any such Town or Borough within the District to be set forth in such Charter the Powers and Provisions in this Act contained . . . ."

political factions within the Court Leet, the police commissioners, and the vestry. Besides the Tories' objection to the extension of the voting franchise to "ten-pound voters,"[3] there was widespread fear that the unlimited power to tax vested in the borough councils by the Municipal Reform Act would result in administrative extravagance and an increase in taxation.[4] Several of the outlying townships that had become part of the parliamentary borough in 1832 raised the same issue in arguing against their inclusion within a greater municipal borough, although they had become dependent on Manchester as the heart of a large and growing urban complex whose political subdivisions were less and less distinct. It is a moot point whether there were in fact any substantial variations in rates within the parliamentary borough, with the exception of Chorlton-upon-Medlock, whose police rate was an unusually low 9d. in the pound. Rather, the fact that all but two of the townships in the parliamentary borough had obtained their own forms of local government within the last two decades must have militated against surrendering local autonomy to Manchester. As Table 11 shows,

Table 11. Principal Local Taxes in Manchester and Surroundings—1835

	Local Act	Popula-tion 1831	Voting Franchise	1835 Assessed Value (£)	Poor Rate[a]	Police Rate	Highway Rate[b]	Total Rate
Manchester	1792	142,026	£16	429,814	2s.	1s. 6d.	10d.	4s. 4d.
Cheetham	—	4025	—	21,406	n.a.	—	21d.	2s.+
Beswick	—	248	—	n.a.	n.a.	—	30d.	3s.+
Ardwick	1825	5524	£30	21,400	16d.	18d.	20d.	4s. 6d.
Chorlton-upon-Medlock	1822	20,509	£4	58,844	4d.	9–12d.	20d.	2s. 10d.
Hulme	1824	99,624	£25	25,262	20d.	18d.	20d.	4s. 10d.

[a] Calculated from James Wheeler, *Manchester: Its Political, Social, and Commercial History, Ancient and Modern* (London: Whittaker, 1836), pp. 344–345. The estimate for Chorlton is incomplete.

[b] Owing to lack of data, the figures for the outlying townships have been estimated on the basis of the ratio between their average expenditures for 1851–1872 and those of Manchester. See Arthur Redford and Ira S. Russell, *History of Local Government in Manchester*, 3 vols. (London: Longmans, Green, 1940), 2:306–307.

[3] The minimum property requirement under the Police Act was £16.

[4] Unlike previous local acts, which had set an upper limit on the taxing prerogatives of local authorities, the Reform Act simply stated that councils were "hereby authorized and required from Time to Time to order a Borough Rate . . . to be made within their Borough" (paragraph 92).

the differences in the tax rate between Manchester and its outlying townships were slight. This was because the townships bore a disproportionately heavy share of the cost of maintaining the ever-growing network of major roads leading to Manchester, a situation that persisted until the 1870s.[5]

Yet the effect of differential local taxation on the resistance to annexation cannot be discounted, at least to the extent that the multiplicity of local taxes encouraged the statutory authorities who collected them to defend their vested interests. No fewer than five local rates were levied in eighteenth- and nineteenth-century England: the *county rate*, used to defray the costs of administering justice and keeping the prisons and lunatic asylums; the *highway rate*, raised on a township basis to maintain the King's highways; the *poor rate*, collected on a parish or township basis (according to local circumstances) and used to defray the expenses of both indoor and outdoor relief and of the Court Leet's constables; the *police rate*, used to finance the general administration and the improvements of a town, if a local Police Act had been obtained; and the *church rate* (which in many instances had ceased to be compulsory), used to maintain Anglican churches constructed under the terms of a local parliamentary act.[6] There were great variations in the annual rate of taxation, which fluctuated according to the need for public expenditures. The responsible authorities estimated what their yearly need might be and taxed accordingly: should extraordinary expenses arise, there was no compunction, particularly on the part of the overseers of the poor, in imposing a supplementary rate. Only the police commissioners, and other recent additions to the local administrative structure, were prevented by statute from rating beyond a certain limit, usually 18d. on the pound. Moreover, different deductions were allowed, according to the customs of the assessing body. In Manchester, for example, all private properties were assessed for the poor rate, but only those with an annual value in excess of £4 10s. were liable for the police rate, or slightly over two-thirds of all residential properties in 1838.[7] In the suburban townships, the police rate was levied on £4 properties in Chorlton

[5] See Arthur Redford and Ira S. Russell, *History of Local Government in Manchester*, 3 vols. (London: Longmans, Green, 1940), 2:306–307.

[6] In Manchester, until the nineteenth century, each tax was levied on the basis of a separate assessment. After 1804, the Manchester parish poor-rate books became the common basis for assessing properties.

[7] S. D. Simon, *A Century of City Government*, p. 65.

and on £5 properties in Ardwick and Hulme. The situation was further complicated by the inverse correlation that existed in any one year between the need to spend public funds and the tax base of the community, since the tax base was the rental rather than the rated value of the property:[8] in hard times, the rental value would tend to decrease while the number of poor-relief cases was suddenly magnified. Hence, the need to impose supplementary rates and the reluctance of the peripheral townships to become liable for the support of the disproportionate number of poor in the central city —an attitude not dissimilar to that of American suburbs today.

A more heated issue was the voting franchise that would be extended to all £10 voters within the borough, should incorporation be obtained. Except for Chorlton-upon-Medlock, which enjoyed an unusually low franchise of £4 and some of whose voters would be disfranchised by incorporation, the other townships, including Manchester, would find their electorate increased substantially by incorporation. Although it was generally agreed that Cobden's castigation of current institutions as anachronistic was correct,[9] there was no consensus on the desirability of incorporation. The Tories would have been content with an extension of the police commissioners' power as a substitute, since this would have prevented the lowering of the voting franchise; the Radicals opposed incorporation on the ground that the £10 franchise was undemocratic and insisted that they would accept nothing less than universal suffrage. When the Privy Council was asked to recommend that the borough be incorporated, three of the parliamentary borough townships were excluded,[10] and the "corporators" presented a peti-

---

[8] Nonresidential uses were assessed on the basis of a complicated formula that took into account the amortization of the construction costs, the area of the building, and a charge for movable equipment.

[9] In a public speech on February 9, 1838, Cobden stated that although "it is due to the character of this important borough that its chief municipal officers should be a body popularly chosen, instead of being nominated by the lord of the manor's Court Leet . . . the old state of the government of Manchester is so decrepit and worked out, that it has actually fallen to pieces. . . . Whether you adopt a Corporation Act, or the extension of your Police Acts, or whatever change you intend, a change you must have; for the old state of things cannot exist any longer."

[10] Bradford, Harpurhey, and Newton. Only the exclusion of Newton, with a population of over 5000, presented problems later on: it evaded many of the reform bylaws while becoming a populous low-income district of Manchester.

tion with only 11,780 signatories, as opposed to the anticorporators' 32,000. The majority of the signatures on both petitions were eventually declared fraudulent, and there was never a clear-cut majority for the incorporation that was finally granted in October 1838.[11]

The early years of the Manchester borough council were difficult ones. Its right to govern was opposed by the Court Leet's officers (the boroughreeve continued to be elected in competition with the new mayor), by the churchwardens, who refused to produce the rate books, and by the police commissioners, who denied the new corporation access to the Town Hall. In spite of the fact that 30 out of the 48 councillors were elected in the nine Manchester wards, the borough council had little to say on the business of the out-townships, which continued to be governed by their own police commissions and vestries. It was not until 1842, when Manchester's charter was confirmed by the Borough Charters Confirmation Act (5 and 6 Vict., cap. 111), that the borough council was able to collect the borough rates from the churchwardens and to negotiate with the various police commissioners for the transfer of their powers to the council.[12] Even then, the administrative organization of the borough remained exceedingly complicated and fragmented. Figure 23 shows the four overlapping administrative districts responsible for Manchester and its vicinity; the Chorlton Poor Law Union, which included three of the borough's townships (Chorlton, Ardwick, and Hulme); the Manchester Poor Law Union, which included Manchester itself and Cheetham, as well as ten other townships not included in the municipal borough; the parliamentary borough, which represented local interests in London; and the municipal borough itself. The municipal borough was fragmented even more by the willingness of the borough council, when it was granted jurisdiction over an out-township, to appoint "a separate committee for that township to carry out the pro-

[11] Although paragraph 141 of the Municipal Reform Act did not specify that a majority of residents need petition for incorporation, there was evident concern within the Privy Council that a minority charter not be granted. This is demonstrated by the gerrymandering of the petitions pro and con undertaken by Captain Jebb, who inquired into the petitions on behalf of the Privy Council. See S. D. Simon, *A Century of City Government*, pp. 85 ff.

[12] Chorlton-upon-Medlock and Ardwick transferred their powers in 1842, Manchester in 1843, Hulme in 1845, and Cheetham in 1851.

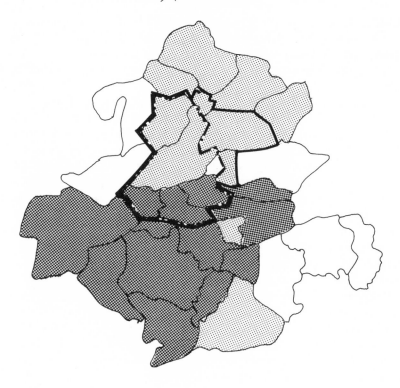

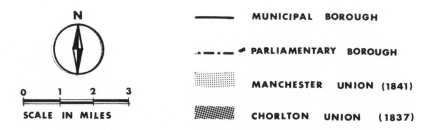

	MUNICIPAL BOROUGH
	PARLIAMENTARY BOROUGH
	MANCHESTER UNION (1841)
	CHORLTON UNION (1837)

Figure 23. Administrative Districts in Manchester—1845

visions of the local Police Act."[13] Therefore, each township retained considerable administrative autonomy, including the power to levy its own rates.

Once its charter had been confirmed, the borough council turned its attention to solving the problems it had inherited from its predecessors. A series of acts were obtained from Parliament that would broaden the borough's statutory powers and release it from judicial dependence upon Salford,[14] establish a borough-wide nuisance committee to enforce the by-laws pertaining to industrial pollution (particularly smoke),[15] establish a free port to promote commercial activities by reducing the high bonding charges Manchester merchants had to pay in Liverpool,[16] and unravel the financial tangle of the police commissioners' various Improvement Committees.[17] Two years later, in 1846, the rights of the manor were purchased for £200,000 and the Court Leet was dissolved, finally freeing the reformed council from an embarrassing relationship with an older, competing jurisdictional body.

Once its authority had been upheld by the courts and its ability to tax demonstrated, the borough council prepared to carry out its responsibilities under the charter. Nine committees were formed to cope with the borough's business: a General Purpose Committee, which acted as an *ad hoc* executive body in between plenary sessions of the council; a Watch Committee, responsible for the new consolidated day and night police forces; a Finance Committee; a Judicial Committee; an Improvement Committee; a Gas Committee, which replaced the gas directors; a Paving and Soughing Committee, responsible for sanitation; a Lamp, Scavenging, and Hackney Coach Committee; and a Nuisance Committee, responsible for proposing and enforcing appropriate bylaws.

The first efforts of the council were directed at improving the quality of the police force. Certain economies of scale could be achieved by having a borough-wide force: prior to incorporation, some six hundred men were employed on various police duties at an annual cost of about £40,000, or 3s. 10d. per capita; what was

---

[13] Redford and Russell, *Local Government in Manchester*, 2:74.
[14] Stipendiary Magistrate's Act of 1844 (7 and 8 Vict., cap. 30).
[15] Borough Police Act of 1844 (7 and 8 Vict., cap. 40).
[16] Bonding Warehouse Act of 1844 (7 and 8 Vict., cap. 31).
[17] Manchester Improvement Act of 1844 (7 and 8 Vict., cap. 41).

generally considered improved protection was provided by four hundred men in 1845–1846, at a cost of just over £23,000, or 1s. 11½d. per capita.[18] It should be remembered that these savings occurred at a time when the town was growing very quickly, as renewed Irish in-migration settled outlying districts such as Hulme; they are therefore all the more remarkable when one considers the social problems created by these perennially unemployed migrants.[19]

The borough council's concern with a police force able to ensure public safety was irrevocably tied to the problem of controlling the new urban lower class. Although the relationship between popular unrest and abysmal living and working conditions was rarely articulated by the leaders of local government, or at least not stated as a justification for reform or the extension of its powers, there was widespread fear of the consequences of radical activism. This is evidenced by the opposition at the national level to extending suffrage to the £10 voter as well as by the conservative opposition to incorporation in towns like Manchester. Engels has eloquently summarized the covert struggle between the establishment and the new urban working class:

The question: What is to become of those destitute millions, who consume today what they earned yesterday; who have created the greatness of England by their inventions and their toil; who become with every passing day more conscious of their might, and demand, with daily increasing urgency, their share of the advantages of society? This, since the Reform Bill, has become the national question. All Parliamentary debates, of any importance, may be reduced to this; and, though the English middle-class will not as yet admit it, though they try to evade this great question, and to represent their own particular interests as the truly national ones, their action is utterly useless. With every ses-

---

[18] Calculated from various data cited by Redford and Russell, *Local Government in Manchester*, vol. 2, Chapters 16 and 17. The comparable costs for the London Metropolitan Police were 2s. 10d. per capita.

[19] Like all English industrial towns in the nineteenth century, Manchester had a high crime rate, and its slums were breeding grounds of antisocial behavior as well as disease. (See Engels's descriptions in *The Condition of the Working Class in England in 1844* [London: Allen & Unwin, 1920], pp. 45 ff.) Yet there seems to have been marked improvement in the administration of the police force between 1840 and 1843, as shown in the crime statistics gathered by Léon Faucher: "Somme toute, l'ordre apparent a gagné à Manchester. Depuis l'établissement de la nouvelle police, les rues sont plus tranquilles, sinon plus sûres." *Etudes sur l'Angleterre*, 2 vols. (Brussells: Wouters frères, 1845), 1:198.

sion of Parliament, the working-class gains ground, the interests of the middle-class diminish in importance.[20]

The improvement of public services other than the police force, although certainly not of a less pressing nature, was undertaken more slowly. During their last thirteen years in office (1830–1844), the police commissioners had finally started the enormous task of paving the streets in the township's new developments, largely as a result of the disastrous cholera epidemic of 1832. Four hundred and eighty streets had been paved and sewered at a cost of £12,000 beyond what could be recovered from abutting property owners.[21] Yet another 450 streets were still unpaved and unsewered. In spite of an annual expenditure of £5000 for scavenging, only the streets of the central business district were cleaned weekly, the poorer districts (a majority of the borough) having their *main* streets cleaned only once a month. The inadequate water supply—just over 2 million gallons for a population of about 320,000 in 1845—obliged more than half the borough to rely upon such unsafe sources as rain water, polluted wells, and even water drawn directly from the rivers, and also precluded the sewering of the town. The Manchester and Salford Waterworks Company provided water a few hours a day to only 23 percent of the borough's houses,[22] and its rates were not conducive even to the most elementary sanitary measures. Its basic charge was 10s. a year, to which was added a surcharge of 5s. for a private water closet; water closets shared by up to ten households were assessed at 2s. 6d. per household.

It is to the credit of the borough council that it attempted to solve all these problems simultaneously, as soon as the new police force had improved public safety in the borough. Using the profits from the gas works (£31,700 per annum in 1843, even though the charges had been more than halved in the last twenty years) and

20 *Condition of the Working Class*, p. 17.

21 "Under the local Police Act, the [Paving and Soughing] Committee had no right to enforce the paving and sewering of any street until one half of it had been built up . . . . When the paving and sewering were completed, the cost could be recovered from the occupiers or owners, each being liable to pay according to the frontage of his house or property." Redford and Russell, *Local Government in Manchester*, 2:144.

22 Of the borough's 46,477 houses in 1847, 28 percent were supplied by street taps that, in the poorer districts, served a radius of a quarter of a mile, and 49 percent had no supply at all. Ibid., p. 177, and S. D. Simon, *A Century of City Government*, p. 350.

monies borrowed under the terms of the Improvement Act of 1844, thirty-three miles of sewers were built within the township alone between 1844 and 1848. This was as much as the police commissioners had constructed in the preceding fourteen years. Progress was also being made in paving working-class streets in all the outlying townships, which were overspending yearly for this purpose. During the summer months of 1847, a general cleaning campaign was undertaken, and at least 3000 tons of night soil and refuse were carted out of the town at a net cost of £5500—a shattering testimony to the inadequacy of normal services.[23] Simultaneously, an effort was made to enforce some minimum standards of sanitation in the cottages of the working class. The Police Act of 1844 had authorized the borough council "to compel the owners of existing houses, as well as of all houses . . . hereafter erected, to provide such [sanitary] conveniences . . . as shall be considered by the Council." The council had passed a bylaw in 1845 requiring a separate privy for each new house and had decided to enforce an older regulation of the police commissioners that no street or court could have a clear width of less than eight feet. Between 1845 and 1847, the borough's Building and Sanitation Committee ordered alterations made to 3640 houses (almost 8 percent of the housing stock) and the construction of privies, raising the ratio from one privy per thirteen dwelling units to one for every three.[24]

The enforcement of minimum standards of light and air was more difficult, given the costs of applying them to existing properties and the problems posed by developers, who were not subject to any compulsory approval of their plans and could only be brought to account for ex post facto violations of the bylaws. By

[23] There was a general improvement in the scavenging of the town after this first effort. In 1848–1849, for instance, £9560 was spent on removing refuse, and the night soil removed from the borough's privies was sold to farmers in the area for £4500.

[24] The cost of a new privy was £3 to £10. (S. D. Simon, *A Century of City Government*, p. 288.) The reluctance of landlords to comply with this requirement can easily be understood by comparing the required investment to the rental income derived. A survey of working-class family expenditures in 1841, for example, shows that the average weekly rent was 4s. 6½d. (16.5 percent of income). The cost of installing a privy for each dwelling unit was therefore the equivalent of 13 to 44 weeks' rent, a considerable expense. William Neild, "Comparative Statement of the Income and Expenditure of Certain Families of the Working Class in Manchester and Dunkinfield," *Journal of the Statistical Society of London* 4 (April 1842): 320 ff.

1851, violations in 11 streets, 10 courts, and 23 passages had been brought to the attention of the committee, and some 15 passages had been compulsorily opened through old properties to provide better ventilation. Although this was a noble effort, and a stronger action than had ever been undertaken by the Court Leet or the police commissioners, it was obviously unequal to the magnitude of the problem. The lack of adequate administrative mechanisms or even of an awareness of the need to control the activities of private developers permitted the spread of slum properties until the last decades of the century. "The speculative builder was free to build whatever type of house he thought would command a ready sale."[25]

The most extensive investments undertaken by the Manchester borough council were efforts to provide an adequate supply of water to the borough and to dispose of sewage without further polluting the rivers, whose water was still necessary for industrial processes. In 1847, an inquiry was held by the borough council to find ways of increasing the water supply and bringing it under municipal ownership and control. After rejecting several proposals by private companies,[26] the council sponsored its own legislation, the Manchester Corporation Waterworks Act (10 and 11 Vict., cap. 203; 1847), which enabled it not only to purchase the franchise and assets of the Manchester and Salford Waterworks Company but to undertake a vast construction project in Longendale, twenty miles east of Manchester. Work was started in the fall of 1848, and by 1851 the first stage was completed, at a cost of £347,737. A reservoir of 135 acres had been built, with a capacity of 809 million gallons; 20 miles of pipeline and tunnels had been completed, and 50 miles of piping had been laid within the borough. The waterworks company was purchased for £537,978, and the borough's water supply was doubled. Encouraged by the relatively modest cost and by the success of this difficult engineering venture, the council decided to expand the works immediately, using the profits of its gas works to provide additional working capital and

[25] E. Simon, "Housing and Civic Planning," in Harold Laski, W. Ivor Jennings, and William A. Rabson, eds., *A Century of Municipal Progress* (London: Allen & Unwin, 1935), p. 203.

[26] See Redford and Russell, *Local Government in Manchester*, vol. 2, Chapter 19 for a description of the various schemes proposed, their relative merits, and the borough council's opposition to them.

Table 12. *Water Supply in the Borough of Manchester*

	1841	1845	1851	1855	1861
Population[a]	311,263	360,000	420,716	440,000	492,720
Water supply (gpd x 1000)	1432	2037	5000	8000	12,500[e]
Cumulative development cost (£)	—	—	885,715	1,298,311	1,600,000[d]
Gallons per capita	4.6	5.6	11.9	18.2	25.4
Development costs per capita	—	—	42s.	58s.	64s.
Percent of houses supplied with water	n.a.	23.0	n.a.	n.a.	n.a.
Basic rate per house	10s.	10s.	6d./£[b]	6d./£[b]	8d./£[b]

[a] Including Salford, which obtained its water from Manchester.
[b] Rates are per pound of assessed valuation.
[e] Estimated.
[d] Estimated (£166,264 of this amount came from profits of the gas works).

pledging the borough rate as guarantee for necessary loans.[27] The extent of the Manchester water supply is summarized in Table 12, together with its costs. By 1876, when over £2,500,000 had been expended, the borough's water supply amounted to 21 million gallons per day,[28] over 80 percent of the houses were supplied, and several of the southern suburbs, in addition to Salford, were fully or partially connected to the Manchester waterworks. Although the Waterworks Committee had been forced to increase its rates in 1862 to accumulate sufficient capital to extend the supply, it had stopped depending upon the transfer of funds from the gas works. More important, the cost of water to the consumer had been substantially reduced. In the 1840s, a house assessed at £10 would have paid 10s. for a sporadic supply and an additional 5s. for a water closet; in the 1850s, the same house had an uninterrupted supply for 5s. and, even after the increase in the rate, paid only 10s. 5½d. per year for an unlimited supply.

[27] "Between 1851 and 1861, half the gas profits went to help pay for the waterworks . . . ." S. D. Simon, *A Century of City Government*, p. 351.
[28] This figure, representing 35.5 gallons per capita, is not radically different from the pre–World War II figure of 46.0 gallons per capita, which included much more extensive industrial uses.

CHAPTER TEN

The Failure of Local Government

The preceding review of the evolution of municipal government in Manchester and Liverpool over a century reveals the failure of local institutions to respond to changing conditions, to provide such needed public services as police protection, an adequate water supply, and minimum space and sanitary standards in housing: in short, to ensure the health, safety, and general welfare of the population. Although it is true that inadequate public services were typical of the time,[1] criticism is justified to the extent that the resources and powers available were sufficient to have averted the abominable living conditions of the new urban lower class. For example, the Manchester police commissioners were able to borrow and invest £52,000 in nine years to construct England's first municipal gas works; the Market Street Improvement Commissioners spent over £323,000 on 2.3 miles of downtown streets between 1821 and 1845; and once the borough council started taking an active interest in the town, it had no difficulty in purchasing the manorial rights for £200,000 or in borrowing more than £885,000 to acquire the Manchester and Salford Waterworks Company and to construct the first expansion of the town water supply. The Liverpool corporation, endowed with even greater financial resources, thanks to its initial investment in the dock estate, was able to pursue its original policy of channeling public funds into the extension of the port, enabling

---

[1] In 1844, the Health of Towns Commission reported that out of England's 50 "large towns," scarcely 1 had "good" sewers and 6 a "good" supply of water.

it to defend its economic position and capture an increasing share of the country's shipping. In view of the evident financial capacities of the local authorities in Manchester and Liverpool, it is a wonder that so little attention was paid to the array of problems generated by rapid urbanization.

In my introduction, I said that certain institutional structures were necessary for effective planning and for the development of public policies that would satisfy community goals. These were: an awareness on the part of government of the forces shaping the community and the translation of these forces into specific issues suitable for community discussion; the existence of a forum appropriate for community discussion and of channels through which community choices could be transmitted to government; sufficient resources, financial and administrative, to enable government to carry out policies designed to implement the communal choices; and appropriate channels for keeping the community informed, giving it the opportunity to reevaluate its original choices and to decide whether to support their translation into governmental policies. Remembering that the populations of Manchester and Liverpool had limited means to impress their desires upon local government, it is still evident that a breakdown occurred within the planning structure as I have outlined it. Although the breakdowns in Manchester and Liverpool were essentially identical, the reasons for them are different and reflect the differences between the institutional and administrative frameworks of the two towns.

THE AWARENESS OF CHANGE

Even a casual survey of late eighteenth- and early nineteenth-century writing reveals an awareness of the shifting balance between rural and urban populations; of the economic, social, and demographic forces at work; and of the living conditions created by rapid urban growth. The demographers of the period, although sometimes possessed of curious ideas about demographic causality,[2]

[2] The earliest study of social conditions in Manchester was undertaken in the 1770s by Thomas Percival. He traces the increase in its working-class population to an unusual source: "A Physician, of the first rank in his profession, has suggested to me, that tea may be considered as a powerful aphrodisiac; and he imputes the amazing population of China, amongst other causes, to the general use of it." *Observations on the State of Population in Manchester* (Manchester: privately printed, 1789), p. 45.

understood the population explosion and its repercussions upon food costs and wages, as well as the relation between the migration of rural populations to the new industrial towns and the growth of urban pauperism. These attributes of the new industrial age were discussed at length in Parliament, where the bulk of legislation was aimed at preventing any political disturbances that they might cause.

In addition to such generalized observations as were found in the reports of various committees of the House of Commons, a great deal of additional knowledge about local conditions was available. But in spite of their being relatively well informed, almost all the members of local government displayed a lackadaisical attitude toward public action, at least while they sat in their official capacity. In Liverpool and Manchester, individuals were engaged continuously in private charitable enterprises designed specifically to alleviate the distress of the urban lower classes; at the same time, these individuals were, more often than not, public figures of some importance, sitting on various committees and boards whose approach was weak and shortsighted. In Manchester, for example, the relation between the lack of the most rudimentary sanitary facilities and the spread of epidemics had been pointed out to the police commissioners on several occasions. Yet, when faced with constructive proposals by one of their own members[3] or by their own Board of Health, the wealthy and educated men responsible for local government sat idly by, although several of them were active political reformers. In spite of their genuine compassion for the victims of industrialization, nineteenth-century reformers were usually ambivalent in attributing responsibility for the destitution of the urban working class. Their criticism of the factory owners or of local authorities was mitigated by their readiness to blame the weak moral fiber of the poor for some of their misery. Gaskell's study of the manufacturing population of England[4] is a typical example of this ambivalence.

The moral, social, and domestic relations of the immense portion of the productive population of the kingdom, now engaged in manufactures, present a picture, as strange and as deeply interesting, as any in the whole circle of the history of mankind. To the philanthropist—to the

[3] See Dr. Ferriar's proposal for public housing in 1805, p. 152.
[4] Peter Gaskell, *The Manufacturing Population of England* . . . (London: Baldwin and Cradock, 1833), pp. 3-4.

man anxious for the well-being and social happiness of his species—it is one calculated to fill the mind with sorrow and fear. It has been little attended to, and still less understood. Remedies are wanted—are loudly called for: but before they can be efficiently applied, the disease must be studied; mere empiricism, even when founded on the purest motives, is dangerous; and when the interest and happiness of a multitude are at stake, a clear and distinct understanding of its wants and failings should precede any attempt to satisfy the one or rectify the other.

This demand for remedial action, tempered by a cautionary note against haste, is followed by the usual depressing rendition of living conditions in Manchester, drawn largely from the findings of Dr. Kay and from parliamentary reports. But Gaskell then goes on to demonstrate that many of these deplorable conditions were the direct result of the nefarious influence of the Irish migrants upon the Lancashire workers.

The introduction of a low Irish population into Manchester and the surrounding manufacturing towns and districts, has unquestionably aided very materially the destruction of domestic virtues and orderly habits in the operatives. The disregard to home comforts, which renders the Irish cabin a blot upon the history of its country, is exhibited still more strikingly when seen in the midst of a large town; and it has, unfortunately, found ready imitators in a class of the community, prepared for its adoption, in some degree, by poverty, ignorance, want of morality, and a growing indisposition for home, generated by a system of labour which, by separating families, and by exhausting their physical energies by incessant application, rendered them ready to fly, for temporary relief, to the gin-shop, the beer-house or the whiskey dealer.[5]

What Gaskell did not mention, of course, was that the proliferation of the "Irish cabins" that he deplores was due to the unfettered greed of private developers and the unwillingness of local government to restrain them. In spite of the information at its disposal, or perhaps because of the irresolute manner in which it was presented, local government simply did not find it necessary to formulate broad policies to meet the needs of rapid urbanization.

THE ABILITY TO ACT

There is no doubt that municipal authorities in Liverpool and Manchester were endowed with sufficient resources to have under-

[5] Ibid., p. 127.

taken public works beneficial to the population at large, and particularly to the poor, without raising additional taxes. In the case of the Liverpool corporation, it is clear that the magnitude of the sums invested in creating and enlarging the dock estate—monies that were borrowed on the surety of the corporate estate—together with the ever-increasing revenues derived from the port and the town dues, would have enabled it to raise whatever capital was needed to carry out the improvements authorized under the various local acts. Even in Manchester, the lack of a source of revenue whose yield expanded with the mercantile growth of the town would not have prevented the financing of required public works from current revenues.

Figure 24 offers a comparison between *actual* and *potential* municipal expenditures and revenues in Manchester, showing what might have been done in order to ensure a minimum standard of health and safety for the inhabitants. The period plotted runs from 1815, when the police commissioners had succeeded in asserting their authority under the terms of their difficult first years in office, to 1855, when the borough had acquired the size and characteristics that it retained until well into this century. The revenues plotted include only those funds at the disposal of municipal authorities, exclusive of poor relief and the salaries of public officials. The sudden acceleration in public expenditures after incorporation is clearly visible, both for normal operating costs and for public works. The rapid increase in public-works expenditures after 1840 was largely due to the purchase of the Manchester and Salford Waterworks Company and to the extension of the water supply that I have already described.

It should be noted that this comparison of potential and actual expenditures links cumulative expenditures with revenues, although this budgetary approach is somewhat contrary to the funding procedures of the time, which tended to consider, at least in principle, each public-works expenditure as a separate and, it was hoped, self-financing venture. Street paving, for example, was carried out of current revenues, the abutting owners being asked to reimburse the cost of the work. The gas works, and later the Waterworks Committees, took considerable pride in achieving economic independence in a few years, although the rates they had to charge were prohibitive for the majority of the town's inhabitants

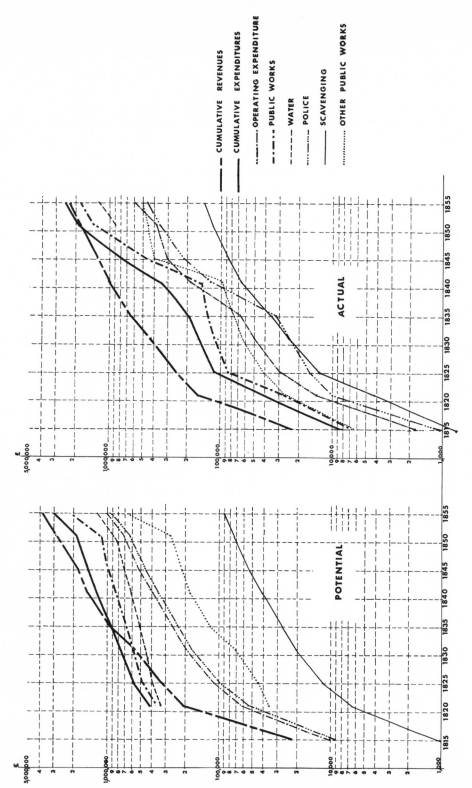

Figure 24. Municipal Revenues and Selected Expenditures in Manchester, 1816–1860

and defeated any broad concept of urban welfare. Yet there was little justification for this procedure, apart from administrative custom. In contrast to operating expenditures (paying salaries, keeping the peace, removing refuse), which had to be financed from current revenues, the very magnitude of public-works investments necessitated borrowing against future revenues. Even in nineteenth-century Manchester, it was common practice to utilize the profits from one municipal venture (the gas works, for example) to fund a deficit undertaking such as the Market Street Improvement Commission, whose outstanding debt was so large that, in spite of substantial transfers from the gas directors, it eventually had to be paid off with monies borrowed by the borough council under the terms of the Manchester Improvement Act of 1844 (7 and 8 Vict., cap. 41). Therefore, it can be argued that, if in the long run an appropriate balance between cumulative revenues and expenditures is achieved, the concept of deficit financing of public works was not alien to a nineteenth-century English municipal situation. The principle of subsidizing needed long-term capital expenditures on the basis of the profits reaped in other municipal enterprises was cited by the police commissioners in 1823, when they applied to Parliament for a monopoly on the right to provide gas to the town.[6]

With the tax revenue at their disposal, the Manchester police commissioners would have been able to provide a respectable level of urban services by 1821,[7] some thirty years before their belated success. Had they gained ownership of the waterworks and not followed the financially disastrous custom of letting out scavenging contracts to private entrepreneurs, they would have realized substantial savings by 1835, which would have allowed the new

[6] See pp. 126–127.

[7] The service population for each municipal activity was estimated separately. For example, the township was taken as the unit for police and scavenging until incorporation, while the actual service area of the Waterworks Committee (including Salford) was used to determine the amount of water needed.

The following cost standards were used: police: 1s. 12d. per capita; scavenging: 19d. per capita, net, assuming the work was undertaken by the municipality and the night soil sold to farmers; water: 12 gallons per capita, with a rate of 6d. per pound of assessed valuation, which is lower than the rate charged by the Waterworks Committee, since it does not include a surcharge for water closets and baths.

borough council, with a minimum of borrowing, to undertake new capital expenditures for education, public housing, or additional improvements. Moreover, considerably more money (£24,000 versus £8000 to £10,000) could have been spent between 1845 and 1851 on street paving and sewer construction. Had the police commissioners decided not to construct their expensive new Town Hall or to undertake the equally expensive alterations in the Market Street area,[8] over £240,000 could have been spent on general improvements, instead of the £40,000 to £50,000 actually spent. Not only would police protection, an adequate water supply, and efficient refuse removal have been available to the whole town, but the excess disposable capital would have provided the means to pave the streets faster, freeing the police commissioners from their financial dependence on the willingness of abutters to reimburse them for their share of the costs. Similarly, the commissioners could have provided public toilets in the dense working-class districts at their own expense, should it have been financially impractical, or politically unwise, to oblige the slum owners to do so.

The funding of this alternative scheme of public expenditures, at least during its first twenty years, would have depended upon the ability of the police commissioners to borrow. In the light of national trends, it is doubtful whether local tax revenues could have been increased significantly, since Manchester's rate was consistently higher than that of its neighboring towns, at least until 1840. Even though the rate declined, after incorporation, to a level com-

[8] The history of the Market Street Improvement Commissioners is a clouded one. They spent almost £324,000 between 1821 and 1845 on the improvement of 2.3 miles of streets in the central business district; of this amount, £65,186 was spent on property acquisition and £111,479 on various other improvements, including demolition of buildings to open new streets, paving, and sewering. An additional £90,000 was spent on interest payments and £49,000 in partial repayment of the monies borrowed. When their accounts were finally audited in 1848, following a ratepayers' petition, no vouchers could be produced for £72,726 spent by the commissioners, and £7539 was totally unaccounted for.

Although their accounts were finally accepted, their plausibility still seems open to question. James Wheeler (*Manchester: Its Political, Social, and Commercial History, Ancient and Modern* [London: Whittaker, 1836], pp. 261 ff.) reports peculiar fluctuations in the cost of properties in the area, suggesting the possibility of favoritism at the taxpayers' expense, especially since no record survives of the disposition costs of excess properties, which the commissioners purchased and resold among members of their own peer group.

parable to, if not actually lower than those of the other townships within the municipal borough, widespread fear existed that any increase in taxes for purposes other than the relief of the poor would be detrimental to the economy.[9] Fluctuations of the poor rate could be justified as the result of external circumstances beyond the control of the local authorities and were probably discounted over several years by the business community because of their supposedly temporary nature. Any increase in the borough rate, however, would have become a permanent cost, a sign of public profligacy to be taken seriously, if not by existing enterprises— which would have found it difficult to move on account of their trained labor force and the capital invested in buildings and machinery—then certainly by new business, whose choice of location had been increased by the extensive railroad system now serving the Manchester area. Even improved tax-collecting techniques and a less generous allowance for exemptions would not have yielded more than marginal increases in revenue. Although only houses assessed at less than £4 10s. were exempt from the police rate, collection was so difficult that for practical purposes only houses valued at £10 and above were included in the tax rolls. Even then, the problems presented by an increasingly mobile, low-income population were such as to prompt the overseers to allow the owners of rental properties assessed at £6 to £20 the option of paying the rate themselves, rather than letting their tenants do so. As an inducement, they were allowed to "compound," that is, they were given a deduction equal to no more than half the rates that would have been collected on all of their properties. In the mind of the overseers, this generous exemption was amply justified, since it ensured a prompter collection of the rate.

Although restricted in their ability to raise additional revenues from local sources, the Manchester police commissioners could have

[9] "The trade of the [Manchester] district had remained depressed since 1847, and there was some fear that ratepayers might be driven out of the borough if the rates went much higher. In 1848, 'the pressure of the times and prevalence of distress' had made it necessary to levy a poor rate of five shillings in the pound in the township of Manchester 'for purposes of the Guardians alone'; and this had indirectly increased the strain upon the finances of the Corporation in 1849–50." Arthur Redford and Ira S. Russell, *History of Local Government in Manchester*, 3 vols. (London: Allen & Unwin, 1940), 2:195–196. See also the *Manchester Guardian*, September 22 and December 6, 1848.

borrowed the capital needed to carry out public works. In their study of English business cycles, Gayer, Rostow, and Schwartz have pointed out that, with the exception of short periods when subjective judgments caused individuals and private bankers to make their assets as liquid as possible, availability of capital was characteristic of the postwar period. In spite of the fluctuations of the discount rate, the absence of prescribed reserves governing the lending policies of the Bank of England and of private banks tended to minimize the influence on the economy of variations in the availability and cost of investment capital: the tightening of the credit market tended to exacerbate the various economic crises, rather than act as their cause.[10] However, at the time when Manchester might have been a large borrower (1815–1831), the private advances made by the Bank of England were declining sharply,[11] while the interest rate was relatively steady at around 5 percent. There is no reason to believe that the facility with which the gas directors and the Market Street Improvement Commissioners of Manchester were able to finance their respective undertakings could not have been matched by the police commissioners, had they been willing to initiate the public works described.

INSTITUTIONAL ESTRANGEMENT

Neither ignorance of local conditions nor a financial or administrative inability to take appropriate action can account for the fail-

---

[10] "Monetary phenomena can be most usefully regarded, in this period, as a reflection of more deep-seated movements." Arthur D. Gayer, Walt W. Rostow, and Anna J. Schwartz, *The Growth and Fluctuation of the British Economy, 1790–1850*, 2 vols. (Oxford: Clarendon Press, 1953), 2:558 ff.

The short-term characteristic of nineteenth-century capital (see Alexander Gerschenkron, *Economic Backwardness in Historical Perspective* [Cambridge: Harvard University Press, Belknap Press, 1962], p. 13) and the sensitivity of the English banking system to subjective interpretations of national and international trends seem to have contributed to the close spacing of the period's economic cycles and the substantial fluctuations in the discount rate.

[11] Gayer, Rostow, and Schwartz, *British Economy*, 2:882. In the 1840s, Britain's annual investable surplus was on the order of £60 million, much of which went into foreign ventures such as the American, Austrian, and Russian railroads. Leland H. Jenks, *The Migration of British Capital to 1875* (New York: Knopf, 1927), p. 126.

ure of municipal institutions in Manchester and Liverpool to deal with the problems of rapid urbanization. Even relatively "destitute" towns such as Manchester (towns lacking a large, revenue-producing corporate estate like Liverpool's) were in fact financially sound. Moreover, Parliament was quite willing to grant local enabling acts for almost any public venture that local authorities might wish to undertake, as demonstrated by the broad powers granted the police commissioners of Manchester and the borough council of Liverpool under their various improvement acts.

One must look instead to the almost total lack of communication between local government and the community as one of the reasons that public resources and powers were not used to guide development. Before Manchester's incorporation, for example, only 8.5 percent of adult males satisfied the minimum property requirement to qualify as voters; and even under the more liberal £10 qualification of the Municipal Reform Act, only slightly over 13 percent of adult males were on the voters' list. In reformed Liverpool, only 10.5 percent of adult males were voters, and other large towns had similar percentages. Considering that the majority of urban assessments (over 70 percent in Manchester) were under £10 in 1838, it is evident not only that the voting potential of the low-income urban working class was practically nil, but that fewer than half of the potentially qualified voters were actually registered. This low registration was due to the widespread practice of compounding and to the length-of-residence requirement of the Municipal Reform Act. Since owners of rental properties assessed at £6 to £20 could choose to pay the poor rate and the borough rate themselves, rather than leaving it to their tenants, many householders were automatically disfranchised. The custom seems to have been prevalent in most urban areas, not only because landlords could charge higher rents on properties whose renters were thus exempt from local taxes,[12] but also because local authorities often utilized compound-

[12] Since abatements of up to 50 percent of the combined value of rental properties were granted under the compounding arrangement, the landlords had a definite pecuniary incentive. Assuming a £10 property, the compounded rate would have been on the order of 6s. or 7s. instead of 10s. 10d. for the Manchester borough rate. A corresponding weekly rent increase of 2½d., or 5 percent of the average weekly rent of working-class families, would not only have made up the rate paid by the landlord but would have yielded an additional annual profit of 4s. or 5s.

ing as a means of withholding the voting franchise from lower-income groups. In 1851, for example, the Manchester overseers recommended to the borough council that they not take advantage of an act extending the voting franchise to all households whose taxes had been paid, whether directly or under a compounding arrangement.[13] The reasons given speak for themselves: the overseers argued that since the borough council, "by compounding voluntarily and by ordinary methods . . . were able to collect more than half of the rates from this class of property, they would prefer to go on as before rather than face the 'serious results which are likely to arise in all corporate towns from such a class of voters.' "[14]

The three-year minimum residence requirement for borough voters, during which time rates had to be paid for two and a half years consecutively, acted as an additional restraint on the ability of the majority of urban residents to influence the policies adopted by municipal government. The lower residence requirements for parliamentary voters, for example, often resulted in higher voter participation.[15] The increasing mobility of labor after the coming of the railroads and the large influx of Irish migrants, particularly in Liverpool and Manchester, made the fulfillment of a three-year minimum residence requirement difficult for a significant portion of urban residents. It should be noted that, with the possible exception of the Irish, this mobile urban labor force did not belong to the lowest social strata, being composed of skilled artisans willing and able to forgo the relative security of the poor relief provided under the

[13] 13 and 14 Vict., cap. 99. This was a "permissive" act, that is, subject to adoption by local authorities.

[14] Shena D. Simon, *A Century of City Government* (London: Allen & Unwin, 1938), p. 434. The quotation is from the *Churchwardens and Overseers Board Book* for January 3, 1851.

[15] The requirements in a parliamentary borough were one year of residence during six months of which the poor rate had been paid. The results of these lower requirements are shown in the following table.

Town	% Parliamentary Voters among Adult Male Residents	% Borough Voters among Adult Male Residents
Birmingham	13.5	9.3
Leeds	14.1	18.8
Liverpool	22.1	10.5
Manchester	15.6	13.3
Sheffield	12.1	16.8

Source: Calculated from S. D. Simon, *A Century of City Government*, p. 429.

Settlement Acts in their search for better economic opportunities.[16] Had they been given the chance, they might well have developed into a relatively stable, educated, and articulate group of spokesmen for the urban masses; as it was, they were automatically prevented from participating in the political process.

To this absence of an electoral base representative of the interests of the community at large must be added a similar lack of participation in public affairs on the part of the urban middle class. While inadequate representation was typical of the time and cannot be judged a priori as contributing to inefficient government, the general unwillingness to serve in public office or to participate in local politics seems surprising in a period when the new middle class was struggling for recognition. Yet this alienation between public officials and the restricted electorate largely drawn from their peers was not only characteristic of the period but related to the coexistence of traditional and emerging institutions. In particular, the onerous duties imposed by unpaid public office, a remnant of the medieval "obligation to serve," did not attract energetic, educated, honest men to positions of responsibility in local government. The tradition was, instead, to attempt to evade, often by dubious means, public service of any kind, as shown by the long annual lists of amercements levied by the Manchester Court Leet upon burgesses failing to appear as jurors or refusing to serve as the court's officers. Not only were the rich willing to pay fines to free themselves from public office, but a brisk trade seems to have been conducted in the sale of bogus records of criminal activity ("Tyburn Tickets"), since, under an act dating back to 1699 (10 and 11 Will. 3, cap. 23),[17] convicted felons were exempted from holding public office.[18]

In Liverpool and Manchester, as well as in other towns, the in-

---

[16] "By the mid-nineteenth century the [tramping] system was very widespread. In 1860, it was in use among compositers, lithographers, taylors, coachmakers, bookbinders, smiths, engineers, steam engine makers, stone masons, carpenters, ironfounders, coopers, shoemakers, boilermakers, plumbers, bricklayers, and various other crafts." E. J. Hobsbawm, "The Tramping Artisan," *Economic History Review* 3, no. 3 (1951):305.

Tramping also "relieved strike funds and provided a means of countering victimization." Ibid.

[17] Repealed in 1827 by 7 and 8 Geo. 4, cap. 27.

[18] The *Manchester Herald* for December 15, 1818, for example, reported that "gentlemen have given upwards of three hundred pounds for [a Tyburn Ticket], because it exempted them from serving."

action of local government can thus be traced to three major causes: (1) the unwillingness of government to utilize its knowledge of developing urban conditions to frame appropriate remedial and preventive policies; (2) the reluctance of even a restricted electorate, selected on the basis of wealth, to live up to its responsibilities, except on the rare occasions when its own interests were threatened; and (3) the inability of a majority of the new urban middle class to influence the tradition-oriented machinery of government. Of these, the first two causes reinforced each other: if the abdication of the electorate allowed the aldermen of Liverpool and the police commissioners of Manchester to construe their role in increasing isolation, the resulting remoteness of local government from political pressures was discouraging to the voters upon those rare occasions when they were moved to act. Hence, the failure of the Liverpool freemen in their attempt to regain control of the corporation and the long and disappointing struggle led by Radical reformers at the meetings of the Manchester police commission and parish vestry. Moreover, the sporadic desire of the middle class to participate in making decisions did not extend to granting the voting franchise to urban newcomers in order to enlarge their ranks. On the contrary, they shared their conservative government's fear that their traditional position of influence, although putative rather than real, would be undermined if the electoral base were broadened. It was safer to endure the shortcomings of familiar ways than to risk the unknown evils of popular suffrage.

THE APATHY OF THE MIDDLE CLASS

The voters' complacent attitude was bolstered by the fact that local government was in the hands of members of their own class, who generally conducted themselves decently enough in discharging their public duties. Local government could not often be accused of neglecting its customary responsibilities. The development of the dock estate by the Liverpool corporation was an enterprise requiring foresight and courage, whose economic benefits were clearly useful to the mercantile community, while the Manchester gas works, and even the limited downtown improvements, were of undoubted benefit to the town's manufactures. Whatever dissatisfaction there was with local government resulted from the allotment of the costs of these ventures, such as the town dues levied on nonfreemen and the high rates charged by the Gas Board. There was no complaint about sharing their benefits, nor about the glaring lack of public concern for sanitary conditions and pauperism. The urban middle class during the industrial revolution was thus unwilling to act, except where public action could bring them direct benefits, such as providing gas to light their factories, their homes, and their neighborhoods; making improvements in the central business district; or responding to conditions that threatened their personal safety.[19] The persistent apathy of the "sixteen-pound voters," whose small number and financial substance should, according to the political theories of the time, have ensured their active and enlightened participation in public affairs, could not be shaken except in the face of the most outrageous abuse of the public trust. In Manchester, the scandal that forced Fleming's resignation and prompted the Radicals to pack the ranks of the commissioners and the parish vestry had been inspired by indignation over the mismanagement of public funds, not by dissatisfaction with the policies of local government, and it resulted in the vigorous but short-lived intervention of otherwise placid leypayers.

Even such liberal reformers as Richard Cobden and Archibald Prentice, both leaders in the fight for the charter and articulate representatives of the new generation of more liberal Whig businessmen who were replacing Tories on the local level, had only a brief interest in local government. In spite of their fiery speeches in favor of democratic suffrage during the struggle for the charter, they did not make an issue of the numerical discrepancy between parliamentary and borough voters or of the fact that compounding by landlords blocked political participation among the urban lower class,

---

[19] "It was the prevalence of sickness, and particularly the danger of the extension of such epidemics as cholera and typhus from the slums to the middle-class districts, which brought about the first attempts to improve matters. The first important sign of any public concern in regard to insanitary conditions seems to have been shown in a memorandum to Parliament by the new Poor Law Commissioners in 1838. In this memorandum they described the appalling sanitary conditions in London, pointing out that epidemics and sickness were the main cause of expenditure on poor relief, and that if they were to be avoided in the future a public health code and measures for dealing with insanitary conditions were essential." E. Simon, "Housing and Civic Planning," in Harold Laski, W. Ivor Jennings, and William A. Robson, eds., *A Century of Municipal Progress* (London: Allen & Unwin, 1935), p. 201.

the very people whose advocates they had been. The same lack of concern permeated other industrial towns and Parliament itself. Although there were several inquiries into the consequences of the Municipal Reform Act, all of which noted with surprise the low level of voter participation, the champions of the act had lost interest. "The Chartists themselves, whose programme included adult suffrage and who might have been expected to take up the question, were not interested in municipal government, and in many cases were actively hostile to the demand for a charter for those towns that were not incorporated under the Act."[20]

Parliament's intermittent concern for local affairs was partly responsible for the slow extension of municipal activities, the deficiencies in municipal performance, and the quality of local services that obtained until the end of the nineteenth century. Whenever the reforming fervor of an individual was aroused, a bill was submitted to cope with the problem at hand, usually on an *ad hoc* basis.[21] But with the exception of the Town Improvement Clauses Act of 1847, which attempted to ensure some uniformity in the language and powers granted under local improvement acts, no attempt was made at the national level to deal comprehensively with the array of similar, if not identical, problems facing the country's urban areas.[22] Devoid of instructions or guidance from London, local authorities were left to handle their individual problems as best they could. It is not surprising that the tendency of the more articulate reformers to gravitate toward London, together with the absence of adequate channels through which the new urban population could make their aspirations known, permitted the traditional

---

[20] S. D. Simon, *A Century of City Government*, p. 438.

[21] For example, the efforts to deal with the problems of public health were undertaken over forty years, in a piecemeal fashion. "Vaccination, the exigencies of Poor Law administration, the four rather alarming epidemics of cholera (1831–33, 1848–49, 1853–54, and 1865–66), the insanitary state of the labouring classes, and the urgent need for a comprehensive registration of sickness and mortality had moved public opinion and Parliament to a kaleidoscopic series of patchwork measures, which included the Poor Law Amendment Act itself, the Factory Act of 1833, the Registration of Births, Deaths, and Marriages Act of 1836, and the Vaccination Act of 1840." George Newman, "The Health of the People," in Laski, Jennings, and Robson, *A Century of Municipal Progress*, p. 161.

[22] For an excellent discussion of the evolving legal concepts that governed the relation between Parliament, local authorities, and the private sector, see W. Ivor Jennings, "Central Control," ibid., pp. 417–454.

oligarchies that controlled local government to fulfill their limited objectives before attempting to satisfy the basic needs of the community at large. Endowed with the economic and administrative means to undertake effective planning, the urban middle class did not hesitate to sacrifice the community interest to its own.

The failure of municipal government during the industrial revolution can, therefore, be ascribed to national political attitudes as well as to local institutional factors that worked against change. Yet it is doubtful whether a broader participation in the political process, either nationally or locally, would necessarily have resulted in better local government. The extension of the voting franchise to the uneducated rural migrants who formed the bulk of the urban working class would have made them the likely prey of demagogues promising immediate benefits, and need not have resulted in the election of public officials with the foresight indispensable to a period of momentous change. In theory, limiting the right to vote to an educated and wealthy elite would ensure an efficient and honest government. The equation of wealth with the ability to make enlightened decisions was simply a recognition of the dangers inherent in the lack of public education, so that the exclusion of the majority of the population from the political process was not the result of an arbitrary decision.

There was a more important cause than limited suffrage for the failure of local government in Liverpool, in Manchester, and in other urban areas: the indifference to urban problems consistently displayed both by local officials and by the restricted corps of voters who belonged to the same mercantile and industrial class as those in power. If it is no surprise that local officials failed to assume responsibility for communal affairs because of their isolation from popular pressures, it is paradoxical that those who were entitled (and expected) to participate in the political process were led to abstain by the relative success of local authorities in responding to their mercantile interests. The development of the Liverpool dock estate, the Manchester gas works, and the downtown improvements carried out in both towns, were successful ventures that satisfied both the government oligarchies and their peers, the middle-class voters. That these undertakings reflected only one facet of the industrial age, its economic opportunities, leaving a host of social problems unsolved, did not seem to have been particularly bothersome to anyone in a position of influence, with the exception of a few reformers. It is one of the inconsistencies of the industrial revolution that its scientific achievements and the social and economic theories that accompanied them—the acceptance of new concepts of social mobility based upon individual achievement, the adoption of more liberal political attitudes, at least toward the middle class—may have militated against responsible and effective urban government.

In his study of the development of public opinion in Manchester, Marshall points out that the political activity of the town's industrialists and merchants during the first decades of the nineteenth century was aimed at obtaining the representation of manufacturing interests in Parliament on a parity with the traditional, agricultural, county interests; at repealing governmental restrictions upon foreign trade; and at ensuring a labor market as free as possible from governmental regulations.[23] The validity of these policies rested on the intricate pattern of international commerce that the economic prosperity of Manchester, Liverpool, and other industrial centers was founded upon. The mercantile sentiments that had prompted Liverpool and Manchester merchants to oppose the war with the American colonies and to deplore the Orders in Council were still motivating their demand for parliamentary reform, the repeal of the Corn Laws, and their opposition to the Factory Acts. But in areas where their own far-flung interests were not involved directly—the adoption of more effective welfare measures, the improvement of municipal services, or even the acquisition of a municipal charter—little concern could be elicited from them. The widening of their traditional world, made possible by an industrial technology requiring ever more distant markets, and by new modes of transportation whose reduced costs and greater speeds forced them to be sensitive to small fluctuations in the demand for goods and the supply of capital at home and abroad, blinded them to the plight of their workers.[24] Indeed, the very breadth of their outlook

[23] Leon S. Marshall, *The Development of Public Opinion in Manchester, 1780–1820* (Syracuse: Syracuse University Press, 1946), pp. 234 ff.

[24] This blindness was not entirely due to class prejudice: the concentration of public works in the central business district, together with the suburban exodus of the rich, allowed the middle-class Mancunian to "go in and out daily without coming into contact with a working-people's quarter or even with workers, that is, so long as he confines himself to his business or to

distracted them from the relatively parochial problems of urban government. The leaders of municipal affairs and their middle-class constituents remained uncontrolled by Parliament and removed from all but sporadic (although at times violent) pressures from the urban masses. Thus they never thought it necessary to engage in a dialogue to frame policies for dealing with the forces transforming their towns nor, in the rare instances when policies were framed, to reevaluate their effectiveness.

It is not my intention to pretend that a historical survey such as this can yield a lesson that is useful today. Yet the apathy that characterized the municipal institutions of Liverpool and Manchester when faced with new social and functional problems created by industrialization can be ascribed to causes that are not dissimilar to those hampering the efforts of our own urban governments to deal with substandard housing, poverty, and the political alienation of the black ghetto. Today, as in nineteenth-century England, awareness of the problem and sufficient means to develop remedial programs are impeded by institutional isolation from the segments of the population whose welfare needs must be met, an isolation that can only lead to the perpetuation of traditional institutional mechanisms. Today, as in the past, the whole system of societal incentives tends to attract imaginative and forceful local leadership to the larger arena of national politics. The federal government, although increasingly concerned with urban problems, is primarily motivated by a comprehensive view of its responsibility that makes it as unresponsive to the finer shades of local problems as the nineteenth-century middle class, preoccupied with its far-flung financial interests.

Indeed, the diversity of functional characteristics and the social heterogeneity that distinguish the modern city and its nineteenth-century predecessor from the older mercantile town suggest that the broadening of the electoral base that has taken place over the last 150 years, although eminently satisfying philosophically, may

---

pleasure walks. This arises chiefly from the fact that, by unconscious tacit agreement, as well as with outspoken conscious determination, the working-people's quarters are sharply separated from the sections of the city reserved for the middle-class; or if this does not succeed, they are concealed with the cloak of charity." Friedrich Engels, *The Condition of the Working Class in England in 1844* (London: Allen & Unwin, 1920), pp. 45–46.

not be sufficient in and of itself to create the dialogue between community and government that my model of the planning process makes a necessary prerequisite to effective action. Paradoxically, this very increase in political participation has only succeeded in diluting the voice of those who are unable to compete successfully within a free enterprise system—at least as long as a modicum of economic growth and social mobility exists. It was hardly accidental that the nineteenth-century increase of the voting franchise in industrial cities did not result in more concern for living conditions in lower-income districts, and that a half century of universal suffrage in the United States has not produced an effective solution to urban problems. In either instance, the middle-class-oriented educational and financial requirements for public office, together with the catharsis of sporadic community consultation, mitigate against the effectiveness of the traditional democratic dialogue between the urban community and its institutions. Nineteenth-century local governments, like contemporary ones, were under no compulsion to articulate issues in a manner specific enough for community discussion and consensus and were selected and assessed on the basis of their general efficiency, a criterion that is inevitably interpreted in different ways by individual segments of the community. Therefore, blanket approval of public policies is almost bound to occur, either because the issues presented are so general that it is difficult to disagree with them or because of the apathy of the voters.

Historically, change in public policy and local administrative institutions seems to have come about only when gross mismanagement or flagrant dishonesty threatened the prerogatives of a group belonging to the decision-making structure or who had interests closely allied to it. The short-lived revolt of the Liverpool freemen, the packing of the Manchester police commission, and the transitional struggle, in both towns, between the reformed corporations and their predecessors are good examples of this process. In other words, change cannot be said to have been forced upon an apathetic local government from without, through pressure from the multitudes whose lives were most dramatically affected by rapid urbanization. The lines of communication necessary for planning were restricted to a particular class and opened only when members of that class became thoroughly dissatisfied with the actions of their peers. Consequently, planning was sporadic and the treatment of the urban masses largely paternalistic. Although participation in community decisions has certainly increased substantially as a result of the upward mobility that has accompanied economic growth over the last century or so, the basic dilemma, to ensure adequate representation for the aspirations of disadvantaged minorities, the modern-day homologues to the Irish factory workers of nineteenth-century Liverpool and Manchester, is still far from resolved.

Selected Bibliography

I. GREAT BRITAIN, GENERAL CONDITION

Ashton, Thomas S. "The Standard of Life of the Workers in England, 1790–1830." *Journal of Economic History* 9 (Supplement) (1949): 19–38.

Ashworth, William, "British Industrial Villages in the Nineteenth Century." *Economic History Review* 3, no. 3 (1951):378–395.

Baines, Edward. *History of the Cotton Manufacture in Great Britain.* London: Fisher, Fisher, and Jackson, 1835.

Beveridge, Sir William. *Prices and Wages in England from the Twelfth to the Nineteenth Century.* London: Longmans, Green, 1939.

Bowley, Arthur Lyon. *Wages in the United Kingdom in the Nineteenth Century.* Cambridge: Cambridge University Press, 1900.

Brownless, P. H. "The History of the Birth- and Death-Rates in England and Wales Taken as a Whole from 1570 to the Present Time." *Public Health*, June–July 1916, p. 219.

Buer, Mabel Craven. *Health, Wealth and Population in the Early Days of the Industrial Revolution.* London: G. Routledge & Sons, 1926.

Chadwick, Edwin. *Report on the Sanitary Conditions of the Labouring Population of Great Britain.* London: H.M.S.O., 1843.

Cole, George Douglas Howard. *A Short History of the British Working-Class Movement, 1789–1947.* Rev. ed. London: Allen & Unwin, 1948.

Colquhoun, Patrick. *A Treatise on Indigence.* London: J. Hatchard, 1806.

———. *A Treatise on the Wealth, Power, and Resources of the British Empire . . .* London: J. Mawman, 1814.

Comber, W. T. *An Inquiry into the State of National Subsistence . . .* London: T. Cadell and W. Davies, 1808.

Dewsnup, Ernest Ritson. *The Housing Problem in England, Its Statis-*

tics, Legislation, and Policy. Manchester: Manchester University Press, 1907.

Drummond, Jack Cecil, and Anne Wilbraham. *The Englishman's Food*. London: Jonathan Cape, 1939.

Eden, Sir Frederick Morton. *An Estimate of the Number of Inhabitants in Great Britain and Ireland*. London: J. Wright, 1800.

Ellison, Thomas. *The Cotton Trade of Great Britain*. London: E. Wilson, 1886.

Engels, Friedrich. *The Condition of the Working Class in England in 1844*. London: Allen & Unwin, 1920.

Faucher, Léon. *Etudes sur l'Angleterre*. 2 vols. Brussells: Wouters frères, 1845.

Finer, Herman. *English Local Government*. London: Methuen, 1933.

Frazer, William Mowell. *A History of English Public Health, 1834–1939*. London: Baillière, 1950.

Gaskell, Peter. *The Manufacturing Population of England* . . . London: Baldwin and Cradock, 1833.

Gayer, Arthur David, Walt W. Rostow, and Anna J. Schwartz. *The Growth and Fluctuation of the British Economy, 1790–1850*. 2 vols. Oxford: Clarendon Press, 1953.

Gilboy, Elizabeth W. "The Cost of Living and Real Wages in Eighteenth Century England." *Review of Economic Statistics* 18 (1936):134–143.

———. *Wages in Eighteenth Century England*. Cambridge: Harvard University Press, 1934.

Habakkuk, Hrothgar John. "English Population in the Eighteenth Century." *Economic History Review*, 2nd ser. 6, no. 2 (1953):117–133.

Hadfield, Ellis Charles Raymond, and James E. MacColl. *British Local Government*. London: Hutchinson's University Library, 1948.

Hammond, John Lawrence and Barbara. *The Skilled Labourer, 1760–1832*. London: Longmans, Green, 1919.

———. *The Town Labourer, 1760–1832*. London: Longmans, Green, 1917.

Hobsbawm, Eric John. "The British Standard of Living, 1790–1850." *Economic History Review*, 2nd ser. 10, no. 7 (1957):46–68.

———. "The Tramping Artisan." *Economic History Review*, 2nd ser. 3, no. 3 (1951):299–320.

Hole, James. *The Homes of the Working Classes, with Suggestions for Their Improvement*. London: Longmans, Green, 1866.

Isaac, Julius. *Economics of Migration*. London: Kegan Paul, Trench, Trubner, 1947.

Keith-Lucas, B. "Some Influences Affecting the Development of Sanitary Legislation in England." *Economic History Review*, 2nd ser. 6, no. 3 (1954):290–296.

Laski, Harold, W. Ivor Jennings, and William A. Robson, eds. *A Century of Municipal Progress, 1835–1935*. London: Allen & Unwin, 1935.

Lipman, Vivian David. *Local Government Areas, 1834–1945*. Oxford: Blackwell, 1949.

Malthus, Thomas Robert. *An Essay on the Principle of Population*. 2 vols. 3rd ed. London: J. Johnson, 1806.

Mantoux, Paul. *The Industrial Revolution in the Eighteenth Century*. Rev. ed. New York: Harcourt, Brace, 1929.

Marshall, T. H. "The Population Problem during the Industrial Revolution." *Economic History Review* 1, no. 4 (1929):429–456.

McKeown, T., and R. G. Brown. "Medical Evidence Relating to English Population Changes." *Population Studies* 9 (1955):119 ff.

Milne, Joshua. *A Treatise on the Valuation of Annuities . . .* 2 vols. London: Longman, Hurst, Rees, Orme, and Brown, 1815.

Moffit, Louis Wilfrid. *England on the Eve of the Industrial Revolution*. London: P. S. King & Son, 1925.

Price, Richard. *Observations on Reversionary Payments . . .* 2 vols. 4th ed. London: T. Cadell, 1783.

Raumer, Friedrich von. *England in 1835*. Philadelphia: Carey, Lea, and Blanchard, 1836.

Redford, Arthur. *Labour Migration in England, 1800–1850*. Manchester: Manchester University Press, 1926.

Redlich, Josef, and Francis W. Hirst. *The History of Local Government in England*. London: Macmillan, 1958.

Rogers, James Edwin Thorold. *A History of Agriculture and Prices in England*. 7 vols. Oxford: Oxford University Press, 1866–1902.

———. *Six Centuries of Work and Wages*. New York: G. P. Putnam's Sons, 1884.

Savage, Christopher I. *An Economic History of Transport*. London: Hutchinson, 1959.

Schumpeter, Elizabeth Boody. "English Prices and Public Finance, 1660–1822." *Review of Economic Statistics* 20, no. 1 (1938):21–37.

Smellie, Kingsley Bryce. *A History of Local Government*. London: Allen & Unwin, 1946.

Stouffer, S. A. "Intervening Opportunities and Competing Migrants." *Journal of Regional Science* 2 (Spring 1960):1–26.

Toynbee, Arnold. *The Industrial Revolution*. Boston: Beacon Press, 1956.

Tucker, R. S. "Real Wages of Artisans in London, 1729–1935." *Journal of the American Statistical Association* 31, no. 193 (1936):73–84.

Ure, Andrew. *The Cotton Manufacture of Great Britain Investigated and Illustrated*. 2 vols. London: H. G. Bohn, 1861.

Vine, John Richard Somers. *English Municipal Institutions*. London: Waterlow and Sons, 1879.

Wales, William. *An Inquiry into the Present State of Population in England and Wales*. London: C. Nourse, 1781.

Webb, Sidney and Beatrice. *English Poor Law History*. 2 vols. Hamden, Conn.: Archon Books, 1963. Originally published from 1927 to 1929.

———. *The Manor and the Borough*. 2 vols. Hamden, Conn.: Archon Books, 1963. Originally published in 1908.

————. *The Parish and the County*. Hamden, Conn.: Archon Books, 1963. Originally published in 1906.

————. *Statutory Authorities for Special Purposes*. Hamden, Conn.: Archon Books, 1963. Originally published in 1922.

Wood, George Henry. *History of Wages in the Cotton Trade during the Past Hundred Years*. London: Sherratt and Hughes, 1910.

Woodward, Ernest Llewellyn. *The Age of Reform, 1815–1870*. Oxford: Clarendon Press, 1938.

Wright, J. F. "An Index of the Output of British Industry since 1700." *Journal of Economic History* 16, no. 3 (1956):356–364.

Young, Agnes Freda, and E. T. Ashton. *British Social Work in the Nineteenth Century*. London: Routledge and Kegan Paul, 1956.

2. LANCASHIRE

Ashworth, Henry. *Statistical Illustrations of the Past and Present State of Lancashire*. Manchester: British Association [1840?].

Baines, Thomas. *Lancashire and Cheshire, Past and Present*. London: W. Mackenzie [1868–1869?].

Britton, John. *A Topographical and Historical Description of the County of Lancaster*. London: Sherwood, Neely, and Jones, n.d.

Chadwick, David. *On the Rate of Wages . . . in Lancashire from 1839 to 1859*. London: W. H. Smith and Son, 1860.

Daniels, George William. *The Early English Cotton Industry*. London: Longmans, Green, 1920.

House, John William. *North-Eastern England*. University of Durham, King's College, Department of Geography. Research Series, no. 1. Newcastle upon Tyne, 1954.

Taylor, William Cooke. *Notes of a Tour in the Manufacturing Districts of Lancashire*. 2nd ed. London: Duncan and Malcolm, 1842.

Wadsworth, Alfred P., and Julia de Lacey Mann. *The Cotton Trade and Industrial Lancashire, 1660–1780*. Manchester: Manchester University Press, 1931.

Walker, Frank. *Historical Geography of Southwest Lancashire before the Industrial Revolution*. Manchester: Chetham Society, 1939.

Young, Arthur. *A Six Months Tour through the North of England*. 4 vols. London: W. Strahan, 1770.

3. LIVERPOOL

Baines, Thomas. *History of the Commerce and Town of Liverpool*. London: Longman, Brown, Green, and Longmans, 1852.

————. *Liverpool in 1859*. London: Longman, 1859.

Black, Adam and Charles. *Black's Guide to Liverpool*. 7th ed. Edinburgh: A. and C. Black, 1879.

Brooke, Richard. *Liverpool As It Was during the Last Quarter of the Eighteenth Century*. London: J. R. Smith, 1853.

Chandler, George. *Liverpool*. London: B. T. Batsford, 1957.

Ellison, Thomas. *The Cotton Trade of Great Britain*. London: E. Wilson, 1886.

Enfield, William. *An Essay towards the History of Liverpool*. 2nd ed. London: J. Johnson, 1774.

Gawthrop, Hugh. *Fraser's Guide to Liverpool*. London: W. Kent, 1855.

Gore's Directory of Liverpool. Liverpool, 1766.

Holford, William Graham, and W. A. Eden. *The Future of Merseyside*. Liverpool: Liverpool University Press, 1937.

Hume, Abraham. *Condition of Liverpool, Religious and Social*. Liverpool: T. Brakell, 1858.

Jones, C. D., ed. *The Social Survey of Merseyside*. Liverpool: Liverpool University Press, 1934.

Lacey, Louis, ed. *The History of Liverpool from 1207–1907*. Liverpool: Lyceum Press, 1907.

Muir, J. Ramsay. *A History of Liverpool*. London: Williams and Norgate, 1907.

————, and Edith M. Platt. *History of Municipal Government in Liverpool*. Liverpool University Press, 1906.

Parkinson, Cyril Northcote. *The Rise of the Port of Liverpool*. Liverpool: Liverpool University Press, 1952.

Picton, James A. *City of Liverpool: Municipal Archives and Records . . . Extract*. Liverpool: G. G. Walmsley, 1886.

————. *Memorials of Liverpool*. 2 vols. London: Longmans, Green, 1875.

Simey, Margaret Bayne. *Charitable Efforts in Liverpool in the Nineteenth Century*. Liverpool: Liverpool University Press, 1951.

Smith, Wilfred. *The Distribution of Population and the Location of Merseyside*. Liverpool: Liverpool University Press, 1942.

————, ed. *A Scientific Survey of Merseyside*. Liverpool: Liverpool University Press, 1953.

Smithers, Henry. *Liverpool, Its Commerce, Statistics, and Institutions with a History of the Cotton Trade*. Liverpool: Thomas Kaye, 1825.

The Stranger in Liverpool. 3rd ed. Liverpool: Thomas Kaye, 1812.

White, Brian D. *A History of the Corporation of Liverpool, 1835–1914*. Liverpool: Liverpool University Press, 1951.

4. MANCHESTER

Adshead, Joseph. *Distress in Manchester*. London: Henry Hooper, 1842.

Aikin, John. *A Description of the Country from Thirty to Forty Miles round Manchester*. London: John Stockdale, 1795.

Ashton, Thomas S. *Economic and Social Investigations in Manchester, 1833–1933*. London: P. S. King & Son, 1934.

Ashworth, Henry. *Report on the Sanitary Conditions of the Labouring Populations*. Manchester: A. Burgess, 1845.

Axon, William Edward Armytage. *The Annals of Manchester*. London: J. Heywood, 1886.

Bullock, Thomas. *Bradshaw's Illustrated Guide to Manchester*. London, 1857.

Darbyshire, Alfred. *A Booke of Olde Manchester and Salford*. Manchester: J. Heywood, 1887.

Frangopulo, Nicholas Joseph. *Rich Inheritance*. Manchester: Manchester Education Commission, 1962.

Hayes, Louis M. *Reminiscences of Manchester . . . from the Year 1840*. London: Sherratt and Hughes, 1905.

Hennock, E. P. "Urban Sanitary Reform a Generation before Chadwick." *Economic History Review* 2nd ser. 10, no. 1 (1957–1958): 113–170.

Kay, James P. (Sir James Kay-Shuttleworth). *Four Periods of Public Éducation*. London: Longman, Green, Longman, and Roberts, 1862.

————. *The Moral and Physical Condition of the Working Classes Employed in the Cotton Manufacture in Manchester*. London: J. Ridgway, 1832.

The Manchester Guide. Manchester: Joseph Aston, 1804.

Marshall, Leon S. *Development of Public Opinion in Manchester, 1780–1820*. Syracuse: Syracuse University Press, 1946.

————. "The Emergence of the First Industrial City: Manchester." In *The Cultural Approach to History*, edited by Caroline F. Ware. New York: Columbia University Press, 1940, pp. 140 ff.

Ogden, James. *Description of Manchester*. Manchester: M. Falkner, 1783.

Prentice, Archibald. *Historical Sketches and Personal Recollections of Manchester Intended to Illustrate the Progress of Public Opinion from 1792 to 1832*. London: Charles Gilpin, 1851.

Radcliffe, William. *Origin of the New System of Manufacture . . .* Stockport: J. Lomax, 1828.

Redford, Arthur, and Ira S. Russell. *History of Local Government in Manchester*. 3 vols. London: Longmans, Green, 1939–1940.

Reilly, John. *The History of Manchester*. London: John Gray Bell, 1861.

Simon, Shena D. *A Century of City Government: Manchester, 1838–1938*. London: Allen & Unwin, 1938.

Timperley, Charles Henry. *Annals of Manchester*. Manchester: Bancks, 1839.

Wheeler, James. *Manchester: Its Political, Social, and Commercial History, Ancient and Modern*. London: Whittaker, 1836.

Index